Hardy's Poetic Vision
in *The Dynasts*

Hardy's
Poetic Vision in
The Dynasts

The Diorama of a Dream

SUSAN DEAN

PRINCETON UNIVERSITY PRESS
Princeton, New Jersey

Published by Princeton University Press, Princeton, New Jersey
In the United Kingdom: Princeton University Press, Guildford, Surrey

Library of Congress Cataloging in Publication Data will
be found on the last printed page of this book

Published with the aid of The Paul Mellon Fund
at Princeton University Press

This book has been composed in Linotype Baskerville

Printed in the United States of America
by Princeton University Press, Princeton, New Jersey

To Laurence Stapleton

ACKNOWLEDGMENTS

MUCH help, personal and institutional, lies behind this book. Those debts which I can acknowledge here must stand for many others.

First, I am happy to have a chance to thank former teachers whose thoughts influenced my thinking about literature and shaped some of the assumptions of this study: the late Lawrence G. Nelson of Sweet Briar College; Warner Berthoff and Isabel MacCaffrey of Harvard University; and L. S. Dembo of the University of Wisconsin. I am indebted to other individuals who contributed their time and knowledge to the progress of this publication: James Gibson of Christ Church College, Canterbury, who read the manuscript with care; Harold Orel of the University of Kansas and editor of the New Wessex Edition of *The Dynasts*, who has generously and patiently corresponded with me on the textual changes in the different editions of Hardy's poem; and Mary Strang of the New York Public Library, who provided me with information and hard-to-find illustrations on the nineteenth-century diorama-theater. Also I wish to thank two of my senior colleagues at Bryn Mawr College who read this work at various stages along the way and offered valuable comments and support: Joseph Kramer, chairman of the Department of English, supplied a genial and discerning perspective on what I seemed to be doing; and Laurence Stapleton directed the dissertation out of which this book grew and shared with me her love of Hardy: to her this book is gratefully dedicated.

I am obliged to the libraries of Bryn Mawr College, Swarthmore College, and Temple University for allowing me to draw extensively on their collections.

My thanks also to the Trustees of the Hardy Estate and to Macmillan, London and Basingstoke, for permission to quote from *The Dynasts* by Thomas Hardy, *The Life of*

Thomas Hardy by Florence Emily Hardy, and the *Collected Poems of Thomas Hardy*; and to Macmillan Company of Canada for permission to quote from the *Collected Poems*.

I would like to thank several foundations for the financial support that enabled this study to come into being: the Danforth Foundation supported my early graduate studies with a Kent Fellowship; the Mrs. Giles Whiting Foundation financed my final year of graduate work with a Whiting Foundation Fellowship in the Humanities; and the Paul Mellon Fund at Princeton University Press has generously subsidized the costs of publication.

And, finally, I want to publish my thanks to my husband Tom, who has been friend, advisor, typist, and babysitter throughout this undertaking; and to our children, Maggie and Frank, through whose young years this work has been such a familiar presence that it is certainly their book too; and to the other members of our extended family for their cheerfulness and understanding.

Susan Dean
Bryn Mawr College
July 1976

CONTENTS

Hardy's Poetic Vision
in *The Dynasts*

THE DIORAMIC VISION

HIGH among the challenges that exercise critics of Thomas Hardy is the "problem" of *The Dynasts*. This vast poem, Hardy's largest and last major composition, is a strangely remote and inaccessible work. Even faithful readers of Hardy are daunted by the marked contrast it presents to his other writings. The well-known novels and tales and lyrics are immediately accessible and alive in subject matter and form. They deal with recognizable ordinary people, offering a close portrait of their deep feelings and anxieties, their work and circumstances, the large outlines and the daily patterns of their lives. In contrast, the leading characters in *The Dynasts* are rulers and generals intent on a war across the Channel on the European Continent. The vast number of such characters, and the brief, quick-shifting scenes in which they appear, make for a lack of substance, a thinness and unreality, to their labors and agonizings, quite different from the nearness and familiarity of the characters in the Wessex stories and tales, who are placed slowly and solidly in their landscapes.

And yet the subject of this poem is one that is familiar to most English schoolchildren and one that was vividly present to Hardy. He was proud of being related to Nelson's flag-captain; had heard tales of "Boney" from childhood; and had thought long about England's role in overthrowing him. These considerations encourage us to assume that whatever it is in the work that sets *The Dynasts* at a remove from the reader, it was put there by Hardy for some peculiar imaginative purpose, a purpose understood by himself and one that we may learn by studying the poem—especially by studying those very features which make for the remoteness.[1]

[1] The assumption that Hardy had an imaginative intention that he

3

At point after point, when we look at the formal features of *The Dynasts* we find factors that explain why many readers—whether with or without special critical expertise—have complained of having failed to be caught up in the poem. One factor is the apparent absence of Hardy's voice. In his stories it is an ever-present force, its ruminating current creating a sense of passing time under which his characters emerge in relief as solid, weathered figures. In *The Dynasts* that narrative voice is divided among the various onlooking phantom spectators and channelled into the prose stage directions.

Then there is the matter of language: Hardy's prose and verse had often been laden with heavy and involuted phrases and home-made locutions, but the power and sincerity and concern in the voice beneath carried the poem or tale onward and carried with it the reader, who tolerated these peculiarities of expression and even grew to like them. But the reader who opens *The Dynasts* finds himself with an assemblage of archaic forms and neologisms and noncewords that is great even for Hardy; and finds that for a few scenes he must work his own way through them until Hardy's voice can establish itself and begin to provide a current of motive and momentum.

But, in my judgment, the feature that most impedes access to *The Dynasts*, even more than the artificiality of the diction and the diffusiveness of the dramatic action, is the strange mixture of the modern and the antiquated that confronts us in the Fore Scene, where we form our first impressions of the poem. I mean the whole supernatural apparatus of the Overworld—the Phantom Intelligences with their spectral names and ghostly powers of vision and swooping visits to the human scene. Here, surely, if we intend to study those factors which contribute to the poem's remoteness, is where we should begin.

Hardy's preface to the drama is partly responsible for the

---

accomplished seems at least as plausible as the opposite assumption, and potentially more interesting.

disorientation we experience when we enter the Fore Scene. In it he states that *The Dynasts* is a work that reflects twentieth-century thought and announces that contemporary belief in scientific materialism ("the Monistic theory of the Universe," Preface, p. viii)[2] is the standard against which he tested what could and what could not go into his poem. Thus, he says, he eliminated from *The Dynasts* all the usual references to divine personages that readers find in tradi-

2 Thomas Hardy, *The Dynasts: An Epic-Drama of the War with Napoleon* (London: Macmillan, 1924), Preface, p. viii. *The Dynasts* was published in three parts: Part One in 1904, Part Two in 1906, and Part Three in 1908. In 1909 Hardy made minor revisions in the poem and the preface for an edition of 1910, published in London. The revised 1910 edition has been the standard edition until the present. Macmillan's 1924 reissue of the poem, which is used in this study, was the first to have a single series of page numbers running consecutively through the three parts. Passages quoted in this study will show citations in the text referring to Part, Act, and scene, followed by page in the 1924 edition, as follows: I,I,i,8. Page numbers may be disregarded by readers using editions with different pagination, such as the forthcoming New Wessex Edition edited by Harold Orel to be published by Macmillan in 1977. (The New Wessex Edition incorporates small corrections—alterations of a word or piece of punctuation—made by Hardy for a special limited edition of 1920, the Mellstock Edition. The wording of passages on which my interpretation is based is in any case the same in both the older and this New Wessex edition.)

I have followed the practice of most critics writing on *The Dynasts* in standardizing some of the many typographical devices employed by Hardy: the miniature type of the stage directions, the italicization of the speeches of the Spirits, the foreign accent marks on "Napoléon" and on other frequently-used names. In such cases the guiding principle was that of an uncluttered page that would not distract the reader. Hardy capitalized all nouns and pronouns referring to the Will. In my own discussion I have capitalized nouns like "Mind" and "Immanent Will," but found it more natural to put pronouns like "it" and "its" into lower case. Terms such as "Unconscious" and "Spirit Intelligences" will appear both ways, in lower case or capitalized, depending on whether, in context, they are being used in a general sense or in the special imaginative sense that the poem gives them. In general, except where it made for awkwardness, I have tried to refer to the Spirits in the singular (e.g., "The Spirit of the Years *says*" rather than "the Years *say*" or "Years *says*") and to use the masculine pronoun "he" for them rather than "it."

tional poems that express the belief of other ages—omitted the divine agents, the celestial machinery, and even all linguistic reference to a first cause as "He." Why, then, do we enter *The Dynasts* through an Overworld, suspended above the human scene, surrounded by Spirits and Shades and Recording Angels? It is hard to see how these spiritual entities are "the modern expression of a modern outlook," as the author claims he meant them to be (Preface, p. ix). Apparently, for Hardy, the materialism of modern science and thought to which he is trying to give imaginative expression does not bind him to a corresponding materialism and naturalism in the imaginative *methods* by which he expresses it. He feels free to introduce non-realistic "contrivances of the fancy" (Preface, p. viii), such as the Phantom Intelligences and their Overworld, in order to deliver his modern outlook.

But as readers with the Fore Scene before us, we may well question Hardy's tactics even if we accept his premise. Even if the anthropomorphic gods of ancient and Christian epic have lost their power and shrunk to mere literary conventions, at least their names and offices have the familiarity of convention and do not estrange us, which is more than we can say of the quaint nomenclature and incorporeal air of the ghostly "contrivances of fancy" in *The Dynasts*. To justify their presence in a modern poem, Hardy's Spirit Intelligences should perform some function that is demonstrably different from the function of the gods whom they have replaced.

A look back at Hardy's Preface gives us some help: these personifications will differ from "Divine personages . . . in antique Mythology" in that they are not "ready-made sources or channels of Causation" (Preface, p. viii). There will be this difference, then: where the old convention imagined figures who could see events and cause them to change, Hardy's new convention will project spirits who have powers of sight only.

The concept of "sight," once we accept it as the basis for

Hardy's invention of a whole set of novel characters, has many important applications. *The Dynasts* not only represents an action, the war with Napoleon, but in addition represents the watching of that action: a double show.[3] Understanding the ways in which the Overworld acts as a distancing and visualizing frame for the action going on in the human world below can give us a perspective on the poem's character of remoteness, and show how it is a consciously chosen effect, designed to serve a deliberate and sustained imaginative purpose.

From this beginning I have undertaken an approach to *The Dynasts* that interprets the poem as vision in action. I have tested this visual approach against Hardy's own critical prose writings: the largely autobiographical *Life of Thomas Hardy*;[4] the critical essays usefully collected by Harold Orel

[3] *The Dynasts* is unique among Hardy's long works in presenting systematically this once-removed view. It is a frequent technique in the lyrics and stories, as we are shown by J. Hillis Miller, *Thomas Hardy: Distance and Desire.*

[4] Florence Emily Hardy, *The Life of Thomas Hardy, 1840–1928.* The biography was published in two volumes: Part One, *The Early Life, 1840–1891,* was published soon after Hardy's death in 1928; Part Two, *The Later Years, 1892–1928,* in 1930. I have used the one-volume edition. Page references to the *Life* will be incorporated in the text of this study.

Richard Little Purdy, in *Thomas Hardy: A Biographical Study,* pp. 265–67 and 272–73, provides the history of its composition and publication. The name of the second Mrs. Hardy on the title page is an "innocent deception," brought about, Purdy speculates, because Hardy's "natural reticence and modesty made impossible any acknowledgement of the work." From his examinations of the working typescript copies in Max Gate papers, Purdy has determined that the account through the year 1918 was written entirely by Hardy, a project probably undertaken during the years 1917–1926; and that even for the four concluding chapters Hardy provided the editorial hand, supplying frequent paragraphs, carrying the biography in synopsis through September 1926, and designating materials to be inserted.

Evelyn Hardy, writing as editor in *Thomas Hardy's Notebooks, and Some Letters from Julia Augusta Martin,* p. 119, adds to Purdy's account this (undocumented) story: "When he was working on his reminiscences, and his wife entered the room, Hardy used to hide the

in *Thomas Hardy's Personal Writings: Prefaces, Literary Opinions, Reminiscences;*[5] and of course Hardy's preface to *The Dynasts*. Passages from those writings which will be cited in this and subsequent chapters provide evidence to support a "visual" reading, as well as evidence against some of the other major critical approaches that have been taken to the poem. Hardy is only one among the many critics and explicators of Hardy, to be sure. But he as much as any other reader may shed fresh light on the obscurity that still screens *The Dynasts*.

Criticism has largely done away with the condescending image of Hardy that reduced him to his provincial origins and "provincial"education: the image of an unfinished earnest autodidact, overwhelmed by scientific ideas and lacking in subtlety and in conscious control over his art. Little by little we have learned not to let apparent defects in his writing close our eyes to its power. Arthur Symons makes the basic observation about the unevenness of Hardy's style: that when it sets forth circumstantial facts of a situation, it is cumbrous, but when it comes to "the impalpable emotion of a situation, we get this faultless and uncommon use of words."[6] Symons explains the phenomenon temperamentally, speculating that Hardy had a natural lethargy that could be shaken off only by a subject that awakened his emotion and therefore his imagination. Herbert Muller noted that the fine net of "new" (ca. 1940's) criticism implied an anti-romantic distrust of emotion that escaped its measure of "soundness," so that as criticism it was unqualified for appreciating the poetic, elemental quality of Hardy's "simple but majestic fictions": "Hardy *exists*, when countless 'sounder' writers are dead."[7] R. A.

---

pages beneath the blotting pad. Yet he agreed that she should be the person to edit his pages and complete his life."

[5] Harold Orel, ed., *Thomas Hardy's Personal Writings: Prefaces, Literary Opinions, Reminiscences.*

[6] Arthur Symons, *A Study of Thomas Hardy*, p. 7.

[7] Herbert J. Muller, "The Novels of Hardy Today," p. 223.

Scott-James suggests that Hardy's prose "pursues its way rhythmically," his effects cumulative.[8] And C. Day Lewis, speaking about the lyric poems, puts into words a principle I think applies to all of Hardy's writings: one must stand back, see the work as a whole, get the total effect: "And with Hardy at his best, it is the poem—the whole poem, not any high spots in it, which makes the impression. . . . If, instead of dwelling upon [spots which are odd, flat and unpoetical], we seek to comprehend the poem as a whole, we find such oddities and flatnesses falling into place."[9] Behind all these remarks there lies the implication that criticism is attempting to face, and come to terms with, a giant.

The Dynasts, because of its character of remoteness that we have described above and because of its apparent singularity among Hardy's writings, still remains an unknown territory, and therefore remains the last major work over which the anti-romantic stereotype of Hardy (at the mercy of ideas, not in control of his art) still looms with some persuasiveness. True, parts of the poem are regularly singled out for their special power, included in anthologies, and praised in general introductions to Hardy. Critics regularly say now that it is the natural sequel to the novels; Scott-James's comment is typical: "the indispensable culmination of his work."[10] But unless the poem is perceived as an imaginative whole, such passing acknowledgments serve only as new stereotypes, substituting for real knowledge. A few critics have, in my opinion, written about the poem in a way that communicates it as an entire poetic experience: Walter de la Mare (1910),[11] Lascelles Abercrombie (1912),[12] Barker Fairley (1919),[13] George Elliott (1928),[14]

8 R. A. Scott-James, *Thomas Hardy*, pp. 19, 28.
9 C. Day Lewis, "The Lyrical Poetry of Thomas Hardy," p. 172.
10 Scott-James, *Thomas Hardy*, p. 35.
11 Walter de la Mare, "*The Dynasts*," in *Private View*, pp. 23–27.
12 Lascelles Abercrombie, *Thomas Hardy: A Critical Study*.
13 Barker Fairley, "Notes on the Form of *The Dynasts*."
14 George R. Elliott, "Hardy's Poetry and the Ghostly Moving-Pic-

9

Arthur McDowall (1931),[15] and Vivian de Sola Pinto (1951).[16] But their remarks on *The Dynasts* were brief—a few pages or a chapter in length; and they seem to have gone ignored or lost. I hope in this study to bring some of their recognitions to bear, with my own, on the task that still confronts readers today, that of obtaining familiar access to *The Dynasts*, with all it holds.

1. IDEAS AS IMPRESSIONS

From Hardy's time until now critics have sought in various ways to overcome the poem's remoteness by denying it. One attempt to tame *The Dynasts* has been to explain its fitness (or unfitness) as an example of one or another of the traditional literary genres. The poem has been viewed as an epic,[17] as a drama,[18] as a mixture of both ("a vast and awkward hybrid"),[19] as a "sublime historic peep-show,"[20] as a movie-script,[21] and even, to Hardy's annoyance, as a puppet-show.[22] But a hint of the poem's imperviousness to

---

ture," and George R. Elliott, "Spectral Etching in the Poetry of Thomas Hardy."

[15] Arthur McDowall, *Thomas Hardy: A Critical Study.*

[16] Vivian de Sola Pinto, "Hardy and Housman."

[17] The following are some of the main critics who have discussed the poem as an epic: Elizabeth Drew, *The Enjoyment of Literature*; Richard Carpenter, *Thomas Hardy*; Samuel L. Hynes, *The Pattern of Hardy's Poetry*; Harold Orel, *Thomas Hardy's Epic-Drama: A Study of "The Dynasts"*; Harold Orel, "Hardy and the Epic Tradition"; Jean R. Brooks, *Thomas Hardy: The Poetic Structure.*

[18] Morton Dauwen Zabel, "Hardy in Defense of his Art: The Aesthetic of Incongruity," p. 143, sees *The Dynasts* as (failed) drama.

[19] Irving Howe, *Thomas Hardy*, p. 157.

[20] Edmund Gosse, "Mr. Hardy's Lyrical Poems," p. 293.

[21] John Wain, "Introduction," *The Dynasts*, by Thomas Hardy, pp. ix–xiv.

[22] Harold Orel, *Hardy's Personal Writings*, p. 144, notes that Arthur Bingham Walkley, literary and dramatic critic for *The London Times*, had proposed, in an unsigned article entitled "*The Dynasts*: A Suggestion" (*The London Times Literary Supplement*, January 29, 1904),

an approach by traditional precedents can be found in the words Hardy uses in his Preface to indicate the nature of *The Dynasts*: "The *Spectacle* here presented *in the likeness of a Drama* . . ." (Preface, p. vii, italics added). Here "Spectacle" is the substantive word, "Drama" only a descriptive term. Later in the Preface Hardy characterizes the poem as a loosely patterned "chronicle-piece," to distinguish it from "a drama strictly contained" (Preface, p. ix). Finally, he describes how it is designed to be a "panoramic show of historical 'ordinates' " that the "mental spectator" must combine, according to his knowledge and sympathy, into "an artistic unity" (Preface, p. ix). These remarks do not describe a work whose genre we can even identify, much less a work that would be helpfully clarified by reference from the particular example to the traditional mode. If they describe anything with which we are familiar, it might be the open form of modern poetry that intentionally demands the reader's involvement for the completion of its design.

Another approach frequently taken to *The Dynasts* has been to look in it for a conceptual system of thought that would reveal what Hardy himself believed, or that would tell us which philosophy was the leading influence behind the poem. Many works of this nature have been written, linking Hardy to such philosophers as Schopenhauer, von Hartmann, Mill, Burke, or Darwin.[23]

---

that Hardy's epic-drama be staged as a puppet-show. This frivolous response so annoyed Hardy that in February 1904 he wrote two letters to the editor to establish the point that *The Dynasts* was intended to be read and was not for the stage.

[23] Some of the main critics who have written on the philosophical sources of *The Dynasts* (and of Hardy's thought in general) are: Helen Garwood, *Thomas Hardy: An Illustration of Schopenhauer*; F. A. Hedgcock, *Thomas Hardy: Penseur et Artiste*; Samuel C. Chew, *Thomas Hardy, Poet and Novelist*; Ernest Brennecke, Jr., *Thomas Hardy's Universe: A Study of the Poet's Mind*; Lionel Stevenson, *Darwin among the Poets*; William R. Rutland, *Thomas Hardy: A Study of his Writings and their Background*; James Granville South-

Hardy's prose contains several warnings against such delving approaches. The word he holds up constantly in them is "impressions":

> . . . the sentiments in the following pages have been stated truly to be mere impressions of the moment, and not convictions or arguments.[24]

> A friend of mine writes objecting to what he calls my "philosophy" (though I have no philosophy— merely what I have often explained to be only a confused heap of impressions, like those of a bewildered child at a conjuring show). (*Life*, p. 410)

> Like so many critics, Mr. Courtney treats my works of art as if they were a scientific system of philosophy, although I have repeatedly stated in prefaces and elsewhere that the views in them are *seemings*, provisional impressions only, used for artistic purposes because they represent approximately the impressions of the age, and are plausible, till somebody produces better theories of the universe. (*Life*, p. 375)

> But being only a mere impressionist I must not pretend to be a philosopher. . . . (1914 letter to Dr. Caleb Saleeby, quoted in *Life*, p. 449)

Elsewhere in the *Life*, Hardy adds that the questions that exercise those who read for his ideas—identifying the probable source of a concept, arguing over claims of priority, debating as to whether the ideas were satisfactory (i.e., "true" or well-chosen) and satisfactorily presented (set forth fairly and coherently)—were tangential matters (*Life*, p.

---

worth, *The Poetry of Thomas Hardy*; Harvey Curtis Webster, *On a Darkling Plain: The Art and Thought of Thomas Hardy*; J. O. Bailey, *Thomas Hardy and the Cosmic Mind: A New Reading of "The Dynasts"*; Orel, *Thomas Hardy's Epic-Drama*; Perry Meisel, *Thomas Hardy: The Return of the Repressed*.

[24] Thomas Hardy, "General Preface," in *Personal Writings*, ed. Orel, p. 49.

319), and were simply inappropriate responses to a "work
. . . offered as a poem and not as a system of thought" (*Life*,
p. 335).

It is not that the ideas are not there in *The Dynasts* and
in the other writings, to be found and explained by scholars.
Throughout the *Life*, Hardy freely records the scientific
and philosophic ideas and books that engage him and even
discusses with some of his correspondents their merit and
their influence upon him. But they are not the central
stimuli to his *poetic* vision. Feeling is central. Thought is
only an adjunct to feeling, or an expression of it, like
meter or "measure"—an attempt to give it a temporary
form of a certain kind.

> The Poet takes note of nothing that he cannot feel
> emotively. (*Life*, p. 342)

> My opinion is that a poet should express the emotion
> of all the ages and the thought of his own.
> (*Life*, p. 386)

> Poetry is emotion put into measure. (*Life*, p. 300)

These statements are corroborated by our experience in
reading the novels, stories, and poems, in which what
strikes us as most central is Hardy's close rendering of the
emotional truth of people—the truth of his own shifts of
feeling as well as the feelings of his characters. But we need
to see how this statement of conscious priority applies to
The Dynasts: how, next to the timeless truth of feeling,
all things—including convictions, including the thought
of one's age—are "mere impressions of the moment."

Hardy's characterization of ideas as "mere impressions"
has generally been disregarded by critics of his philosophy,
who have tended to take it as one of his many attempts to
put up a screen around his private person. But the fre-
quency and care with which he uses the word "impressions"
suggest that the word had a poetic meaning for him, and
that it may have carried, besides its usual sense of temporary

imprints or patterns of correspondence, a special reference to the fleeting and evanescent, even beautiful, nature of all patterns that make their brief impression on the course of life. Even a human life constitutes such a "mere impression of the moment." Hardy notes of his sister after her death: "December 23. Mary's birthday. She came into the world . . . and went out . . . and the world is just the same . . . not a ripple on the surface left" (*Life*, p. 430). Likewise, the most advanced thought of his time might hold its impress for no more than a large moment—an adulthood, a lifetime, or an age—after which it too would yield place to a new impression in a new time, and the world be just the same. Only the "emotion of the ages" endures—indeed is concurrent with—the flow of life.

For our reading of *The Dynasts*, then, Hardy's statements about impressions, the temporary nature of thought, and the timeless nature of emotion, direct us to take lightly and metaphorically even that imposing "Monistic theory of the Universe" which is posted so prominently in his Preface and which is carried through in such skilled detail in the poem. He would not have us fix too solemnly upon it, even as he himself did not fix upon it—"a plausible theory only," he said in a 1904 letter to the *Times*.[25] An approximate impression of this theory (itself an impression) will be conveyed to us in a "panoramic show," by means of scenes that are themselves a series of visual impressions: but all of these impressions are there only to give a temporary structure and pattern and frame to feeling.

2. The Making of a Vision

The shaping of *The Dynasts* as we follow it in the record preserved in Hardy's *Life* is primarily a visual process. Hardy's working notes, kept over the years, give us the rare opportunity to watch the poet widening and deepening his

[25] Thomas Hardy, "*The Dynasts*: A Postscript [2]," in *Personal Writings*, ed. Orel, p. 146.

field of vision according to the demands of his subject, to the point where a number of foci and a balance of perspectives are called on to deal with what is seen.

A word of description is in order first about the biography, which is a major source of reference for this and all studies of Hardy. We have said that it is autobiographical, being Hardy's gathering, within a roughly chronological frame, of the data of his life. But that data baffles the reader who comes in search of the person, Hardy, for it is always poetic and never personal in its relevance. The biographical facts—birth, ancestry, schooling, architectural years, the turn to novel-writing, marriage, travel, sickness, publications, the turn from prose to poetry, and the entry into the period of old age and honor—are external; throughout Hardy views himself with detachment, telling us nothing of the sufferings or feelings of his "subject." The historical matter contained in that chronological frame—memories and documents preserved over the years—is unselfconscious "raw" data: the living words of journal entries, excerpts from letters, memoranda, and dated notes, as they were written in a given "past" situation, keeping the sense of actuality and context. But because that matter has been chosen, censored, edited, and put into an overall shape by the detached Hardy, we have the same fascinating compound of conscious and "unconscious" that we shall see in *The Dynasts*.

Within Hardy's chronological frame, moreover, the data is ordered to show us his mind as a museum, carefully arranged and disclosed by him to posterity. A lumber-room we may call it, in which he has saved the small and large pieces on which his imagination worked. Here are the musical "motifs": loved pieces of classical music, names of dance tunes and ballads and liturgical settings. Here too are thoughts on painting, poetry, literature, philosophy, life, age; here, interesting correspondence with readers about the "meaning" or circumstances of his works; throughout, precise impressions of flora and fauna, scenery,

15

seasons, the weather of a day or an hour; and always, the strange material of human nature: anecdotes, recollections, folklore, gossip, macabre tales. Looking at them from our vantage point, we realize that all of them were preserved and exhibited because they once constituted material for potential compositions, and because they somehow entered into compositions that became reality. As we read, we can visualize how life became art in the poet's mind. Thus, while the *Life* teases and eludes as biography, every page of it has an intense relation to our study of Hardy's imagination.[26]

[26] Robert Gittings, *The Young Thomas Hardy*, pp. 1–6, writes to explain the disparities between Hardy's subjective version of his life in his autobiography and "the facts of the life" as traced from objective documentary evidence by the modern biographer. Gittings' explanation is that the gaps and omissions in the *Life* were motivated by a class-consciousness in Hardy that propelled him to escape his lower-class origins, denying them in his story of himself while drawing on them for his other stories. The "clumsily-connected anecdotes" in the *Life* that seem irrelevant to what Gittings considers "the main themes of his life" (that is, the themes of social class and classlessness) are, Gittings reasons, the result of Hardy's "always uncertain" prose style, further blurred by the poor memory and heavy hand of old age.

Clearly, the view taken by this study differs in most respects from Gittings' theory. It sees Hardy's move from provincial beginnings to a final cosmopolitan classlessness as motivated not so much by economic and social insecurities (although Gittings valuably demonstrates that these conditions were strong and present in Hardy's background) as by a real attraction to the "life of the mind" as an end in itself. Then, as now, persons who were attracted to the life of the mind by accidents of education entered into an invisible community, often unknown to each other, but in touch through the printed word with the ongoing life of thought. By its very nature this community did away with class; membership was free, self-elected, unaffected by one's past or present circumstances except as they affected practically the amount of time and vitality one had for keeping up with thought and expression (see Gissing's *New Grub Street*). Thus, the young architect Hardy who earnestly read the journals recommended to him by his mentor, Horace Moule, was moved less by the fact that the life of letters and culture was associated with social respectability than by the excitement of coming to intellectual consciousness and, later, of bringing all his newly ordered perceptions to artistic expression. Similarly at the end:

The first reference to *The Dynasts* in the *Life* is a description of Hardy's initial encounter with the matter of Napoleon, which was to occupy the same high place in his imagination as the "matter of Troy" and the "matter of Gaul" did for poets before him. It came about accidentally, we are told, when he was a boy of eight rummaging in a closet, and happened across some old periodicals that had belonged to his grandfather and that dealt with the Napoleonic wars: "The torn pages of these contemporary numbers with their melodramatic prints of serried ranks, crossed bayonets, huge knapsacks, and dead bodies, were the first to set him on the train of ideas that led to *The Trumpet-Major* and *The Dynasts*" (*Life*, pp. 16–17). The encounter with history through the medium of colorful, melodramatic prints made upon this young and impressionable boy a *visual* impression.[27] Is it too much to infer that this first glimpse of his subject through melodramatic and, probably,

---

the established author, regularly travelling from Dorset to reestablish cultural and social contact with the present and returning to Dorset to commune again with the past, was not the lonely, unhappy, guilt-haunted man seen by Gittings. He is quite companioned by his memories, his "ghosts," his thoughts, his conversations on the passing scene, by his writing of poems, and his constant thought about poetry.

Hardy himself could be cited to testify that social class and worldly advancement were not for him "the substance of life" (for example, in his comments on the literary productions of the "properly" educated, *Life*, p. 213, quoted in this study, Chapter III, note 7; and in the tone and words of the last stanza of "Your Last Drive," CP, p. 320; and in the basic affirmations of his writings). But such testimony would not count for much to the eye that is predisposed to regard external facts as proofs and to put the burden of proof on words (mere words, rationalizations). In the final analysis, differences of interpretation about inward spirit beneath outward facts cannot be proved. They can only be put next to each other as what Hardy would call "impressions of the unknowable"—alternative or complementary but always partial.

[27] Hardy wrote to a correspondent seeking pedagogical advice that "fairly good engravings, such as those in the *Graphic, Illustrated News,* etc.," would be of great value in setting to work the "powerful imagination" of a child between 9 and 13 (*Life*, p. 159).

set-piece illustrations affected Hardy's handling of his historical material when he later came to write down his version of those events? For indeed the scenes that we picture the most readily and vividly when we think back on *The Dynasts* are remarkably like those traditional paintings illustrative of famous scenes in history that formerly appeared in periodicals and are now found mostly in history readers and on museum walls. The hero's death beneath deck in the *Victory*; the surrender in the snow at Ulm; the dynastic meeting on the barge at Tilsit; the sequence of views at Moscow (as museum paintings of a certain period, or as calendar art, it could make up a triptych entitled "The Lesson of History": "Triumph" at the Hill of Salutation, "Vanity" at the top of the Kremlin, "All to Nothing" in the snowy wastes); the encounter at La Mure near Grenoble; the dozing Emperor reviewing his troops on the Belgian frontier with the edict of proscription nailed to the tree behind him; the last view of spent horse and rider in the moonlit wood at Bossu: all of these views are "historic," which is to say, they satisfy our expectation, rather than startle or surprise it. It is as though we recognize them as having always been in our minds. If they seem to us like familiar, though unconscious, traditions, they must have seemed even more familiar and traditional to the readers of Hardy's time.[28]

This sense—that history in *The Dynasts* is rendered as a series of flat paintings—lies, I think, behind an objection raised by several critics of the poem. They hold that Hardy weakened what could have been the great historical drama that his novels and Wessex lyrics show he was preeminently qualified to write, through his (wrong) choice of not putting all of his powers of imagination into the historical drama as an end in itself. In this view *The Dynasts* suffers by com-

[28] Cf. Henry W. Nevinson, *Thomas Hardy*, p. 60: "These visions seem to me hardly in place within the drama. They are too much like that picture in an old gallery in Brussels—a vision of multitudinous mothers holding up their slaughtered children to Napoleon's face in passionate reproach."

parison to that other epic history about "the war with Napoleon," *War and Peace*. Whether because the metaphysician in Hardy prevailed over the novelist,[29] or because he never organized his reflections about society into some sort of coherent theory of history,[30] or simply because he failed to make full use of the stirring material contained in his historical sources,[31] the historical characters in *The Dynasts* are found to lack the warmth and life of those in Tolstoy's work and even to lack the deeply imagined life of those in Hardy's own best novels. Beneath this view it is taken for granted that Hardy should have intensified the poem's simulation of actuality and dissipated its aura of remoteness.

The answer that this study will hold out to this criticism is that Hardy's "thin" treatment of history becomes clear when it is viewed as part of a visual exhibit, carefully limited, proportioned, and aligned to balance with other components in a fully imagined whole. Readers should not look for a full-bodied experience of human history in *The Dynasts*; just as philosophy in the poem is a "mere impression of the moment," so history in it is also a series of impressions.[32] They are impressions of a past "moment" in human time, one hundred years before the moment early in the twentieth century that happened to provide itself as an interpretive lens, filtering the "emotion of the ages" through "the latest illumination of the time."

[29] Southworth, *Poetry of Thomas Hardy*, pp. 210–12.

[30] J. I. M. Stewart, *Thomas Hardy*, pp. 217–18.

[31] Walter F. Wright, *The Shaping of "The Dynasts": A Study in Thomas Hardy*, pp. 227–28.

[32] Emma Clifford, *"War and Peace* and *The Dynasts,"* p. 43, comments suggestively that Hardy made a remarkably straightforward, even "pedestrian," transferral of the written history in his various sources. See also by Clifford: "The 'Trumpet-Major Notebook' and *The Dynasts*"; "Thomas Hardy and the Historians"; "The Impressionistic View of History in *The Dynasts*." When Clifford's careful, orderly work of inquiry is completed and brought together under one cover, it should provide a basic tool to future study of *The Dynasts*.

Although history was to be only one impression in Hardy's vision and to compose only one layer of his poem, the *Life* testifies that he put great time and care into his labor to achieve historical accuracy and historical immediacy in each of his hundred and twenty-nine this-world scenes. He collected and used a substantial library on Napoleon and the war; consulted materials in the British Museum; addressed historical inquiries to his kinswoman, the daughter of Hardy of Trafalgar; and made repeated visits to sites on the Continent—towns, cathedrals, battlefields—that figured in his story.

It is not too much to call *The Dynasts* the work of a lifetime when we consider the following dates: 1848, his discovery of his grandfather's periodicals as a boy of eight; 1868, his first outline of a poem on Napoleon; 1908, the publication of *The Dynasts,* Part III. During this entire sixty-year period—the almost forty years in which *The Dynasts* was a literary project, and the twenty years before that when the project was only a keen interest—chance and choice kept bringing Hardy into contact with persons who themselves had been in contact with that war. The *Life* records his glimpses of important personages like Louis Napoleon and Palmerston; it notes his regular interviews at Chelsea Hospital with veterans from the Peninsula and Waterloo. There are vivid recollections in it of his own early encounters in Dorset with officers whose uniforms and talk set his imagination stirring. Even more highly charged are the recollections passed on to the boy Hardy by the relatives and neighbors whose lives touched the historic past. His own grandmother could tell him how it felt to be alive and hearing the news of the French Revolution; Dorset people could remember seeing George the Third in the summers when he resorted in their region; his grandfather had joined the local volunteer guard, and others had organized a regular night watch over the Channel shoreline during the period when an attack by Napoleon hung over their coast.

All of these impressions Hardy collected over the years until he was ready to draw them into a web of history that could be called "panoramic," in which he would reweave the color, stir, and sweep of those times, and would treat the components of each scene with as much attention to consistency, perspective, and questions of inclusion as an artist would bring to painting a canvas. But the multiplicity of scene-pictures, the multitudinous cast, required a vast viewing frame. This requirement, we are persuaded after following the evolving vision in the *Life*, is met by Hardy's epic machinery. That machinery is not the clumsy appendage to the drama that it strikes many on first view and that it remains in the settled view of even some leading Hardy critics: to Stewart "impressive and tedious by turns";[33] to Pinion a mechanism that "creaks repeatedly."[34] Rather, it is a basic way of encompassing all the complexity and magnitude, illusion and irrationality, that Hardy had come to see in his subject. The chronological entries in the *Life* show him continually extending the formal limits of his theme. From a single narrative poem on one man, Napoleon, in one battle, the Nile, it grew into a ballad, and then a series of ballads, bringing several actions (and presumably several protagonists) together into an "Iliad of Europe," with Napoleon "a sort of Achilles," acting under compulsion, "a pathetic sight" (*Life*, pp. 57–58, 106, 416). In form it is conceived as a "grand drama" (*Life*, p. 114), a "historical Drama" (*Life*, p. 148), then a "Great Modern Drama" (*Life*, 146), until it became that new thing which Hardy introduces to us in the Preface: "a drama for mental performance," a "panoramic show" for a "mental spectator" who will coordinate and complete its action with his knowledge and imaginative sympathy (Preface, pp. ix–x).

While the form of his drama was evolving, Hardy's thinking about the part of human action in it was becoming

---

[33] Stewart, *Thomas Hardy*, p. 216.
[34] F. B. Pinion, *A Hardy Companion: A Guide to the Works of Thomas Hardy and their Background*, p. 110.

clear. Conscious motive, human knowledge, rationality—
these supposed regulators of human behavior had only
ostensible effect upon men's actions. Rather, these were the
terms that applied: "automatic, reflex movement"; "impulsion"; "forces, emotions, tendencies"; "passivity . . . unconscious propensity" (*Life*, pp. 148, 152, 247, 168). The
view that human behavior is basically non-rational is in
accord with Hardy's other writings, although these words
for it are more uncompromising and technical than we
might have expected. "The characters do not act under the
influence of reason," he says of *The Dynasts* in 1892 (*Life*,
p. 247). What was true of the human individuals in his
provincial and domestic dramas holds all the more strongly
for the mysteries of mass behavior and decisions of state
in a "vast international tragedy" (Preface, p. vii).

We do find in the *Life* one view that represents a development beyond what the novels and stories imagined
about human nature. Hardy tells of becoming increasingly
aware of the fact that in London: "Each individual is conscious of *himself*, but nobody conscious of themselves collectively . . . no consciousness here of where anything comes
from or goes to—only that it is present" (*Life*, pp. 206–07).
This perception of collectivity[35] affected the focus of *The
Dynasts*, widening it from particular persons to "people"
embodied in the figure of Europe. The focus thus widened
inspires two tentative notes that anticipate the famous aerial perspectives in *The Dynasts*:

> 1891: "A Bird's-Eye View of Europe at the beginning
> of the Nineteenth Century. . . ." (*Life*, p. 234)

> 1896: Brussels, Waterloo. "Europe in Throes. Three
> Parts. Five Acts each. Characters: Burke, Pitt,
> Napoleon, George III, Wellington . . . and many
> others." (*Life*, p. 284)

[35] Hardy expresses this insight in different words, "involuntary inter-
social emotions," in *"The Dynasts*: A Postscript [2]," in *Personal Writings*, ed. Orel, p. 146.

Who, if we may assign particular identities to collective mankind, were these "many others?" We recall that only a part of Hardy's labors was with books of history, and that much of his time and effort and curiosity went into talking with people who had parts in the war.[36] These "many others" included, along with the leading characters whom Hardy read about, the soldiers who since his youth had kindled his interest and affection, and the Wessex people with their long local memories. Why were all of these men, great and small, set moving? Why were they and whole nations and an entire age set "in throes," heaved up from the normal everyday course of life and thrown into a "historic" war? What did history achieve with such interruptions of lives and outpourings of blood? It only created "history," transforming little-known, peaceful localities into places famous as scenes of slaughter and transforming obscure people into individuals distinguished for having been combatants, agents, and victims of slaughter: bitter history and false glory.

We feel, after putting *The Dynasts* next to the account in the *Life*, that it was questions such as these that spoke to Hardy in his subject: some such intractable largeness that defied one simple focus and would not let him isolate one great man or a few great men from the whole web of events. There is no central character in the drama who drew out all his sympathies, and therefore ours, as Tess and Henchard did; but, collectively, each character is incorporated in that powerful image of a prone, emaciated human body that depicts "Europe in throes."

[36] This aspect of Hardy's research—that form of impression-gathering which is now called "oral history"—is hard to measure, but I believe that it deserves more than the usual passing acknowledgment and that it should be viewed as bearing imaginative consequences equal to those growing out of Hardy's work with written sources. Himself an historian, R. J. White, *Thomas Hardy and History*, pp. 74–77, does recognize the importance for Hardy of these personal contacts with history which embody the reach of "living memory," a lifetime's length in span.

INTRODUCTION

Thus Hardy's account of the development of his conception of *The Dynasts* educates us to the service performed by the Overworld. We see a necessary point for vision, a platform set back in space far enough to take in the world's wide panorama and to see through its pictured shows down to the living pulse beneath.[37] On that platform are set, as we know from our reading of the Preface, "supernatural spectators of the terrestrial action, certain impersonated abstractions, or Intelligences, called Spirits" (Preface, p. viii). Once *The Dynasts* is interpreted according to a visual design, these inventions of Hardy's fall into place, and pose no further difficulty to our reading. But a preliminary examination of the place of vision in Hardy's thinking can help us to read with more attention and to find more complexity and suggestiveness in those Spirits.

3. HARDY'S THOUGHTS ON VISION

There are many passages in Hardy's critical writing where he seems to say about whatever subject is under discussion, "It is all a matter of vision." One part of the *Life* especially (coming in the years of the 1880's and 1890's, suggesting a preoccupation with vision at that time) contains numerous annotations on the possible variety in points of view. Hardy notes the difference between the subjective views held by someone in an experience and the objective views of a watcher outside.

[37] See Thomas Hardy, "The Science of Fiction," in *Personal Writings*, ed. Orel, p. 137: "A sight for the finer qualities of existence, an ear for the 'still, sad music of humanity,' are not to be acquired by the outer senses alone, close as their powers in photography may be. . . . To see in half and quarter views the whole picture, to catch from a few bars the whole tune, is the intuitive power that supplies the would-be storywriter with the scientific bases for his pursuit." For more about "the whole picture" and "the whole tune," see those pages which have to do with "Dream" in the closing sections of Chapter Two of this study.

Faces. The features to beholders so commonplace are to their possessor lineaments of high estimation, striking, hopeful. (*Life*, p. 186)

That which, socially, is a great tragedy, may be in Nature no alarming circumstance. (*Life*, p. 218)

On returning to London after an absence I find the people of my acquaintance abraded, their hair disappearing, also their flesh, by degrees.

People who to one's-self are transient singularities are to themselves the permanent condition, the inevitable, the normal, the rest of mankind being to them the singularity. Think, that those (to us) strange transitory phenomena, *their* personalities, are with them always, at their going to bed, at their uprising! (*Life*, p. 206)

Not only is there that difference in how the self is perceived, felt by the self to be a hopeful, nobly intentioned subject *over* experience, perceived by others to be commonplace, and subject—like all things—*to* experience. There is also the difference in the objective views held by the watcher of life as his own circumstances change.

I am more than ever convinced that persons are successively various persons, according as each special strand in their characters is brought uppermost by circumstances. (*Life*, p. 230)

Experience *un*teaches.—(what one at first thinks to be the rule in events).

The Hypocrisy of things. Nature is an arch-dissembler. A child is deceived completely; the older members of society more or less according to their penetration; though even they seldom get to realize that *nothing* is as it appears. (*Life*, p. 176)

Hardy accounts for this second difference—that of degrees of visual discernment—by the work of circumstance upon the viewer. Both perceptions of a subject—its interior and its exterior aspects—are necessary and valid, although Hardy indicates his own preference for the penetrating view of sympathy over the distanced view of judgment.

> If you look beneath the surface of any farce you see a tragedy; and, on the contrary, if you blind yourself to the deeper issues of a tragedy you see a farce. (*Life*, p. 215)

> Looking over old *Punches*. Am struck with the frequent wrong direction of satire, and of commendation, when seen by the light of later days. (*Life*, p. 224)

> All tragedy is grotesque—if you allow yourself to see it as such. A risky indulgence for any who have an aspiration towards a little goodness or greatness of heart! Yet there are those who do. (*Life*, p. 296)

Yet for these different degrees of penetration Hardy would cite the combined wisdom, aesthetic and scientific, of the nineteenth century: "the eye sees that which it brings with it the means of seeing."[38] Hardy quotes these words from Carlyle in a critical essay of 1888. As a young man he had expressed the same idea in more simple words that reflect his own poetic concern: "The poetry of a scene varies with the minds of the perceivers. Indeed, it does not lie in the scene at all" (*Life*, p. 50).

Hardy's developed sense of sympathy—which ascribes pre-shaping causes for better and worse, and which keeps always in mind the antithesis between the external view of experience and the internal one—is fully at work in his greatest novels of character, giving power to his compound presentations, from without and within, of Eustacia, Henchard, and Tess. Behind those novels is this perception of the uniqueness of the individual perspective: "Society, *collectively*, has neither seen what any ordinary person can see, read what every ordinary person has read, nor thought

[38] Thomas Carlyle, *The French Revolution*, Part One, Book I, Chapter II, "Realized Ideals"; quoted in Thomas Hardy, "The Profitable Reading of Fiction," in *Personal Writings*, ed. Orel, p. 125.

26

what every ordinary person has thought" (*Life*, p. 224). For Hardy, then, the limitedness built into human vision is not a cause for scorn or despair. His notes in the *Life* on his own changing outlook are not ironic but attentive. It is as though he were putting together over the course of a lifetime a full, rounded view of experience, one that remembered to include in its compound, if not all the possible finite views of experience, since the number would be infinite, then the fact of them all.

Thus, the difference between the physical patterns of material reality and the distortions made of those patterns by the eye and the brain, one remove away, are for Hardy what gives human vision its interest and worth. They are its source of poetry, its creation and replenishment of nature.

> I don't want to see landscapes, i.e. scenic paintings of them, because I don't want to see the original realities—as optical effects, that is. I want to see the deeper reality underlying the scenic, the expression of what are sometimes called abstract imaginings.
>
> The "simply natural" is interesting no longer. The much decried, mad late-Turner rendering is now necessary to create my interest. The exact truth as to material fact ceases to be of importance in art. . . . (*Life*, p. 185)

In these statements, and in the following one, with its James-like[39] metaphor, Hardy establishes his poetics directly in the "inaccuracy" and idiosyncrasy of each human vision.

> As, in looking at a carpet, by following one colour a certain pattern is suggested, by following another colour, another; so in life the seer should watch that pattern among general things which his idiosyncrasy

---

[39] Hardy's image of the pattern in the carpet is dated June 3, 1882; Henry James's story, "The Figure in the Carpet," was published in the collection, *Embarrassments*, in 1896. The use of the figure by two men who knew each other only slightly would seem to be coincidental.

moves him to observe, and describe that alone. This is, quite accurately, a going to Nature; yet the result is no mere photograph, but purely the product of the writer's own mind. (*Life*, p. 153)

It is very much a protestant theory of knowledge and art, thought through down to practical technique:

Reflections on Art. Art is a changing of the actual proportions and order of things, so as to bring out more forcibly than might otherwise be done that feature in them which appeals most strongly to the idiosyncrasy of the artist. . . . (*Life*, p. 228)

Throughout the time that these thoughts about vision and art were being recorded in his notebooks Hardy was busy writing fiction and lyric poems. Studies will show that there was a cross-traffic between poetic theory and imaginative practice.[40] But it is *The Dynasts* that is the culminating result of those years of interest in the idiosyncrasies of human sight.

4. OUR VISION OF "THE DYNASTS"

In discussing the visionary aspects of *The Dynasts* here and in what follows, I will be using the words "poem" and

[40] Especially in *Tess of the d'Urbervilles* (1891) do I find the results of these meditations of the 1880's on the necessity for a subject to be seen from many perspectives. The view of Tess is continually shifting: it includes society's view of her and her own view of herself; it sees her as a latter-day "peasant" ruined by an "aristocrat," but also as a descendant of aristocrats who suffers the wrong formerly inflicted by her ancestors; it sees her as a part of nature, and apart; it includes the partial perceptions of her held by d'Urberville and Clare; and it surpasses all the perspectives above with the view voiced by the narrator, who, by putting on and taking off his own several "Spirit" voices, demonstrates how deeply his imagination is engaged by this "pure woman." It was these constant shifts of perspective which Lionel Johnson protested in *The Art of Thomas Hardy*, pp. 209–55, but his own troubled response paradoxically shows them to be the source of the novel's power.

"drama" in certain special but, I hope, consistent ways. "Drama" is used as a term for the historical show that is panoramically presented on the terrestrial stage in one hundred and twenty-nine scenes. When we join to them the Fore Scene and the After Scene, with all the possibilities for meaning that are added by this reach toward ourselves through the presentation of other spectators removed from actual involvement in that history, then the larger, more inclusive term "poem" is used.

The visual term "perspective" will be used somewhat more loosely. In certain contexts it will mean "point of view" or "how it seems": as, "from the perspective of the Spirits" or "from the perspective of the humans toiling below." But in the overall scheme of this study it is generally meant substantively as referring to the material of vision, "what is seen," what *part* of the field of vision is laid open. Conflating several dictionary definitions has yielded one that will work for us: *perspective*, an aspect of life viewed from a particular standpoint (in this study, the standpoint of abstract intelligence looking back on the past to find some meaning emergent in experience). There seemed to be four main perspectives or "aspects of life" to consider in Hardy's vision, each of which is treated in one of the four chapters of this study. In each chapter the visualizing method, the recording eye of the poem, will belong to the Spirit Intelligences; yet that eye will not have to stand still upon the Overworld platform, but will shift and move, now close, now far, to deliver a full account of the aspect examined in that chapter.

The Phantom Intelligences give utterance to the major responses to life voiced by the mind—humanity's mind, Hardy's mind, the reader's mind. Hardy wrote in the *Life*, when he was developing his conception of these spectral figures:

> Abstract realisms to be in the form of Spirits, Spectral figures, etc.

The Realities to be the true realities of life, hitherto
called abstractions. The old material realities to be
placed behind the former, as shadowy accessories. (*Life*,
p. 177)

"The old material realities" are represented in the shadow-
show down on the terrestrial stage. But since, as we saw in
the passages quoted above, vision was more "real" to Hardy
than the material phenomena that stimulated it, the Spirits,
representing the responses made by human intelligence to
experience, are more "real" than the facts of history staged
before them. We can understand how they are "abstract"
by picturing them in terms of the waves of energy that are a
manifestation of the pulsations of the Will in the poem:
thus, they are the impressions brought by waves that have
travelled as far as possible from their original impact in
phenomena. These impressions are "collective": that is,
they represent intellectual positions contributed to by many
individuals through the ages. The shadow-patterns of
phenomena disappear before one's eyes; the world of abstract mental patterns is as dateless as the human mind:
there the oldest debates still pulse and hum in the emptiness
of space, drawing on new material only to exemplify their
views, and only rarely admitting into the dialectic a new
idea from the realm of time.

In our discussion of this abstract debate, the Spirit of the
Pities represents, as an ideal, charity, and, as a mental faculty, the sympathetic imagination that enacts charity. The
Spirit of the Years represents the ideal of objectivity as it is
approximated in the mental disciplines of the sciences,
philosophy, and history. The Recording Angel is the historical record; the Spirit of Rumour registers the first
reverberations set off by events, before these impressions
have settled into the permanent record. The Spirit Sinister
is read as though it were called the Spirit Cynical: it is the
voice of disappointed idealism, which looks for a malevolent
pattern behind events, just as the idealistic Spirit of the

Pities longs eventually to see a benevolent pattern there. The Spirit Ironic is the faculty that sees, as do the Spirit Sinister and the Pities, incongruity everywhere, but whose sight is content with that incongruity and looks for no pattern behind it. The Shade of the Earth is the voice of nature, of laboring matter, of flesh that is woven into existence to feel and to suffer until it is dissolved back into nescience.

But we miss the full suggestiveness of the Phantom Intelligences if we are satisfied with having put into words our own working definitions for each Spirit. Hardy warned his readers that *The Dynasts* would require the active involvement of the mental spectator. The Preface said, we recall, that the "panoramic show" enacted on the terrestrial stage would be "a series of historical 'ordinates' (to use a term in geometry): the subject is familiar to all; and foreknowledge is assumed to fill in the junctions required to combine the scenes into an artistic unity" (Preface, p. ix). What applies to the hundred and twenty-nine scenes of the *drama* I have taken to apply also to the *poem* that is framed and extended toward us by the Fore Scene and After Scene. There too a series of ordinates is presented to the reader, these being the responses the human mind has made to the experience of history. Again it is up to us, as mental spectators, to combine them into unity and meaning. As in geometry, certain guides to imagination have been set up by the poet in designing the poem; but the design is deliberately left to be completed in our minds, as each of us accomplishes the act of perception and artistry that Hardy set in motion.[41]

[41] I believe I have found one critic who has taken the Overworld design of the poem, as I have, to be deliberately incomplete. Barker Fairley, "Notes on the Form of *The Dynasts*," p. 415, sees that the poem gives the reader not a statement of poetic commentary but pieces of poetic commentary that he must put together into a statement. Fairley finds precedents for this openness of form in the choruses to *Antigone*, *Prometheus Bound*, Shakespeare's loosening of dramatic

31

When the various Overworld views are drawn into the mind and woven into a concluding pattern, each conclusion will differ because, as we know from Hardy the critic, each reader's mind differs. Is the drama of history an evil joke, as the Spirit Sinister would see it? Or is it a vast and entire illusion, as the Spirit Ironic wonders? Is it what the Spirit of the Years maintains, a web of intricate patterns whose patterning has no purpose or conscious direction, other than its own random activity? Is it what the Spirit of the Pities envisions, an open-ended, unfinished process of creation in which an informing consciousness of fairness has begun to stir?

The reader may give weight to any one, or to any combination, of these explanations. One possibility is to point to evidence in the poem of the growing assurance of the Pities,[42] and to conclude that *The Dynasts* comes down on the side of the "evolutionary meliorism" that Hardy declared elsewhere was a view he personally held at times. He commends the responsible realism of this position in his Preface to *Late Lyrics and Earlier* (1922) and illustrates it with a line from his poem, "In Tenebris": "If way to the Better there be, it exacts a full look at the Worst."[43] At one point, late in the *Life,* he uses the term "meliorist" to describe himself *(Life,* p. 387); and in a 1907 letter to Edward

stringencies, and the form of *Faust*; then puts all precedents aside. "*The Dynasts* . . . increases also the potential of dramatic expressiveness. [In] *The Dynasts* . . . explicitness [i.e., commentary or, in our terms, 'ordinates of vision'] takes its widest reach." And, p. 403: "No comprehensive piece of literature was ever so discontinuous as this epic-drama." (Fairley made this statement in 1919, just before Pound, Eliot, and Joyce published *their* "discontinuous" works.)

42 Some of the main critics who take this "optimistic" interpretation are: Amiya Chakravarty, *"The Dynasts" and the Post-War Age in Poetry*; Bailey, *Thomas Hardy and the Cosmic Mind*; Roy Morrell, *Thomas Hardy: The Will and the Way*; F. R. Southerington, *Hardy's Vision of Man.*

43 Thomas Hardy, "Preface," *Late Lyrics and Earlier*, in *Personal Writings*, ed. Orel, p. 52.

Wright included in the *Life* he sets forth the process by which meliorism might take place in the universal Will, and claims the idea as his own (*Life*, p. 335).

But it is also possible to find that the poem bears out the skeptical agnosticism of the Years,[44] since Hardy is careful to keep separate the poem as a whole from the particular views of any of the observers—even from the Pities, with their final song of hope.

This study, because it interprets the poem as a vision freely left to be completed in each spectator's mind, combines both readings. The position taken here is that, in the poem's presentation of the Spirit views, all (but especially the two leading ones of hope and skepticism) are equally valid—or invalid. Our particular reading happens to follow the general lines of the "hopeful" reading, but argues that the grounds for that hope exist as a possibility in the poem, not as a necessity.

Hardy himself, after writing *The Dynasts*, made various comments on its interpretation. In the 1907 letter to Edward Wright mentioned above, in which he discussed the idea that the mass of the Will might eventually become conscious of itself and ultimately sympathetic, he is proud to have arrived at that notion independently of other thinkers —if coincidentally with them (*Life*, p. 335). Yet, a few years later, during the gloom of World War I, he is able to be satisfied for the opposite reason—that he had not retained any of the "Good-God theory" in the concept of the First

---

[44] The following are some of the main critics who make this skeptical or "pessimistic" interpretation of the poem—and of Hardy—after taking *The Dynasts* into account: Abercrombie, *Thomas Hardy*, p. 205; Bonamy Dobrée, "Thomas Hardy," p. 19, "nullity"; Orel, *Thomas Hardy's Epic-Drama*, pp. 83–84; Pinion, *A Hardy Companion*, p. 115. See also Eleanor Chilton and Herbert Agar, *The Garment of Praise: The Necessity for Poetry*, pp. 311–24: the authors concede that the hope expressed by the Spirit of the Pities in the After Scene probably does represent Hardy's own hope; but he must be joking, they think, to entitle such wan hope "meliorism"—perhaps inflicting on us one more of his "little ironies."

Cause of things shown in *The Dynasts*—and he reflects that it might be well for Europe, now in a "present infamous and disgraceful state" despite some thousands of years of belief in a "God of Mercy," to give some trial to the "theory of a Goodless-and-Badless God (as in *The Dynasts*)" (*Life*, pp. 375–76). Just as Hardy, speaking of the Will as an idea, could derive from its neutrality different possibilities at different times, so he could speak about the conclusion to his poem. In 1914 (again during World War I) he commented to his wife that if he could have foreseen the coming of that convulsive war, "he would probably not have ended *The Dynasts* as he did end it" (*Life*, p. 368). He adds that his belief in "the gradual ennoblement of man" was undermined and a contrary notion strengthened, that "the never-ending push of the Universe was an unpurposive and irresponsible groping in the direction of least resistance" (*Life*, p. 368). His long-held assumption that the Napoleonic struggles had dispelled the "ardent romance" and "bluster" of war that had for so long taken in mankind was destroyed in 1914, he said (*Life*, pp. 365–66). But a remark he made before the war, in a 1908 letter to Edward Clodd, is wiser, and should, I think, supercede all comments which read "optimism" or "pessimism" into the poem's conclusion: "Yes: I left off on a note of hope. It was just as well that the Pities should have the last word, since, like *Paradise Lost*, *The Dynasts* proves nothing" (Appendix III to *Life*, p. 454).

If, as in our general interpretation and particular reading, the poem's hopeful conclusion is located in the active mind of the reader, that hopefulness can be carried far. For it is a basic assumption of the poem that the world can improve only if there comes about an increase in consciousness. By analogy, if consciousness is awakened in the mind of the reader—if he comes to share the Pities' urgent sensitivity to the world's need for conscious sympathy and "fairness"—then the mental universe is itself a little more awake, and evolutionary meliorism is not only a future possibility but, in one small instance, a present accomplishment. Per-

haps that is the dawn that the Pities turn to hail at the end
of the After Scene: the hope for an awakening and enlightenment in ourselves, just on the other side of the Overworld
and the poem.

The main objection that has been raised against *The
Dynasts* from the time of its publication until now is that
the Spirits, with their anatomizing vision of blind force and
their constant refrain upon its meaning, will not let the
Napoleonic story engage us, will not let us forget that its
end is foreknown and predetermined, not only before we
came to read it in our century or as it happened in the early
nineteenth century, but since the beginning of time. Thus
the critical consensus has been that the Overworld blocks
out whatever drama was inherent in the history dramatized
on the world stage below, so that all that remains is spectacle—though that spectacle a considerable one. (Here
critics have divided, giving more, or less, but always some,
praise to the intense visualization of action.) Our interpretation uses these same terms differently: the world is the
spectacle, and the Overworld, instead of being an obstruction, is the bridge that enables spectacle to become a dramatic act of perception and creation.

Any one approach, however far it may take us into a
poem, necessarily leaves ground uncovered as it makes its
particular way. As one example of necessary omission, the
visual lines of this study allow for discussion of the poem in
a visual sense only; much more remains to be said about the
texture and sound of the poetry.[45] But partial as this
particular approach may be, I believe I have established a
case for it as a method of access to *The Dynasts*: demonstrating in this introduction that Hardy thought about

---

[45] Some of the older commentaries on Hardy's verse are still the most
helpful for the reader seeking an appreciative understanding: Edmund
Gosse, "Mr. Hardy's Lyrical Poems" (1918); Arthur McDowall, *Thomas
Hardy* (1931); Edmund Blunden, *Thomas Hardy* (1941); C. M. Bowra,
"The Lyrical Poetry of Thomas Hardy" (1946); C. Day Lewis, "The
Lyrical Poetry of Thomas Hardy" (1951).

vision in certain ways that do have imaginative bearing on *The Dynasts*; and documenting in the chapters that follow the extent to which *The Dynasts* can usefully be understood as an enactment of vision.

An understanding of the workings of Hardy's imagination in this poem may and should take us nearer to a larger understanding: that of "the unity and wholeness of Hardy's vision, regardless of the genre in which he chose to write"— the study of which Helmut Gerber considers to be one of the major tasks still to be achieved in Hardy criticism.[46] Even as this study was being written, meanings that emerged from it suggested congruences with Hardy's other works. The shorter poems and the very titles of his volumes of poetry acquire a new resonance after *The Dynasts* has made one sensitive to Hardy's interest in the relativity of appearances, perspectives, perception, and vision. "Dream" is another prime example: it is impossible to read casually Sue's speculation in *Jude* that the First Cause worked like a somnambulist, or in *Tess* that the heroine moved in a kind of dream, or to pass over the word "dream" in any of the lyrics, after finding that word to be so heavily charged with poetic significance in *The Dynasts*. And so this study can lead to many more.

5. The Diorama

With so many features of the poem to be discussed in terms of vision, we require, like Hardy, a frame upon which to view them separately, in some sort of orderly sequence, and also to picture how they work together, interweaving in the mind to form a poetic whole. Hardy himself in the drama gives us the metaphor we have taken to structure this study: "And their great Confederacy dissolves like the diorama of a dream" (Semi-chorus II of the Pities, II,i,vii,168).

The diorama is an optical exhibit, housed in a cubicle

[46] Helmut E. Gerber and W. Eugene Davis, *Thomas Hardy: An Annotated Bibliography of Writings About Him*, "Introduction," p. 18.

with a viewing frame on the front. As on a conventional stage, there are stage borders and wings leading to an opaque backcloth. The diorama achieves an additional dimension of depth by placing a series of translucent veils between the fore-frame and the back-cloth. When colored lights positioned above are played upon and through these veils, they create vivid optical illusions in which apparently solid views disappear into one another and then reappear at will.

As the Oxford English Dictionary informs us under its entry for "diorama," the diorama had entered the English scene in 1823, before Hardy was born.[47] "The Diorama, invented by Daguerre and Bouton, was first exhibited in London, 29 Sept. 1823, the building being erected in Regent's Park. It was patented in 1824 by J. Arrowsmith, No. 4899. . . . 1823. Ann.Reg.309. It is called the Diorama, and the idea is borrowed from the panorama. 1824. J. ARROWSMITH Spec. Patent No. 4899 (title) An improved mode of publicly exhibiting pictures . . . which I denominate a 'diorama.' "

As a word, "diorama" seems to have entered literary use about a decade or so after its introduction into the language by Arrowsmith. Hardy probably missed encountering it in its early appearances under the variant forms of "dioramic" and "dioramist": "1831. BREWSTER *Nat. Magic* iv. (1833) 66 The same picture exhibited under all the imposing accompaniments of a dioramic representation. . . . 1834. HOOD *Tylney Hall* (1840) 246 Here an indignant dioramist raves at a boggling scene-shifter."

But he would have encountered it in some of the later literary entries that the dictionary records: "1872. GEO. ELIOT *Middlem.* liii, The memory has as many moods as the temper, and shifts its scenery like a diorama. . . . fig.

[47] These entries, definitions, and examples of usage for "diorama," "dioramic," and "dioramist" are taken from *The Oxford English Dictionary*, Compact Edition (New York: Oxford University Press, 1971), Vol. I, p. 732.

1876. L. TOLLEMACHE in *Fortn. Rev.* Jan 117 Literature is able . . . to give a diorama of what it depicts, while art can give only a panorama. . . . 1881. *Daily Tel.* 27 Dec., well-managed dioramic effects depicting a terrible storm with thunder and lightning."

Hardy definitely knew *Middlemarch*; he could have read the *Daily Telegraph* in some of his regular visits to London; he might or might not have come across Tollemache's suggestive remark in the *Fortnightly Review*. But what matters more, none of these quotations carry equivalents or definitions for "diorama." They assume that the general reader of that time would have recognized the invention that is referred to, without the explanation we need today. Hardy could still make this assumption when he used the word in *The Dynasts*.

Whether or not Hardy was thinking of the diorama when he gave form to the vision of his poem is not important to this study. All we need to do is to show that the figure offers a clear scheme and useful terms for envisioning what is at work in *The Dynasts*. But, as it happens, Hardy does in fact put into his poem a long passage in which the diorama can be felt as a presence behind us, demonstrating the virtuosity and range of its dissolving views. Perhaps he is enjoying a silent, allusive joke between himself and the knowing reader; perhaps the diorama is accidental and unconscious. At any rate, as the passage below will show, if the thing that is at work is not a diorama, it is very like one.

The passage occurs in the stage directions for the battle of Puebla Heights at Vitoria in Spain (III,ii,ii,367–68). Up until then the point of vision from which the drama is seen (by the Phantom Observers, with the reader watching over their shoulders) has shifted freely and almost playfully—now far, up in the sky, now near, into closed rooms and corners. Suddenly the perspectives that have been so freely at play are pulled together into one clear, demonstrative sequence, as though in a bravura display of all the different ways in which an object can be looked at, and is looked at, in the imagination of this poem. In discussing this passage I shall insert parenthetical explanations of the way in which each different view represents a major perspective in the poem's field of vision.

First we are shown the "normal" view of humans acting.

DUMB SHOW

All the English forces converge forward—that is, eastwardly—the centre over the west ridges, the right through the Pass to the south, the left down the Bilbao road on the north-west, the bands of the divers regiments striking up the same quick march, "The Downfall of Paris." (III,ɪɪ,ii,368)

Then a voice breaks in on the stage directions and changes the view.

SPIRIT OF THE YEARS

You see the scene. And yet you see it not.
What do you notice now?

There immediately is shown visually the electric state of mind that animates WELLINGTON, GRAHAM, HILL, KEMPT, PICTON, COLVILLE, and other responsible ones on the British side; and on the French KING JOSEPH stationary on the hill overlooking his own centre, and surrounded by a numerous staff that includes his adviser (sic) MARSHAL JOURDAN, with, far away in the field, GAZAN, D'ERLON, REILLE, and other marshals. This vision, resembling as a whole the interior of a beating brain lit by phosphorescence, in an instant fades again back to the normal. (III,ɪɪ,ii,368)

This is the anatomizing perspective Hardy uses to disclose, beneath the activity of the human drama, the force that directs all action—the force referred to by philosophers as "determinism" and called by Hardy in the poem "the Will," or "It." Hardy's master-image for it, a sleeping, animating brain, embodies two contradictory truths: an organism that is dreaming that it is a consciousness; and yet an organism that is unconsciously, beneath its dream, a network for blind, random, electric impulses. Like electricity, the Will is hard to visualize, more easily seen in the patterns and changes it effects. It works through the genetic and historical and social influences that shape every human being, his possibilities and impossibilities. To this inner shaping are added other figuring or disfiguring pressures from outside, which are easier to recognize as circumstantial, such as coincidence and chance. In Hardy's fiction the Will was viewed from this indirect and removed angle because his main focus was on the human lives that are shaped under pressure and revealed under pressure. But in this perspective of *The Dynasts* the focus is upon the Will in both its direct and its indirect manifestations. Sometimes it is manifested in the popular will that is courted by statesmen and generals. Sometimes it shows itself in the currently fashionable in opinion, dress, entertainment, manners. Sometimes it is present in a given character's sense of urgency toward one policy rather than toward another, a tendency in which reason has no part, except to be brought in after the fact for purposes of rationalization. Sometimes it is the resistance set up by a character to the general current, establishing a countercurrent. But underlying all these effects, and empowering them, it is primal Energy, which gives life to all living things and form to all bodies, which urges on all patterns and brings about all consequences.

The stage direction in our Vitoria-paradigm then shifts from energy back to substance, returning us to the usual, body-seeing human perspective and showing us one army, more animated, prevailing at Vitoria over another, less animated. We understand, now, why one army wins and the other loses. They think it is through their own effort, wit, and energy, but this "thought" is an illusion. Their very lives and fates are being dreamed by a mind asleep.

But, earlier in the same stage direction, before either of

these two views were set in motion, the scene had been pictured in two still different perspectives. The first can be called the likeness-revealing perspective. When it looks at man, it is reminded of the rest of creation as well. When it looks at other living things, it is reminded of man. Hardy links human and other phenomena at point after point, again and again, usually through similes in the prose descriptions. But perhaps the link that is the most suggestive is the one shown here, in which he pictures the shape of a human hand in the massive contours of the earth, and thus makes us feel earth as a living thing:

> By degrees the fog lifts, and the Plain is disclosed. From this elevation, gazing north, the expanse looks like the palm of a monstrous right hand, a little hollowed, some half-dozen miles across, wherein the ball of the thumb is roughly represented by heights to the east, on which the French centre has gathered; the "Mount of Mars" and of the "Moon" (the opposite side of the palm) by the position of the English on the left or west of the plain; and the "Line of Life" by the Zadorra, an unfordable river running from the town down the plain, and dropping out of it through a pass in the Puebla Heights to the south, just beneath our point of observation—that is to say, towards the wrist of the supposed hand. The left of the English army under GRAHAM would occupy the "mounts" at the base of the fingers; while the bent finger-tips might represent the Cantabrian Hills beyond the plain to the north or back of the scene. (III,ii,ii,367–68)

This perspective is followed by another that is quite different. This fourth perspective focusses on the distinctness, quiddity, uniqueness of each thing, where the interweaving perspective highlights what things have in common. With no more than a change in paragraphing Hardy silently makes the full shift in perception.

(. . . while the bent finger-tips might represent the Cantabrian Hills beyond the plain to the north or back of the scene.)

From the aforesaid stony crests of Puebla the white town and church towers of Vitoria can be described on a slope to the right-rear of the field of battle. A warm rain succeeds the fog for a short while, bringing up the fragrant scents from the fields, vineyards, and gardens, now in the full leafage of June. (III,II,ii,368)

It is as though the phenomena noted in this last perspective had just crept onto the edges of the viewer's consciousness, but not into the center of his concern. They register on the frame of the senses—fragrant scents, sounds of leafage, colors and angled surfaces. But their existence, and their presence, is coincidental. They make an "impression" on the neutrally recording consciousness, which records that impression without attaching to it any comment. Unnoticed, or not commented upon, by the actors and watchers of the drama, they are presented for us to notice and make of them what we will.

The dioramic effects in the passage above are unique in *The Dynasts,* in that nowhere else in the poem will we see them displayed in such close sequence. But they should give us a glimpse of the variety and beauty that can be achieved through such shifts in mode and point of view, and make us the more willing to use the diorama as a mechanism for looking closely into the poem's vision.

Let us suppose, then, that we have before us a model of a diorama-theatre and that we can project onto its boxed stage these four main visual perspectives of *The Dynasts.* We will then have a picture that makes clear the logic of the sequence of chapters that follow. At the back of the stage hangs the view to infinity, the impenetrable veil behind all the other dissolving veils. On this backcloth Hardy has imagined an evolving brain weaving tissues of itself, whose extending and retracting fibers are the phenomena of life

(Chapter One). At the front of the stage move the fleshly characters of the drama, solid to their own eyes, but mere shades to us, who are always reminded of the view through them to the back of the stage. The human beings who are agitated and energized by the Napoleonic struggle occupy the stage center, and are made known to us by their speech and actions (Chapter Two). On either side of them, linked by the poet's imagery and narrative detail, are other natural phenomena related to them by their mutually shared condition of total dependency upon the Will that lies in back of them all (Chapter Three). And along the periphery, on the diorama's viewing frame, are phenomena that seem to be there for some different reason, or for no reason. Their dependence on the all-defining Will, while not denied, is not exposed to the diorama's full dissolving light. These phenomena, which compound the spectacle with their seeming-free existence, are indications that the immense creative energy beneath the poetic universe is weaving many dramas in dimensions not yet exhibited, not yet dreamed of (Chapter Four).

6. DIORAMIC VISION

We come back to the remoteness and flatness, the lack of drama, that, as noted, is the traditional objection that has been brought against *The Dynasts,* and the quality that has done most to obstruct wider appreciation of the poem. Does looking at *The Dynasts* primarily as a vision, and looking at that vision as though it were a diorama, provide an answer to that criticism; or does it only restate it, after all, in new, visual terms? Hardy himself in the poem voices what we might call the informed criticism of his diorama. The words he uses for it—"spectacle," "exhibit," "display," "demonstration," "scene," "pictures of the play," and "show" (every kind of show: puppet-show, lantern-show, phantasmagoric show, "curst" show, "galanty"-show, "idle" show, and "forthshowing")—are all flat, static ones. They suggest magic shows, optical illusions designed to divert and to fool the simple with their "effects" and "impressions." Is it not a real problem with Hardy's dioramic poem that it holds up to us an image that is static—that sleeping brain—while dazzling our eyes with life-like optical effects and illusions of movement? True, the theatre-box, the system of illumination, the whole structure and conception, are beautiful and ingenious. But as with all ingenious toys that offer the illusion of living movement, the time must come when its effects become repetitive, its illusion guessed, and it is proved to be a lifeless machine after all, and a limited one.

How can a diorama, which is an arrangement of flat painted surfaces to give the appearance of depth and movement, answer this objection? The answer lies in the fact that what begins in an arrangement of surfaces becomes a free-standing object of art and a freeing act of vision.

The Dynasts, as this study assumes, and as Chapter One will attempt to prove, is first of all a poem: an expressive structure that uses prose and verse to create a rounded image that reinforces itself in every word and detail. There is a purposeful relationship that functions between the poem's underlying brain-image and the visual techniques by which the scenes are presented and stage directions silently noted, between the Overworld and world of time and space, and the optical exhibit that moves and shows all: a relationship the reader can recognize because it comes alive in his own eye and mind. Another extension of this mental-optical relationship is the poem's dioramic system of lighting, whose changing illumination will be described in Chapter Two: the solid view, the anatomizing view, and, shading between these, the dissolving view, in which all judgments on actions, all distinctions of persons, all living things themselves, are subdued to the status of a dream of the mind. These and other extensions of the poem's image (followed in Chapters Three and Four) create so intricate and unified a network connecting the poem's various surfaces and perspectives that the poem pulls together before

44

our eyes its own separate system and universe. Thus it achieves an autonomous existence, independent of circumstances, independent of the dioramist and the viewer, the autonomy of art. It has become a source for our impressions, and a place to which we may come again to renew or to adjust them.

The poem Hardy has achieved is, therefore, a rounded object, possessing facets and depths whose interest and beauty are not exhausted after their illusion, the logic of their joining, is perceived. But, in addition, *The Dynasts* is a poem for the mental spectator, in whose mind it is fulfilled—in the unpredictable, open-ended, collaborative way we have described—as a drama. In all seeing, flat surfaces outside the eye reflect waves of light to the eye; but it is only then, when the waves are focussed, inverted, and projected back onto a corresponding visual field, and there, in the depths where they are interpreted, that vision takes place. There the intellectual drama is continued to its unpredictable resolution, in a theatre that corresponds to the model Hardy holds up to us.

We bring to *The Dynasts* minds long since shaped into broad types and subtle individualities by our histories, the shared and the private, that part of it we are aware of and all the rest we can never know. What we see in the poem, what we discover and help to create, will vary with each reader and the circumstances of each reading. We can cite Hardy's own words to the would-be seer as the charter for our idiosyncratic visions: ". . . the seer should watch that pattern among general things which his idiosyncrasy moves him to observe, and describe that alone . . ." (*Life*, p. 153).

Certainly the reading of *The Dynasts* offered in this study has been shaped by the history that has elapsed since the poem was published. A chronological reading of Hardy criticism tells us that such has ever been the case. We carry the memory of our lifetimes, which almost touch the end of Hardy's lifetime, when he reflected on the hope at the close of his poem in the light of the First World War. We must

45

say of the ensuing world history that we have experienced that we do not seem to have succeeded in doing better, although perhaps we do know a little better. But that is ambiguous evidence: does it confirm hope, or despair? Also, we bring to the poem our contemporary interest in the relationship between mind and body, the conscious and the unconscious, and the possibility of traffic between the two. Recent events, too, have forced us to become more sensitive to the mutual dependence of all life on this planet. Thus educated as readers, when we arrive at *The Dynasts* it is as though Hardy had looked ahead to our experience and had waiting for us a vision that could take us into its imagination, even as it so easily and beautifully encompassed worlds extending into all dimensions of space, up to the stellar reaches and down to microscopic galaxies, even as it set afloat the human mind also as one more world in the whole wondrous immensity.

Our literal translation, into the terms of contemporary biology and physics, of the time-honored microcosm-macrocosm metaphor, is frankly anachronistic—although I do not think Hardy would have disapproved. He might, however, have wondered at how much we make in this study of the suggestive correspondence between our own mind and the poem's "mind," its Overworld consciousness dreamily, musingly, poised over dreaming unconsciousness. If that emphasis would seem to him idiosyncratic, then what we have described as his peripheral perspective might seem even more to merit that term. He would recognize the substance of what is seen in it—the "little things" and "unbid sights" that creep in along the edge of vision and draw away some of the attention that would be centered on "death's dyed stage." But he might have been surprised at the power we find in them to irradiate.

Here we shall call in a last comment of Hardy's on vision —a comment that applies specifically to the reader and critic:

The [proper critical] aim should be the exercise of a generous imaginativeness, which shall find in a tale not only all that was put there by the author, put he it never so awkwardly, but which shall find there what was never inserted by him, never foreseen, never contemplated. Sometimes these additions which are woven around a work of fiction by the intensive power of the reader's own imagination are the finest parts of the scenery.[48]

His concluding sentence may carry a trace of irony—Hardy had to suffer much from being misread. But from all he wrote about seeing, and all he gave us of his seeing, I believe he would have stood on his words, and would have had us stand there too.

[48] Thomas Hardy, "The Profitable Reading of Fiction," in *Personal Writings*, ed. Orel, p. 112.

ONE

THE ANATOMIZING LIGHT

1. "Key-Scene to the Whole":
The View Presented in the Six Transparencies

THE light of the diorama penetrates and makes transparent all of the seemingly solid organisms in the exhibit until it falls upon the organism behind all—the impenetrable web that is the "key-scene to the whole" (Fore Scene, 6). This key scene depicts an enormous brain underlying and animating the whole material universe. Though some of its projections beat to its pulses with more stress than others, all things move and have their being by its rhythms. All kinds of space—mental, terrestrial, extra-terrestrial—are at the same place, because upon that one brain. All the other categories by which humans organize phenomena—time and cause and composition and motive—are only thoughts of that brain, manifestations of its life-beat or "Will."

This is to state bluntly a defining metaphor that is presented with consistent tact in *The Dynasts*. Hardy keeps before us the uncaptureability of the life-force he pretends to capture in light and shadow at the back-scene of his diorama.

> The PRIME, that willed ere wareness was,
> Whose Brain perchance is Space, whose Thoughts
>   its laws,
> Which we as threads and streams discern,
> We may but muse on, never learn.
>   (General Chorus, Fore Scene, 7)

It is (italics mine) *"like* the lobule of a Brain," he says when he first introduces the image; and, in the passage above, "perchance." When the brain next appears directly, "there

48

is again beheld *as it were* the interior of a brain *which seems to* manifest the volitions of a Universal Will" (Stage directions, I,i,vi,36). Subsequent displays continue in this openly tentative, approximating fashion: the network of "currents and ejections" behind masses of humanity is "brain-*like*" (Stage directions, I,vi,iii,118); penetrating vision brings into view the *"films or* brain-tissues" of the Immanent Will (Stage directions, III,i,i,330); the electric state of mind that animates English forces in Spain and fails to animate French ones is revealed in a vision *"resembling as a whole* the interior of a beating brain lit by phosphorescence" (Stage directions, III,ii,ii,368). Thus there is a tentative and approximate, wondering kind of film over Hardy's image for the life-force.

THE metaphysical image is presented through the six transparencies that are revealed at strategic intervals in the action. Each contributes its layer of suggestion to the whole image and its shading to the scene in the drama against which it is projected. This discussion will follow the sequence of those transparencies in pointing out the elements Hardy incorporated into his image of the unconscious brain.

The first transparency appears in the Fore Scene (pages 6 and 7), when the drama taking place on Europe is about to be opened to the phantom intelligences "scene by scene." Beneath the far view of "the spectacle of Europe's moves," beneath the closer view of "writhing" peoples, is revealed an x-ray "anatomy of life and movement" that takes the shape of a single organism. The movement is described first by the Spirit of the Pities in a layman's vocabulary: "Strange waves . . . like winds grown visible"; winding, retracting, looking as fragile as gossamers but in fact irresistible, and bearing men's forms on their coils. The Spirit of the Years translates this report into a more scientific, properly anatomical vocabulary: ". . . fibrils, veins,/Will-tissues, nerves, and pulses of the Cause. . . ." Through these bodily organs the Will labors: "These are the Prime Volitions...."

In the second transparency (I,1,vi,36) the same "preternatural" vision that we beheld before the terrestrial drama as an abstraction is now revealed through the context of a particular earthly situation, to show its implications for individual lives. Napoleon's coronation at Milan is an important scene, for it is the first time we actually see him in the drama and it is at the decisive moment when he assumes for himself the symbol of empire and destiny, forswearing the libertarian ideals in whose name he came to power. Ironies are shown behind ironies: the cathedral prelates are constrained to crown Napoleon, and constrained, moreover, to pretend to do so as though by free choice; Napolean crowns himself even as he claims to bend to God's will; and the Pities blame Napoleon's "active soul, fair freedom's child" (I,1,vi,33) for advancing along this hypocritical course; when in reality, according to the transparency-slide brought in by the Years, all of the actors in the scene are passive, and all are unconsciously like the prelates, constrained to act as though by free choice.

The third transparency emphasizes the cruel, crude aspects of the brain's control. This view is shown by the Years in order to correct the Pities' impulse to pray to the Will for some alleviation of the suffering that will come in the battle of Austerlitz.

SPIRIT OF THE YEARS

> Again ye deprecate the World-Soul's way
> That I so long have told? Then note anew
> (Since ye forget) the ordered potencies,
> Nerves, sinews, trajects, eddies, ducts of It
> The Eternal Urger, pressing change on change.

At once, as earlier, a preternatural clearness possesses the atmosphere of the battle-field, in which the scene becomes anatomized and the living masses of humanity

50

transparent. The controlling Immanent Will appears therein, as a brain-like network of currents and ejections, twitching, interpenetrating, entangling, and thrusting hither and thither the human forms. (I,vi, iii,118)

The language of the stage-directions and of the Spirit of the Years enforces the fact that these ordered potencies cannot be addressed as a person and entreated for mercy. The harsh verbs ("twitching," "entangling," "thrusting") indicate not only power but overriding power; the list of the parts of "It," presented without a break to show the relentlessness and totality of the pressures ("potencies/Nerves, sinews, trajects, eddies, ducts"), demonstrates that the humans have no place to hide, as well as no one to pray to.

This is the most harshly and negatively put of the transparencies, but the Spirit Intelligences do not seem here as sensitive to its harshness as we might expect. The Pities do in fact pray again later in the drama to the Will. And at this very point the Ironic Spirits sing a song in which they take the Years' last words, "pressing change on change," and, giving the image of pressing a surprisingly positive twist, compare the Will to "some sublime fermenting vat":

SEMICHORUS I OF IRONIC SPIRITS

Heaving throughout its vast content
With strenuously transmutive bent
Though of its aim unsentient. . . .
(I,vi,iii,119)

They go on to sing that this transmutive process has worked prodigally from as far back as consciousness can remember:

SEMICHORUS II OF IRONIC SPIRITS

He of the Years beheld, and we,
Creation's prentice artistry
Express in forms that now unbe

SEMICHORUS I OF IRONIC SPIRITS

Tentative dreams from day to day;
Mangle its types, re-knead the clay
In some more palpitating way; . . .

(I,vi,iii,119)

The image of artistry introduced here is striking: the sublime fermenting-vat, "strenuously transmutive," shaping its
tentative dreams, then crushing them, then rekneading them
in new trembling outlines. Even with its wastefulness this
kind of creative determinism is much easier to accept than
that mechanical determinism which merely twitches human
forms hither and thither. The change lies in the addition
of "fermenting vat" to "pressing change on change" and of
the word "transmutive" to the transparency picture of
"strenuously."

The fourth transparency gathers up the suggestions from
the Spirits that the brain is an unconscious artist. Napoleon
is about to cross the Niemen into Russia, and the Pities are
moved to wonder how he could make so self-destructive a
decision.

SPIRIT OF THE YEARS

I'll show you why.

The unnatural light before seen usurps that of the
sun, bringing into view, like breezes made visible, the
films or brain-tissues of the Immanent Will, that pervade all things, ramifying through the whole army,
NAPOLEON included, and moving them to Its inexplicable artistries. (III,i,i,330)

The shift from a biological and mechanical emphasis is ac-
companied by a shift in language: the body organs that
clotted together into a lobule have here become brain-tissues, films like gauzes moving on a mysterious loom; and
where the unconscious brain's omnipotence had resided in
its totalitarian power, now that omnipotence lies in the in-
explicability of its artistry. The implications of the new

quality in the unconscious brain are liberating for man. The harshly, assertively scientific mode reduced brain and man to an object. Seeing the universal brain poetically as another artist elevates brain and man to being subject as well as object. To partake in artistry may not be quite the same as to be entirely unconditioned; yet there is something about art, some "inexplicable" cooperation between inner and outer fulfilment, the nature of the material and the nature of the design, that satisfies freedom. With this transparency Hardy has brought into play in the drama two complementary vocabularies for describing the brain and two modes of looking at it. We will be able to think of both these vocabularies when the poem uses words to do with weaving—web, loom, fabric, threads, strands, spinning, knitting, mending, patterning—for by now Hardy has made us perceive a similarity between the processes of biology and art, and between the wet tissues in flesh and the tissues in the dry artifact we call cloth.

Transparency five, shown behind the Dumb Show of the battle of Puebla Heights in Spain, reveals how the animating Will makes some of its projections potent and others ineffective, impotent.

> There immediately is shown visually the electric state of mind that animates WELLINGTON . . . and other responsible ones on the British side; and on the French KING JOSEPH stationary on the hill overlooking his own centre, and surrounded by a numerous staff. . . . This vision, resembling as a whole the interior of a beating brain lit by phosphorescence, in an instant fades again back to the normal. (III,ii,ii,368)

The logic that the first five transparencies have contributed to the drama up to this point is that men are to be understood as totally subsumed in the Will's "mechanized enchantment" (Spirit of the Years at Borodino, III,i,v,344). But at Albuera a new note is introduced by the Spirits—a sense in which men can be seen as partly dissociated from

53

the "causal coils in passionate display" (II,vi,iv,299) that has been the spectacle of this drama. It is the sense that perhaps they, too, like the Will behind them, move in a dream.

SPIRIT OF THE PITIES
. . . On earth below
Are men—unnatured and mechanic-drawn—
Mixt nationalities in row on row,
    Wheeling them to and fro
In moves dissociate from their souls' demand,
For dynasts' ends that few even understand!

SPIRIT OF THE YEARS
Speak more materially, and less in dream.
(II,vi,iv,299)

The sixth transparency puts that dream-sense before us. Once again the Spirit of the Pities is being corrected by the Years for identifying too closely with the strained feelings of one of the human actors—here, Wellington in his crisis at Waterloo.

SPIRIT OF THE YEARS
        Know'st not at this stale time
That shaken and unshaken are alike
But demonstrations from the Back of Things?
Must I again reveal It as It hauls
The halyards of the world?

A transparency as in earlier scenes again pervades the spectacle, and the ubiquitous urging of the Immanent Will becomes visualized. The web connecting all the apparently separate shapes includes WELLINGTON in its tissue with the rest, and shows him, like them, as acting while discovering his intention to act. By the lurid light the faces of every row, square, group, and column of men, French and English, wear the expression of those of people in a dream.

54

SPIRIT OF THE PITIES
Yes, sire; I see.
Disquiet me, I pray, no more!

The strange light passes, and the embattled hosts on
the field seem to move independently as usual.

(III,vii,vii,505)

As matter, the shapes in the tissue are totally taken up in
the whole; as energized consciousness, there is some part in
each shape that, while it is being moved, is "discovering his
intention" to be moved—some unmoved part that carries
on that observing and discovering, some part that is apart
from the dream itself, so that it can be said to be *in* a dream.

These, then, bluntly stated, are the characteristics of the
recurring image of the unconscious brain-web that dominates the drama. It is the object of its own predictable scientific laws of matter and force and thus can be described
in scientific vocabulary; it subjects matter to certain spontaneous, unpredictable processes of creation and thus can be
spoken of in poetic language; and it dreams, a mental phenomenon that, both science and art agree, is essential to the
body's creation and renewal.

This much is true of the brain-image itself. But there are
other respects in which that key image to the whole opens
up the drama for the reader. The spirits, as projectors and
viewers of the diorama, present the picture of a great unconscious brain. But this is not the whole picture: the spirits
themselves form part of the total image that we see. They
are faculties of consciousness that have evolved from the
great unconscious center, drawing life-energy from its darkness and beating to its rhythms. They are always "ITS
slaves" (I,vi,viii,137) at base, and "at most" its "accessory"
and "bounden witness of Its laws" (I,i,ii,15). Grounded
in the brain, yet at their tips they are able to circle, bend
and sway over the dark matter beneath them, and to commune together over the meaning or meaninglessness of it all.

The composite image of both together, unconscious and

55

conscious, resembles man's brain. Indeed, I read the two, the universal and the human brain, as being interchangeable. The Spirits sing of having been projected from two sources:

CHORUS (aerial music)
Yea, from the Void we fetch, like these,
And tarry till That please
To null us by Whose stress we emanate.—
Our incorporeal sense,
Our overseeings, our supernal state,
Our readings Why and Whence,
Are but the flower of Man's intelligence;
And that but an unreckoned incident
Of the all-urging Will, raptly magnipotent.
(I,VI,viii,137)

But the human mind from which they have flowered is but a film on the Universal Unconsciousness; and so I believe that this particular ambiguity works, as do the "Gauzes or screens to blur outlines" that Hardy recommends in his Preface (xi), to blur the macrocosm and the microcosm into one.

The poem as a whole, with its phantom-audience and diorama-drama, is designed to be experienced in the mind of the human being who reads it. The Overworld is where the intelligences, "spirits," sit and express the human reader's views of life outside of and inside of himself, a conscious and unconscious body.

When the two worlds are given this "free" interpretation and viewed as two layers of the human mind, *The Dynasts* is opened up and revealed to be a new poem, holding in itself possibilities for life, fluidity, and suggestiveness unexpected by the modern reader. And, conversely, when those worlds are interpreted literally and narrowly, as they have been by most critics, as conventional renditions of the levels of heaven and earth in the old epics, then one is perplexed by the fact that Hardy wrote a poem in the epic-tradition of Homer and Milton without attaining the suspense and the suspension of disbelief of those epics. That perplexity has characterized the majority view of *The Dynasts*. But there are a few critics who have interpreted Hardy's two worlds in ways that approximate or corroborate the reading offered in this study, and I will cite them here in order to gather into one place what is to date a minority opinion.[1]

Bonamy Dobrée asks whether, in the passage quoted above, the Spirits are flowers thrown up by "Man's intelligence" or by the Will; and concludes that we never quite know, but that this "indecision" "irks" our thought, left free in this way by Hardy, into "further activity."[2] Two other critics, Walter de la Mare[3] and Vivian de Sola Pinto,[4] go beyond Dobrée in decisiveness. They identify the Intelligences as aspects of the reader-spectator's intelligence, and, on the basis of that identification, predict that *The Dynasts* will be adopted by future generations as a work in advance of its time because of the modernity of its theme of consciousness and the originality of its treatment of that theme. As to treatment, both critics agree with Barker Fairley[5] that this dramatic portrayal of shifts of consciousness (Fairley describes it as making the implicit explicit;[6] de la Mare, as the fusion of the subjective mode of fiction with the objective mode of drama)[7] is the single most remarkable feature of *The Dynasts*, representing Hardy's imaginative contribution to the advance of modern literature. Pinto goes on to note that the unconscious Will combines with the Over-

---

[1] An historical overview of minority opinions on Hardy, and of the changes in majority opinion, is supplied by Gerber and Davis, *Thomas Hardy: An Annotated Bibliography*.

[2] Bonamy Dobrée, "*The Dynasts*," pp. 113–14.

[3] Walter de la Mare, "*The Dynasts*," in *Private View*, pp. 24–25.

[4] Vivian de Sola Pinto, "Hardy and Housman," pp. 52–53.

[5] Barker Fairley, "Notes on the Form of *The Dynasts*," pp. 401–15, passim.

[6] *Ibid.*, p. 415.

[7] De la Mare, "*The Dynasts*," in *Private View*, p. 24.

world and that the two together make up Hardy's "masterly portrayal of the structure of the modern mind."[8] And when D. H. Lawrence analyzes the character of Clym Yeobright in his *Study of Thomas Hardy*,[9] he seems to be pointing to this same imaginative correspondence of the human and the universal unconscious in Hardy. Clym was blind to attempt to calculate a moral chart for life from the surface of life because—and here follows the Laurencian co-relation: the mysterious resonance of Clym's own heart was as far removed from his thinking, talking, and knowing as the stars and the whole stellar universe are from any chart of the heavens. Just as knowledge and chart are co-related, so are heart-within and universe-without.

The last critic in this group is Katherine Anne Porter, who, talking not about *The Dynasts* but about Hardy's work as a whole, draws that correlation even more tightly into a common identity, and expresses in two paragraphs what this chapter will argue is contained in the special terms and details of *The Dynasts*:

"He did believe with a great deal of commonsense that man could make the earth a more endurable place for himself if he would, but he also realized that human nature is not grounded in commonsense, that there is a deep place in it where the mind does not go, where the blind monsters sleep and wake, war among themselves, and feed upon death.

"He did believe that there is 'a power that rules the world' though he did not name it, nor could he accept the names that had been given it, or any explanation of its motives. He could only watch its operations, and to me it seems he concluded that both malevolence and benevolence originated in the mind of man, and the warring forces were within him alone; such plan as existed in regard to him he had created for himself, his Good and his Evil were alike the mysterious inventions of his own mind; and why this

8 Pinto, p. 53.
9 D. H. Lawrence, "Study of Thomas Hardy," p. 418.

was so, Hardy could not pretend to say. He knew there was an element in human nature not subject to mathematical equation or the water-tight theories of dogma, and this intransigent, measureless force, divided against itself, in conflict alike with its own system of laws and the unknown laws of the universe, was the real theme of Hardy's novels; a genuinely tragic theme in the grand manner, of sufficient weight and shapelessness to try the powers of any artist."[10]

Originating from the unconscious mind (of mankind, of the poet,[11] of the reader, of the Universe), the Spirits have come into consciousness at different stages of life and with different stages of life and with different angles of intelligence. The Spirit of the Years, the oldest and highest projection, can see the farthest, looking back to the "germ of Being" (Fore Scene, 2). When the Will sets forth in time and space one of the ribands of its "web Enorm," the Years can see as a whole the design the drowsing knitter is playing out "in skilled unmindfulness," even before that design is accomplished in time. He can picture entire webs spun out from the unconscious brain; he can imagine the reach of all the webs fringed together out into the gulfs of nothingness; and he can even concentrate and "visualize the Mode" (Fore Scene, 6) of how brain's spinning works, eyelessly making and unmaking. But he cannot see what is contrary to his own long mental experience, and so he cannot imagine the Will's ever changing, and he cannot imagine, except intellectually, what it feels to be living in the flesh.

For this reason, the Spirit of the Pities, youngest of the Intelligences and "lowest" in the sense of being the least able to have a high, generalizing perspective, is the most important of the phantom intelligences. He has the closest

[10] Katherine Anne Porter, "Notes on a Criticism of Thomas Hardy," pp. 157–58.

[11] Hardy once wrote that what he liked about the late Wagner (and about late Turner and other artists in their final, mature phase) was the disclosure of the inmost recesses of idiosyncrasy, the "spectacle of the inside of a brain at work like the inside of a hive." *Life*, p. 329.

sense of body and its feelings of pain and of free, heavy responsibility. He is the one who corrects Year's "correct" but reductive terms for men ("mannikins," "jackaclocks," "jacks," "homuncules," etc.):

> They are shapes that bleed, mere mannikins or no,
> And each has parcel in the total Will. (Fore Scene, 4)

Because of his closeness to the body and its feelings, he is able to perform the act of sympathetic identification that is Imagination's basic leap. The story of the Napoleonic drama belongs to the Spirit of the Years. The basic method in which it is bodied forth with all its sensations, sufferings, and sense of life as well as of death, and the intuitions that bodily experience uniquely yields, is adapted to the faculties of the Spirit of the Pities. His very shortsightedness, his plaintive need to ask at time helplessly, "Where are we? And why are we where we are?" (above the Russian army in the snows of Lithuania, III,i,ix,352), result from his intensity of vision, recreating what it is like to live life in another's body—or what it is to live in one's own body, taking the mind outside the wall of the skull and the limits of purely conceptual experience.

These two are the poles of Intelligence. The other spirits are shades, more or less, between these, whose voices contribute perspectives that it would be out of tone or character for the two main intelligences to express but that are needed to bring out aspects of the drama and to give a sense of roundedness to the intellectual debate. As distinct voices, they speculate about the pulsions of the Will. Separately and in chorus they muse in wonder upon its rhythms and make those rhythms into song.

THE final impression of the brain image, after the three parts of the drama have been played before it and the viewers have been left in the overworld, is of roundness.

There is the roundness, first, of the debate. In the Fore Scene (p. 2) the Pities ask if it may not be thought that the consciousness of the Will may at some future point awaken, and the Spirit of the Years replies no, not according to his way of thinking. In the After Scene the same question and answer are exchanged, with the same basic positions of hope and skepticism expressed, even though the weight of authority has shifted between the two speakers and the Spirit of the Pities is able to charm the Spirit of the Years with his hymn of how the Will should be, and to open his mind to the thrill of a stirring in the air which is *"like* (italics mine) to sounds of joyance" (After Scene, 525). But each Intelligence, while informing the others, has maintained the integrity of his own point of view.

Then there is the circularity of paradoxes that the poem seems constructed to cup so that they roll endlessly: dream and reality. Who is awake to the Truth, the Years or the Pities? Who is locked in a dream based on showings, the Pities or the Years? (Spirit of the Years, After Scene, 522). Is the hope of waking an illusion, or, rather, is the certainty of never-waking, of ever-dreaming, the illusion? And who knows, anyway, in this performance of gauzes and screens, anatomies and transparencies and strange lights, in which spectral phantom intelligences are held to be the true realities and human bodies are supposedly display figures, what is real and awake and what is dream?

> As once a Greek asked I would fain ask too,
> Who knows if all the Spectacle be true,
> Or an illusion of the gods (the Will,
> To wit) some hocus-pocus to fulfil?
> (After Scene, 524)

Is not this presentation of a solid world as though it were a "fixed foresightless dream" (III,vii,viii,517) itself a conjuror's trick?

How very skillful and thorough a conjuring-trick it is we begin to appreciate when we study how all the anomalous features of its presentation, its strange "effects," cooperate to make us experience *The Dynasts* as though we were dreaming it. Two early critics, Walter de la Mare and George R. Elliott, have tried usefully to account for some of the means by which Hardy achieved this sense of illusion in the poem.

There is, first, the swiftness of the scene-changes. As Elliott puts it: "the folk and their rulers pass and repass before us in 130 [sic; should be 129] scenes each of which is so clearly drawn as to fascinate the eye, and so swift and insulated as to give us just that sense of unreality which is in the author's heart."[12] The vaporous curtains that close each scene accord with the disembodied nature of dream, and contribute a dream's sense of inevitability. De la Mare notes: "stealthily and hitchlessly the scenes clear, brighten, fade, and close; out of the 'unapparent' voices speak."[13] De la Mare holds that while this dreamlike mode of visualization remains faithful to the history that it sets out to present (preserving its manifold outlines), it succeeds in bathing all in "an atmosphere of pure imagination, an imagination with the powers of a creative, all-seeing spectator to whom the whole complex drama is but a succession of mental phenomena."[14]

Then there are the dreaming characters. (We recall that in the sixth transparency each combatant at Waterloo was shown "acting while discovering his intention to act" and wearing, in the lurid anatomizing light, "the expression of those of people in a dream.") De la Mare continues: the prospect of Hardy's characters acting out their parts in a hypnotic trance is itself hypnotizing to us, so that, "whatever our wonder and delight or horror and revulsion may be in surveying his vast spectacle, we are very rarely stirred out of the trance. . . . We are in thrall to a dream—and to a dream that comes at times very near to crossing the border-line of nightmare."[15] Elliott agrees: "The whole is the vivid

12 George R. Elliott, "Hardy's Poetry and the Ghostly Moving-Picture," p. 288.
13 De la Mare, "*The Dynasts*," in *Private View*, p. 26.
14 *Ibid.*, p. 24.   15 *Ibid.*, p. 25.

and naive architecture of a dream. . . ."[16] It is our dream of a dream.

So the shadowy images reflect and repeat themselves and the paradoxes echo, and Hardy has created the perfect circular container for them, a sealed perpetual-motion box. For the brain-image is a circle too: "the dreaming, dark, dumb Thing" (After Scene, 524) shaped like a lobule; the antennae-like projections hovering above, watching its weavings, bending over to weave in and out among them. Around all we may imagine the orb of a skull. Against its bone-case reverberate the sounds of the aerial music from the consciousness, the dreamy monotonic mumming speech of the actors (Preface, x–xi) and the "curiously hypnotizing" pulse-rhythms of the unconscious. Through its darkness

> . . . ghastly gulfs of sky,
> Where hideous presences churn through the dark—
> Monsters of magnitude without a shape,
> Hanging amid deep wells of nothingness.
>
> (After Scene, 522)

are interwoven limitless threads of light and shade. It is a wonderful image.

And, finally, there are the meanings circling from the interchangeability of the universal and the human brains: the helplessness to date of the Universal Intelligence to bring the rule of force under the control of wise governance, and man's helplessness; the Universe's tentative creativity, and man's; nature being the same in both.

These new meanings are the result of our reading so much into Hardy's crucial ambiguity (see the Final Chorus, I,vi, vii,137, already discussed) as to what is the actual base of the "flower of man's intelligence" whose murmurings we hear in the poem as the various Spirit Intelligences. For the first set of correspondences with which we fill the space left undefined by Hardy (universal brain is human brain, and

16 Elliott, "Ghostly," p. 288.

spirit consciousness is our consciousness) leads us on to the next set of correspondences between human-universal actions and the human-universal Unconscious (both being body, lying at the base of thought).

The meanings stirred up by this "free" reading should shift the poles that have traditionally defined critical discussion of Hardy's view of the universe and man. It has become a truism to say that for Hardy there is a tragic flaw in the universe but not in man.[17] The corollary drawn by some critics is that if man is innocent, Hardy must fix responsibility on something outside him—on society, or the Universe.[18] Guerard expresses perhaps the strongest version of the view—and reaction against it—that Hardy makes too much of a case for humanity. He is troubled by the implication in Hardy that people get a "raw deal" from life: such extenuating sympathy, he holds, is too indulgent to man (especially to that strong tendency toward self-indulgence in every reader) to allow us to see Hardy as a tragic artist of the first order.[19] But in our reading, the tragic flaw runs through a much larger subject than is commonly stated, and individual man, society, and the universe suffer the same condition of being victim and victimizing. Thus it becomes harder to fix poles of blame and extenuation, and the famous pity, which now happens to include man, becomes a larger and more mysterious matter, and it is less possible to consider it a movement of self-indulgence. Further, there are certain terms that are too often put into service as opposing alternatives in discussions of Hardy: man vs. "It" (the source of life); man, here, vs. nature (other living things) out there; the innocent urge to be happy that all of Hardy's main characters have, vs. the more culpable indifference to the pain brought on others by this urge when a

17 Bonamy Dobrée, "Thomas Hardy," p. 23.

18 Examples of this conclusion can be found in C. M. Bowra, "The Lyrical Poetry of Thomas Hardy," p. 241; R. A. Scott-James, *Thomas Hardy*, p. 25; A. J. Guerard, *Thomas Hardy*, pp. 156–58.

19 Guerard, *Thomas Hardy*, pp. 158–59.

less sympathetic character follows it out; the destructiveness located in the depths of the human unconscious, along with the power to repair and create that also lies there (despair next to hope, pessimism alongside meliorism); and even that invidious set of opposites, "heart versus head"—both being only different terms for "sentience." Simply by blurring the base of intelligence in *The Dynasts*, seeing two layers of reference rippling conterminously like gauzes of a diorama, we can erase old lines and bring into play new ones.

2. THE VISUALIZING OF OTHER SCENES

While the transparencies appear in only six scenes, Hardy keeps his key scene in mind as he presents the other scenes. For the brain-metaphor, I hope to show, is behind two basic methods by which Hardy moves his point of observation, between scenes and within scenes.

It is an established commonplace for readers of *The Dynasts* to observe how remarkably Hardy anticipates the techniques of the camera[20] and sound track in his aerial perspectives and free deployment of space, as well as in his intense visual and auditory effects. But, on reflection, most readers have agreed with Hardy's explanation that his imagination operated more freely by not having to be limited to any "material possibilities of stagery" (Preface, x), and have concluded that these remarkable effects would lose their potency in being translated into any other medium than the mental one they make vivid and "eminently readable" (Preface, x). Certainly it would be interesting to transpose onto film the layers of the diorama, and to put the techniques of the modern camera to the test of Hardy's aerial perspectives. But even if *The Dynasts'* potent effects could be satisfactorily transferred to that medium or to any other than the printed page, the mind would still be the best theatre for its visualization since the poem is *about* the mind.

---

[20] The camera, too, was another of Daguerre's optical devices, developed by him after the diorama.

The first point to make about Hardy's aerial perspectives in *The Dynasts* is that they go even beyond the needs of the action in their virtuosity and daring. One example of his command of space can be found in the Dumb-Show description of Marie Louise's progress to France.

> The observer's vision being still bent on the train of vehicles and cavalry, the point of sight is withdrawn high into the air, till the huge procession on the brown road looks no more than a file of ants crawling along a strip of garden-matting. The spacious terrestrial outlook now gained shows this to be the great road across Europe. . . .
>
> The puny concatenation of specks being exclusively watched, the surface of the earth seems to move along in an opposite direction, and in infinite variety of hill, dale, woodland, and champaign. . . .
>
> The tedious advance continues. . . . Our vision flits ahead of the cortege to Courcelles. . . . Here the point of sight descends to earth, and the Dumb Show ends.
>
> (II,v,v,278–279)

A sensational manipulation of visual focus and sound occurs in stage-directions describing the retreat from Quatre-Bras.

> The focus of the scene follows the retreating English army, the highway and its margins panoramically gliding past the vision of the spectator. The phantoms chant monotonously while the retreat goes on.
>
> (III,vi,viii,482)

Here, from the end of the coronation-scene at Milan, is a scene-closing for a movie maker:

> The scene changes. The exterior of the Cathedral takes the place of the interior, and the point of view recedes, the whole fabric smalling into distance and becoming like a rare, delicately carved alabaster ornament. The city itself sinks to miniature, the Alps show

afar as a white corrugation, the Adriatic and the Gulf of Genoa appear on this and that hand, with Italy between them, till clouds cover the panorama. (I,ɪ,vi,37)

And here are two scene settings that work their will with the English Channel:

> A view now nocturnal, now diurnal, from on high over the Straits of Dover, and stretching from city to city. By night Paris and London seem each as a little swarm of lights surrounded by a halo; by day as a confused glitter of white and grey. The Channel between them is as a mirror reflecting the sky, brightly or faintly, as the hour may be. (II,ɪ,ii,149)

> From high aloft, in the same July weather, and facing east, the vision swoops over the ocean and its coast-lines, from Cork Harbour on the extreme left, to Mondego Bay, Portugal, on the extreme right. Land's End and the Scilly Isles, Ushant and Cape Finisterre, are projecting features along the middle distance of the picture, and the English Channel recedes endwise as a tapering avenue near the centre. (II,ɪɪ,v,197)

The process of "smalling" something into distance, or turning the English Channel on end, seems to have been undertaken for pleasure, as an end in itself.

Scene-settings like these make two points: the first and general one is that the earth is bigger than the self-important little human dramas played upon it (such as the two within-door scenes—the Coronation at Milan and the reception at the Marchioness of Salisbury's—which precede these skiey views). The second point is that, to the intelligences (intelligences of the life force and of man),

> What are Space and Time? A fancy!—
> (III,ɪ,iii,339)

By means of "vision's necromancy," the "compacted whole" of the global web of things can be turned around and shown. What the Spirits promise in the Fore Scene they perform during the sequence of the drama.

> We'll close up Time, as a bird its van,
> We'll traverse Space, as spirits can,
> Link pulses severed by leagues and years,
> Bring cradles into touch with biers;
> So that the far-off Consequence appears
> Prompt at the heel of foregone Cause.—
>
> (Fore Scene, 7)

The dramatic action itself they cannot touch. Is it any wonder, then, that they flaunt the freedom of maneuver that is allowed them, and show that in the sphere appointed to it the mind is lord over phenomena? Intelligence can display the parallels between the diplomatic messages between England and France or between the proclamation Napoleon makes to his army as he sets forth into Russia, and the Russian counter-proclamation. Intelligence can make art out of these two discernings of similarity, picturing the one as an antiphonic chant that shuttles over a now darkening, now brightening, mirror between two patches of city-light; and making the second into a kind of fugal chorus of leaves stirred by a wind and answered by a countering "Distant Voice in the Wind." Part of the brain's freedom, then, is to have the power of making infinite connections between separated experiences, and to exercise it with pleasure: here at least is music out of dissonance, here is room for moving where elsewhere there is only the being-moved.

But, while the poem's vision connects, tilts, and moves scenes about freely, this unrestricted movement is exercised *outside* of scenes, where it does not violate their inner order and integrity. *Inside* of scenes the eye of observation operates under certain restrictions imposed upon it by the poet. It is positioned at a certain place and perspective that is clearly announced to the reader in the initial stage directions, and is fixed in that position for the duration of the scene. From its base it records sights and sounds of what is being said and done onstage, as well as other sensations from the action and the environment—weather, time of day, off-stage noises and flashes, furnishings, etc. In short, within the drama's action the poet's imagination restricts itself to the physical equipment of the five senses and the record-keeping brain that a perceiving human being carries inside his skull.

Once its base, angle, and focus are set, the observing mind records the waves that strike its senses, and its record consists of these physical "impressions" *only*. It is as though when he came to write *The Dynasts* Hardy were carrying out the following memorandum he had written to himself in 1892, during a time when he was jotting down ideas for his "Napoleon drama": "We don't always remember as we should that in getting at the truth, we get only at the true nature of the impression that an object, etc., produces on us, the true thing in itself being still, as Kant shows, beyond our knowledge" (*Life*, pp. 247–248).

Examining the presentation of action within scenes in *The Dynasts*, we find that it does indeed report "only the true nature of the impression" of objects, etc., and that it does so with great fidelity. Mass actions are reported according to physical sensations: dust raised, light reflected from weaponry, and sounds heard through the distance. Napoleon's army entering Spain is discerned by the "whitey-brown tilts of the baggage-waggons" dragged laboriously up the mountainside, "their lumbering being audible as high as the clouds" (II,ii,i,181). At Wagram, ". . . the positions and movements of the Austrian divisions . . . appear on the plain as pale masses, emitting flashes from arms and helmets under the July rays" (II,iv,iii,235). "You see their metal gleaming as they come," says the Austrian Emperor (II,iv, iii,241) as he watches in fascination the final and victorious French charge at Wagram; at that very moment the "columns glimmer" of the Archduke John as he comes up, too late. At Salamanca, "a cloud of dust denotes the English baggage-train" (III,ı,iii,334). At Vitoria, "whiffs of grey smoke followed by low rumbles show that the left of the English army under GRAHAM is pushing on there" (III,ıı, ii,368). At Waterloo, Wellington gauges the opposition from hints given by sensations:

> The noonday sun, striking so strongly there,
> Makes mirrors of their arms. That they advance
> Their growing radiance shows. Those gleams by Marbais
> Suggest fixed bayonets. (III,vı,viii,481)

Later, ". . . the position of the battalions is revealed only by the flashing of the priming-pans and muzzles, and by the furious oaths heard behind the cloud" (III,vıı,vii,507).

It is a tasking and sometimes involuted procedure to keep the poem's eye of observation a scientifically objective and impersonal instrument registering only a succession of "impressions" of reality. When the observing eye is used to present a scene and to note the presence of life at the rear of that scene, an aperture must be provided beforehand:

> At the vacant end of the room (divided from the dining end by folding doors, now open) there are discovered the EMPEROR NAPOLEON . . . and attendant officers. (II,ı,viii,170)

> At the back of the cellar is revealed, through a burst door, an inner vault . . . (II,ııı,i,206)

Sometimes this presentation of evidence together with the circumstances of evidence can result in some peculiarly heavy, involuted expressions:

> The truth of this intelligence is apparent.
> A low dull sound heard lately . . . has increased . . .
> (III,vı,v,474)

> His tall, stern, saturnine figure with its bronzed complexion is on nearer approach discerned heading the charge (III,vıı,ii,490).

It begins to be discovered at the front that a regiment
of hussars . . . have deserted . . . (III,vii,vii,508).

Regular expressions of this sort, impersonal notations of
the evidence of sensation, have a cumulative effect. There
are places, in the prose which sets forth the drama, where
Hardy drops his visualizing mode and simply says that
something really took place, without first filtering it as
spectacle through a viewing eye. (The death scene in the
cockpit of the "Victory" [I,v,iv] is an example: at the opening, "The wounded *are lying* . . ." and "NELSON is lying . . ." [italics mine].) But we do not notice such excep-
tions; what we do notice, rather, is a sentence like this one,
taken from the stage directions for one of the scenes at
Waterloo: "The wind occasionally brings the smoke and
smell of the battle into the encampment, the noise being
continuous" (III,vii,v,498). Here it is "the noise" that is
continuous, not, one inference away from sensation, something like "the battle yet continuing." A precise, carefully
empirical statement like that one, and the hundreds of other
statements setting forth the *sensations* of actions in the
hundred and twenty-nine earthly scenes, persuades us that
the recording eye that envisions this drama for us is an
instrument that keeps consistently and scrupulously to the
raw data of experience.

Inferences must be made from sense-data, by the characters in the drama and by ourselves as we read. The effect
of seeming-scientific objectivity established by the point of
observation makes us constantly aware that they are just
that—inferences and conjectures only, "the true thing itself
being still, as Kant shows, beyond our knowledge."

But even with this awareness we necessarily and actively
engage in the guesswork that is involved in getting at the
truth of events and that is left to us by Hardy's presentation
of events as sense-phenomena. For example, when the stage
directions give details of the state of health of characters
who have leading roles to play in the drama, we readily

infer that these details are "material," that they may be read in the light of the diorama's dissolving view. We see them as rough indicators of the active presence of Will in a character, and thus as providing an index to that character's likely effectiveness. The physical details of Napoleon and Pitt are noted with particular faithfulness whenever those two characters appear; and so we may, and do, view them as composing graphs of physical decline that show the Will gradually withdrawing and having done with what were its two main instruments during that period of history. In this manner the drama itself enacts the scientific method of studying history: conjecture is invited and required by the data supplied in the prose stage directions and scene descriptions, and succeeding events of the drama either sustain or overturn those conjectures.

As we noted earlier, the observing and recording eye of *The Dynasts* works under another limitation. In each earthly scene that it witnesses it is located upon a fixed base, a situation that makes it less free than the ordinary human brain, which can move as the actual participant in the scene moves. "What's toward in the distance?" the Spirit of the Pities asks after the battle of Puebla Heights (III,II,ii,369), and the Spirit of the Rumours describes what he sees down on the road to Vitoria—the flight of civilians, the accidental shelling of the throng, the pressing forward of the English from the left, and the retreat of the enemy, who "Pass rightwise from the cockpit out of sight" (III,II,ii,369). But the point of observation does not attempt to follow the French past the cockpit, even in imagination, for its purpose is to record the physical phenomena that make up an experience, and to report what is observed through the hazy atmosphere, the din and confusion.

And it does seem that Hardy arranges many of his scenes so that his camera will record haziness and limited clarity: not only the desired object of vision, but what inundates and obscures it. The scene of the battle of Jena, for instance, opens with a description of the fog in the hazy October dawn, in which the observing mind briefly glimpses Napoleon exhorting his soldiers, but soon can catch only the sound of his words through the mist. There follows a brief Dumb-Show describing the French attack and victory. Then the Prussian Prince Hohenlohe comes within range of the observing eye, where he is observed sifting from conflicting reports the disastrous news that the French have also been victorious at nearby Auerstadt. The scene closes as it began, emphasizing confusion and blindness.

> The October day closes in to evening. . . . The crossing streams of fugitives strike panic into each other, and the tumult increases with the thickening darkness till night renders the scene invisible, and nothing remains but a confused diminishing noise, and fitful lights here and there.
> The fog of the morning returns, and curtains all.
> (II,ı,iv,160)

Or again, after the afternoon battle of Salamanca ending in victory for the English, the point of observation is held in place on into the night to record the conversation of Wellington and his officers. Their exchange could just as well have been staged in a separate scene set within a tent; but Hardy seems to have been interested in the precise effect of having us experience the characters as voices in the darkness. "Their disordered main body retreats into the forest and disappears; and just as darkness sets in, the English stand alone on the crest, the distant plain being lighted only by musket-flashes from the vanishing enemy. In the close foreground vague figures are audible in the gloom" (III,ı,iii,337). "VOICE OF WELLINGTON," "VOICE OF AIDE" the ensuing speeches are labeled; and when the speakers pass offstage into the darkness, they are described in the stage directions as "talking shapes."

Narrowing or obscuring the aperture of the eye of observation in this way makes other senses have to be exercised in order to discern the course of events. This fact is the source of the suspense in some of the drama's indoor scenes in which the attention of the actors and of the recording intelligence is straining toward events outside that are cut off from view. In his chamber in Madrid, for instance, the Prince Godoy disposes one by one of his women and himself while the angry mob is heard and glimpsed through a window as it surges outside and finally breaks in to seize him. In a room in the interior of the Kremlin, a shocked and agitated Napoleon debates tactics with his staff while light from the conflagration without flaps into their window and leaping heat cracks the very windowpanes.

In Marie Louise's apartment in the Tuileries, first the royal family and later the abandoned servants debate on how to save themselves while the allies close in upon them; the conversations are carried on to the sounds offstage of weeping and expostulations, a shriek descending the stairs and fading out, and the approaching blare of military marches as the Allies draw near. In all of these scenes, the boundedness of the camera to one spot captures the trapped positions of the protagonists inside and the raw messages of their senses as the noose outside is drawn more tightly around them.

True, a point of observation placed in the situation of a trapped and straining protagonist is a common method of producing suspense, but in *The Dynasts* Hardy's systematic use of the bound focus is uncommon for any writer, even for himself. Only one other work suggests itself for comparison—his early novel, *Under the Greenwood Tree,* subtitled "A Rural Painting of the Dutch School," whose each scene was presented as a kind of still portrait, with careful attention given to the description of lighting, composition, and perspective, after which the elements in the composition would stir and carry on with the action. But in that early work the reader and author were allowed to move freely beyond the limits of the visual frame set up at each scene's opening; in *The Dynasts* we see only what passes inside the immovable viewing frame of each scene. Hardy, looking back on the viewing limits he set upon himself in the drama, describes them thus in a 1922 letter:[21]

> . . . you have to remember that the events generally in *The Dynasts* had to be pulled together into dramatic scenes, to show themselves to the mental eye of the reader as a picture viewed from one point; and hence it was sometimes necessary to see round corners, down crooked streets, and to shift buildings nearer together than in reality (as Turner did in his landscapes). . . .
> (*Life*, p. 417)

Clearly, then, suspense was not always Hardy's chief motive for placing restrictions on "the mental eye of the reader." Some other interest is at work in the scene on the eve of Austerlitz, when Napoleon's dictation and conversation with his Marshals inside the tent is recorded from outside, until he emerges into the night air and progresses through his adoring soldiers. The same is true in Berlin following upon the battle of Jena, when the news of the Prussian defeat arrives in the form of bulletins nailed up in a central courtyard. The point of observation is placed at a distance from the court, in a room shared by three Berlin ladies who choose to strain and peer through a magnifying glass to make out the succeeding announcements rather than to go outside and read the bulletins with other citizens. At Vienna, too, Marie Louise in the gallery holds her friend Neipperg from running down to the saloon below to learn what disconcerting news has arrived, preferring to puzzle out the news from a distance. And, finally, when staging the interview between Napoleon and Alexander at Tilsit, Hardy sets the point of observation not within the floating pavilion, where the events of consequence are

---

[21] In this letter Hardy was responding to the comments of a reader who had written to ask about certain points that had puzzled him in Hardy's description of Berlin at the time when Napoleon had entered it in triumph (II,i,v and vi).

taking place, but on the shore. The observing eye then looks down on raft and water and riverbanks at a distance too far for sound; and so the exchange is presented first in dumb show and then at second hand through the whispers of English spies.

The result of these extra restrictions on the point of observation is multiple. First, the point of observation holds in its purview not only the reverberating action, but also its effect on the surrounding atmosphere: in the vocabulary of physics, which is a major strand of the poem's imaginative language, it records not only the impulse but the waves it sets off. Secondly, the observing eye seems to be sharing, as the Pities in their sympathy would do, the earth-bound limitations of men who must look helplessly upon the great events that will have profound bearing upon their own lives. And, finally, the fixed eye seems to invite attention to the consistent and steady and remarkably informative way it works even while it is kept to its appointed limits. The scene overlooking the battlefield of Ligny is an example of the power of this tool. By locating the prospect "from the roof of the windmill of Bussy," Hardy is able to show how much one point of observation can do with immediate phenomena.

> At this moment hoofs are heard clattering along a road that passes behind the mill; and there come round to the front the DUKE OF WELLINGTON, his staff-officers, and a small escort of cavalry.
>
> WELLINGTON and BLÜCHER greet each other at the foot of the windmill. They disappear inside, and can be heard ascending the ladders.
>
> Enter on the roof WELLINGTON and BLÜCHER, followed by . . . others. Before renewing their conversation they peer through their glasses at the dark movements on the horizon. WELLINGTON'S manner is deliberate, judicial, almost indifferent; BLÜCHER'S eager and impetuous. (III,vi,v,471)

. . . Exeunt from roof WELLINGTON, BLÜCHER and the rest. They reappear below, and WELLING- TON and his suite gallop furiously away in the direc- tion of Quatre-Bras. (III,vi,v,473)

The consistency of this technique of presentation is what is so remarkable here. Recording-work such as this makes us appreciate what a strong instrument the skull-camera is: able without a shift or tremor to discriminate and register sensations from far and near, and delivering to the mind's ordering centers the most sensitive impressions from the wealth of phenomena outside.

But for the characters in the drama, struggling for the perfect vision to work "their" wills, the instrument is hardly strong enough, given all the impediments to vision they have to labor under. There are the many fogs, nights, sun hazes, and clouds of dust and gunpowder mentioned earlier as being the common conditions of battle-scenes. There is the problem of connected events taking place at great distances from each other—since for men of flesh space seems real and what happens seems of pressing urgency. And there is the "tangle of intentions" (Hardy's expression in a footnote regarding his interpretation of Villeneuve, I,ii,ii,41) that is so hard for a man to see around in himself, and even harder for others to judge.

Thus in many scenes the foreground of the stage is occu- pied by characters straining to perceive. Beacon-keepers and sentinels peer into the distance; generals and emperors squint, with desire or dread, through field-glasses. Ministers such as Pitt try to mark and face the lourings of the times, to read their "full significance" despite their own human "lackings" of omniscience (I,i,iii,20). A Collingwood is able to divine a Napoleon's true intent, while a Mack, chosen for his farsightedness, hazards and loses all through "stark sightlessness" (I,vi,iii,116). The uncertain reports of strag- glers, couriers, deserters, spies; even the uncertain informa- tion of rumors and premonitions; a foreign-language news-

77

paper; barely legible placards—all such hieroglyphs are seized upon by human beings reaching out for intelligence. The many towers and windmills and ridges and window-views to which watchers climb are the attempts of flesh to gain the aerial and distance-dissolving position of the Spirits. Reading alongside these straining protagonists, with the drama's point of view consistently burdened with the limitations that mortal senses labor under, is an exercise in sympathy, worthy of the Pities, for how difficult it is to perceive clearly the drift of events and to make the proper choices.

But another development takes place as these phenomena are recorded through the drama: a gradual shift from uncertainty to, if not certainty, then a de-emphasis on uncertainty. Once Napoleon passes the apogee of his military career (II,III,ii,215), phenomena that previously had signified the gaps in men's perceptions of events continue to appear but no longer mean so much. At the battle of Vitoria fog and rain are noted, but they do not "figure" in the drama. Obscurity and uncertainty are falling into the background now, for a pattern is beginning to emerge in which the English steadiness of purpose will prevail and the French will falter and lose heart.

Or, later, when the news comes to Casterbridge that Napoleon has escaped from Elba and returned to Paris, there is a gap in the news report that in earlier uncertain times would have given pause to the hearers and to the reader, for in times of great stress any gap can let in bad news. But the widespread tension has relaxed by the time of Part III— shrinking to the area around Belgium; and so a missing piece in the report of the London guard to the country people causes no questions: "Next, the telegraph from Plymouth sends news landed there by *The Sparrow*, that he has reached Paris, and King Louis has fled. But the air got hazy before the telegraph had finished, and the name of the place he had fled to couldn't be made out" (III,v,vi,452).

It seems that, for the people acting in the drama and for our intelligences beholding it, the feeling of being tiny pieces in the hands of senseless turbulent forces changes to a feeling that destiny (i.e., design) is working. Perhaps we may use in our explanation one of the metaphors from physics used in the Fore Scene by the Years:

> Our scope is but to register and watch
> By means of this great gift accorded us—
> The free trajection of our entities.
>
> (Fore Scene, 2)

It is as though all, in the drama and outside it, watched a body round the high point of its trajectory: the mind has a sense of the general shape that the rest of the path will take, and it is only a matter of watching to see how the details will work out. Viewed in the largest sense, the designs of the Immanent Will may add up to no overall pattern, go nowhere. But the forces themselves, be they little waves or large trajectories, do follow some laws of dynamics; and the particles of matter, depending on their composition (a Wellington in contrast to a Napoleon), are governed by some laws of duration. Thus it is that in Part III of *The Dynasts* the reader's historical knowledge of what happened after Elba is supported by a change of emphasis within the text, from a stress on the question of where the Will will light next, to a demonstration of how the Will works through different materials with different principles of magnetism (a Wellington in contrast to a Napoleon). We will consider this latter emphasis in Chapter Two of this study, which deals with the poem's near perspective on human beings. Here it is enough to say that the experience of this shift in emphasis is delivered through the consistent method by which Hardy positions and restricts the point of vision within each scene, so that it strictly records sense phenomena. Thus Hardy's presentation gives us in its "modern," "scientific" way that dateless mythlike experience of the fulfilment of design that we look for in a work of art.

To sum up: in this important matter of the visualization of the scenes of the drama, Hardy's technique is intensely imagined, complex but consistent with itself, and in suggestive correspondence with the key image of the poem.

3. IMPRESSIONS OF THE ENERGIZING OF MATTER

The brain image is linked significantly to what is shown on the stage, as well as to how it is shown. The anatomizing light makes visible the vital connections between matter, the stuff of life, and energy, the activating force that impels it to move to various pulsations, rhythms, and patterns. One shape that matter takes is flesh. In the Fore Scene the brain is a physical organ, pulsating flesh, and its creations or extensions of itself in the drama are flesh too. The word "flesh" occurs often in the drama, usually in a statement about its vulnerability. Guns riddle human flesh (I,i,i,11), set open "quaint red doors" in sweating fells (II,vi,iv,300), "punch spectral vistas" through bodies (II,vi,iv,299). English ships being loaded for Spain "gulp down their freight/ Of buckled fighting-flesh . . ." (II,ii,iii,195). A "huge elastic ring/ Of fighting flesh" contracts around Leipzig (III,iii,ii, 383–84). When Napoleon reads that in the eyes of the Universe he has no right to exist and is liable to public vengeance, his "flesh quivers" and he turns as though expecting to be stabbed in the back (III,vi,i,454). It is insane for this soft, easily punctured substance to be exposed to battle-fire:

> It nulls the power of a flesh-built frame
> To live within that zone of missiles . . .
>
> (III,vii,viii,512)

And the Spirit Sinister points out the crucial distinction between consciousness and flesh, between going through an experience vicariously in the mind and going through it actually in the flesh.

> One needs must be a ghost
> To move here in the midst 'twixt host and host!
> Their balls scream brisk and breezy tunes through me
> As I were an organ-stop. It's merry so;
> What damage mortal flesh must undergo!
>
> (III,vii,vii,509)

Flesh must undergo not only damage, but pain. As the Pities were the first to point out, what the Years call "flesh-hinged mannikins" are "shapes that bleed, mere mannikins or no . . ." (Fore Scene, 4), and by an intolerable antilogy, the mannikins feel (I,iv,v,77).

The fact that matter is kindled into feelings and consciousness does not open the door to a non-physical soul or let the the spirit-flesh dualism into Hardy's "Monistic theory of the Universe" (Preface, viii). Rather, when matter is energized into form it is "sentient," and possessed of feelings, sensitivity, and identity; and when those forms are taken apart, "decomposed," then feelings, consciousness, and identity are no more. A dumb show from the battle of Leipzig shows what in this poem lives are at their base—temporarily charged bits of matter: "So massive is the contest that we soon fail to individualize the combatants as beings, and can only observe them as amorphous drifts, clouds, and waves of conscious atoms, surging and rolling together . . ." (III, iii,ii,383). All flesh shares this physical base. Surgery on a human soldier is little different from "opening innerds at a pig-killing" (III,vii,v,499). And a dead soldier's glassy stare, as though he still had a mind after death to get sight of the battle, is, like everything else, physically explained: "Lots of dead ones stare in that silly way. It depends upon where they were hit" (III,vii,v,499).

The murderous battles of the Napoleonic war provide ample opportunity for human forms to return to mere matter, lose their identity and decompose into the elements. From Albuera and Waterloo come these two examples of how furiously men were driven to batter each other down to the last "conscious atom."

. . . The lines of the Buffs, the Sixty-Sixth, and those of the Forty-Eighth, who were with them, in a chaos of smoke, steel, sweat, curses, and blood, are beheld melting down like wax from an erect position to confused heaps. Their forms lie rigid, or twitch and turn, as they are trampled over by the hoofs of the enemy's horse. (II,vi,iv,300)

The streams of French fugitives as they run are cut down and shot by their pursuers, whose clothes and contracted features are blackened by smoke and cartridge-biting, and soiled with loam and blood. Some French blow out their own brains as they fly. (III,vii,viii,515)

. . . At last they are surrounded by the English Guards and other foot, who keep firing on them and smiting them to smaller and smaller numbers. (III, vii,viii,516)

The elements themselves do the work of decomposition when the French Army retreats from Moscow (III,i,ix,353–54). The snow literally appals, covers the army with a pall. Just as it confounds, pours together to one, the colors of the landscape, so it pulls off minute parts of the mass, rapidly snuffs out the fallen men's lives, and straightway transforms them into grave mounds. Pine trees loom up over the army, ravens hover over the living to feed off the dead, and in the awful silence "The sky seems to join itself to the land." "And where is the Grand Army?" asks Marie Louise (III,i,xii,362). "Gone all to nothing, dear," says Napoleon (III,i,xii,363). This is only partly true: the Grand Army is no more the energized mass it was; its form has been taken apart, its particles separated and decomposed, its living fire snuffed out; but its matter has been caught up into the enfolding matter of Nature, dust is again dust.

The many catalogs in *The Dynasts* are another way of breaking matter down. Even those things considered greater than the sum of their parts, catalogs say, are only the parts in the last analysis. A catalog in the battle of Albuera gives the composition of that fundamental fighting unit, a soldier, and of that compound of soldiers, a division.

> . . . Hot corpses, their mouths blackened by cartridge-biting, and surrounded by cast-away knapsacks, fire-locks, hats, stocks, flint-boxes, and priming horns, to-gether with red and blue rags of clothing, gaiters, epaulettes, limbs, and viscera, accumulate on the slopes, increasing from twos and threes to half-dozens, and from half-dozens to heaps, which steam with their own warmth as the spring rain falls gently upon them. (II,vi,iv,301)

The portable contents of the city of Vitoria show what civilization breaks down to:

> With the going down of the sun the English army finds itself in complete possession of the mass of wag-gons and carriages distantly beheld from the rear—laden with pictures, treasure, flour, vegetables, furni-ture, finery, parrots, monkeys, and women—most of the male sojourners in the town having taken to their heels. . . .
>
> The road is choked with these vehicles, the women they carry including wives, mistresses, actresses, dancers, nuns, and prostitutes, which struggle through droves of oxen, sheep, goats, horses, asses, and mules—a Noah's ark of living creatures in one vast procession. (III, ii,iii,370)

Under pressure, value breaks down to fact: a masterpiece of Spanish art is used for the paper it is painted on, and a priceless canvas is cut up to make a soldier a poncho.

The Durnover band, also, if viewed with an anatomizing eye for physical components, can be broken down in a cata-log. "The Durnover band, which includes a clarionet, ser-pent, oboe, tambourine, cymbals, and drum, is playing 'Lord Wellington's Hornpipe' " (III,v,vi,449).

And finally Napoleon himself is tabulated in effigy: his "innerds . . . a lock of straw from Bridle's barton," his outward parts "of a' old cast jacket and breeches from our barracks here. Likeways Grammer Pawle gave us Cap'n Meggs's old Zunday shirt that she'd saved for tinder-box linnit; and Keeper Tricksey of Mellstock emptied his powder-horn into a barm-bladder, to make his heart wi' " (III,v,vi,450). When the flames burn the mommet through to the fire-stuff at its center, all is blown to smithereens. This will be the physical end of Napoleon and of all men, even without the push of sympathetic magic.

MATTER in the drama often reveals the presence and direction of the Will by the wave-patterns of energy that register on its surface. They suggest images from the scientific thread of language in the transparencies: electric or magnetic or propulsive forces. These images do not hold still; they are like suggestive patterns the Will throws up to the surface of its current, often one pattern turning up in several bodies, or one suggestive image bursting into another. It is possible to consider these displays of energy under three categories: rhythm, heat and light, and explosive force.

The transporting power of rhythm and music is a force Hardy keenly appreciated. Many of his prose narratives turn on scenes in which the pulse of dance music beats down people's reserve and inhibitions and seems to lift their bodies temporarily into some ecstasizing universal power. For Hardy church music also had a power, beyond the logic or illogic of its texts, to take men's consciousness back to the time of youth when they were lifted together as a congregation to its solemn joyful harmonies. In his lyrics and narratives he usually supplied the names of the liturgical pieces and dance tunes, a tendency that seemed to fit with his adopted role of local historian, Scott's antiquarian, interested in all details in his reconstruction of the past.

84

But in *The Dynasts*, where the changing moods of peoples and the changing allegiances of nations figure so largely, song titles provide an evocative tracing of the Will's rhythmic movement of people's enthusiasms. Hardy first uses this device at a café in Vienna midway through Part II, when nationalistic sentiment against Napoleon's imperialism, ignited by the example of England, is beginning to stir in Spain and Austria as well:

> Dancing-rooms are lit up in an opposite street, and dancing begins. The figures are seen gracefully moving round to the throbbing strains of a stringband, which plays a new waltzing movement with a warlike name, soon to spread over Europe. The dancers sing patriotic words as they whirl. (II,III,v,229)

The running thread reappears some acts later at the Prince Regent's fete at Carlton House, and from here on when we are given the names of the tunes in fashion they immediately suggest the prevailing mood of the moment, a mood to which they are both response and stimulus: "The Regency Hornpipe"; "Speed the Plough"; "The Copenhagen Waltz"; "La Belle Catarina"; "Down with the French."

The titles touch lightly on concerns, great and small, being moved by the Will: to the Prince Regent (just after a view of the King's misery) and to his intrigues with the "belles"; to the realization growing all over Europe, with the victories in Spain, that the French can be beaten and to the hope that swords may soon be beaten into plowshares. Afterwards the technique used in this scene appears at celebrations, on the field, and even on Durnover Green at Casterbridge.

But the most extended display of music and rhythm in the drama occurs at the Duchess of Richmond's ball on the eve of Waterloo. As was true elsewhere, the titles of the dance tunes suggest current enthusiasms; the people dance

85

out together "The White Cockade," "Hungarian Waltz," "The Hanoverian Dance." As always, the tunes vary, but the music that sets the pulse and pattern is the Will's. Then the dancing is paralyzed by the news that battle is imminent. In the rhythm-notes of the Générale the beat of the Will, Necessity, is heard *directly*: "Suddenly there echoes into the ballroom a long-drawn metallic purl of sound, making all the company start" (III,vi,ii,460). (Here Hardy achieves a brilliant effect by writing in the musical notation of the Générale, its steady, one-toned insistent beat, as though to make visible the experience in the form of pure energy.) "The loud roll of side-drums is taken up by other drums further and further away, till the hollow noise spreads all over the city" (III,vi,ii,460). The officers and ladies dance one last dance. For once they are fully conscious that for the space of this movement life is a dance that closes with death.

COUNTRY DANCE: "THE PRIME OF LIFE"

The sense of looming tragedy carries emotion to its climax. All the younger officers stand up with their partners, forming several figures of fifteen or twenty couples each. The air is ecstasizing, and both sexes abandon themselves to the movement.

Nearly half an hour passes before the figure is danced down. Smothered kisses follow the conclusion. The silence is broken from without by more long hollow rolling notes, so near that they thrill the window-panes.

SEVERAL

'Tis the Assemble. Now, then, we must go!

The officers bid farewell to their partners and begin leaving in twos and threes. When they are gone the women mope and murmur to each other by the wall, and listen to the tramp of men and slamming of doors in the streets without. (III,vi,ii,461)

Everyday common sense is given its chance to criticize the fact that music carried to such intensity can so intoxicate human beings that they lose themselves to it and often have the whole course of their lives changed by the experience, a phenomenon that occurs more than once in Hardy's writing. A mother catechizes her daughter as to the number of dances she had, and their names. What is remarkable, the daughter *remembers*: "Enrico," the "Copenhagen Waltz" and the "Hanoverian," and the "Prime of Life."

ELDER LADY

It was very foolish to fall in love on the strength of four dances. (III,vi,iv,469)

. . . How do you know what his character is, or if he'll ever come back? (III,vi,iv,470)

But "character" and "coming back," while real questions whose force will show as time passes, carry little weight in those rare extraordinary times when people are seized by "pulsion" and share briefly in the universal rhythm. What is demonstrated at the ball, at once so historic and "phantasmal" (Hardy's footnote, III,vi,ii,454), is a pure version of the many-versioned dance that people lost themselves to in the age of Napoleon.

In contrast with these group-phenomena, the central and dominating figure of Napoleon, so often shown standing alone, seems to be immune to the pulls that move ordinary men. He holds apart from the ball at Cambacérès, disdaining to lose himself in frivolities with the "motley crew" (II,v,i,253,254). But this individual too bends to a dance, "turns toe," as Madame Metternich archly puts it (II,v,i, 258) to marriage with Marie Louise. If he does it stiffly, refusing to "unbrace" himself from stately considerations (II,v,i,253), then that befits one who is

. . . as the brazen rod that stirs the fire
Because it must.

(III,vii,ix,521)

87

When we look for energizing patterns of heat and light, we find that "the brazen rod that stirs the fire" requires frequent contact with the fire. Napoleon is positioned beside a fire, or wanting to be, in at least eight scenes: Ulm, Austerlitz (scene iii), Austerlitz (scene v), Astorga, Courcelles, Borodino, Tuileries, Leipzig. We might not note this as worth remark except for the number of times that Hardy has the man, not given to casual remarks, speak about the cold.

> Come near and warm you here. A glowing fire
> Is life on these depressing, mired, moist days
> Of smitten leaves down-dropping clammily,
> And toadstools like the putrid lungs of men.
>> (I,iv,v,75)

> 'Tis good to get above that rimy cloak
> And into cleaner air. It chilled me through.
>> (I,vi,iii,116)

> Let there a fire be lit: ay, here and now.
>> (II,iii,ii,210)

One gets more chilly in a wet March than in a dry, however cold, the devil if he don't!
>> (II,v,vi,279)

One would imagine that for such a man life could seem a series of warm centers with cold open-air spaces in between, and that his secret of survival was to be recharged at each fire with heat to last over the long interstices.

It may be useful to insert a digressive paragraph here that "places" Hardy. This bare-animal need for life-heat (shelter and fuel and clothing and food and the warmth of affection, and the insurance that these will be supplied on through the cold stretches of time) is a peculiar awareness that we find also in Dreiser, that other "determinist" who has often been compared to Hardy. And while Napoleon is unusual among Hardy's characters in having so symbolic a need to such a pronounced extent, the two writers share an awareness of how simple and basic men's human needs are, and how complex and thick are the pressures that push against and with those needs and "determine" men's choices. And both are alike in expressing strong sympathy with men for "having" to choose according to the needs they were born with—the universal one for life-heat as modulated by their life-circumstances and their individual constitutions.[22]

But in the metaphysics of *The Dynasts*, Napoleon, the direct instrument of the Will, is in his physical make-up more sensitive to heat and cold than is any other character, and, it is suggested, with good reason. It is purposeful coincidence that Napoleon is quite in the grips of a cold and his faculties numbed at the time of the battle of Borodino, so that as Rumour reports, "on this much-anticipated day / Napoleon's genius flags inoperative" (III,i,v,344). Perhaps the pull toward heat was one of the factors, along with "policy," for his desertion of the remnant of the Grand Army in the snows of Russia; Hardy shows him hurrying to the fireside once back in the Tuileries.

Other men are described as showing warm blood in their countenances. (For example, the Austrian Emperor's "fresh-coloured face contrasts strangely with the bluish pallor of NAPOLEON'S . . ." [I,vi,v,122]). Napoleon's face, at whatever stage of his career we see him, is always pale and ashen. Other men find in Napoleon their light and illumination. This charismatic kindling is poetically enacted in the darkness of the night before Austerlitz, when the French soldiers spring up as Napoleon walks along them, and promise their general victory on the morrow:

> They gather into wisps the straw, hay, and other litter
> on which they have been lying, and kindling these at

---

[22] An imaginative affinity between the two writers may have been felt by Dreiser himself, if we may take as evidence the tribute he wrote to Hardy the novelist in Harper & Brothers' *Thomas Hardy, Notes on His Life and Work*, p. 15; and his remarks on Hardy the poet published in an article by William White, "Dreiser on Hardy, Henley, and Whitman: An Unpublished Letter."

the dying fires, wave them as torches. This is repeated as each fire is reached, till the whole French position is one wide illumination. The most enthusiastic of the soldiers follow the Emperor in a throng as he progresses, and his whereabouts in the vast field is denoted by their cries. (I,vi,i,113)

And this is how Napoleon also seems to perceive himself at the end of his trajectory, as a source of light for other men:

> Great men are meteors that consume themselves
> To light the earth. This is my burnt-out hour.
> (III,vii,ix,520)

Men are either fated with this igniting quality, or not. Joseph Bonaparte's progress to Madrid, for example, "was glorious as a sodden rocket's fizz!" (II,ii,vi,200).

What, then, lights up the spirits of the man himself? For he is a human being as well as a manifestation of energy. In *The Dynasts* it seems to have been a personal belief in the useful public image he wished to construct of a family unit, legitimated and sanctified by church and state, and continuing into the future.

> . . . his great end, a strong monarchic line.
> (Metternich, II,v,iii,268)

> Disclose ourselves to the good folk of Paris
> In daily outings as a family group,
> The type and model of domestic bliss
> (Which, by the way, we are).
> (Napoleon to Marie Louise,
III,i,xii,364)

The few times in which we see Napoleon's countenance change its cold pallor occur in connection with his urge for this domestic project. At his wedding, his face for a rare moment "shines with joy," then suddenly "blackens as if the shadow of a winter night had fallen upon it" (II,v,viii,

287) when he notices that the Italian Cardinals have stayed away from the ceremony, thus refusing to recognize the union. He tries to "be as bright as ever" but his face cannot cast off "the sombre expression which settled on it" (II,v, viii,288–89). The union and issue once achieved, the warm image of the family has the power to brighten even the deepest darkness. When everything, even suicide, has failed him:

> A letter is brought from MARIE LOUISE. NAPOLEON reads it, and becomes more animated.
>> They are well; and they will join me in my exile.
>> Yes: I will live! The future who shall spell?
>> My wife, my son, will be enough for me.—
>>> (III,iv,iv,415)

But Marie Louise does not join him in his exile, and after his escape from Elba she does not answer his call to her to come to France to establish a regency.

The urge to be a settled bourgeois "household father" (Josephine, II,ii,vi,204) is a natural counterdrive to his restlessness for empire. When talking to Josephine, Napoleon presented "policy" and "private joy" as opposites (II,ii,vi, 204), but attempted to consolidate them in his second marriage. Ironically, by that attempt he loses both empire and affectionate domesticity.

Hardy suggests in Part Two, by interweaving scenes involving the marriage question (starting with scene viii, Act I) with others showing French losses in Spain, that perhaps the urge for domesticity drew away energy from Napoleon's drive for conquest. The Spirit of the Years comments on the Emperor's decision to relinquish personal command of the campaign in Spain and return to affairs in Paris:

> SPIRIT OF THE YEARS
> More turning may be here than he designs.
> In this small, sudden, swift turn backward, he
> Suggests one turning from his apogee!
>> (II,iii,ii,215)

Hardy follows history in showing that Napoleon's dynastic concern worked to destroy the empire in the precipitately on-and-off marriage-and-alliance arrangements with Russia and Austria. But he contributes his own interpretive touches to the story by showing Napoleon's genius as a general—the famous gift for concentration upon his battle-object, and instantaneous assessment of odds—weakened by his sentimentality as a father. Twice (II,IV,iii,298, and III,I,iv,341) he hears of Wellington's success in Spain; each time he most strangely pushes the fact to the side of his mind with the remark, "No matter," and each time what *does* matter is the bright and brightening fact of his son. And so Wellington grows with his army from a nuisance to a menace to the worthy adversary who overthrows him.

Even after Napoleon's empire is lost at Leipzig, the Spirits suggest, domestic happiness might have made a difference in his fortunes. But, in an irony Hardy must have appreciated, the domestic happiness that weighed so much in the hazard of the empire proved to be a phantasm, dissolving from Napoleon's reach at the end when he turned to it for shelter and warmth. The drama shows that it was the rejected wife who remained tenderly and unselfishly attached to him till death, while "thin persuasion" (III,IV, ii,401) was enough to keep the second one aloof and averse. The story of the two marriages, of the wrong choice made out of a desire for an heir, could have been one of Hardy's psychological studies in *A Group of Noble Dames*; and in its ironic reversal of fortune it could have been one of the *Wessex Tales*. But, finding this story in Napoleon, Hardy is able to show how the Life Force weaves private and public threads into its tapestry:

> Had he but persevered, and biassed her
> To slip the breeches on, and hie away,
> Who knows but that the map of France had shaped
> As it will never now! (Spirit Ironic, III,v,iv,442)

It is strange to consider that this tale of the loss of private joy and of policy, with all its wide-spreading repercussions for the rest of men, gains rather than loses in pathos when it is translated into the terms of heat and light running through it. So many threads were destroyed in the web of life—not because of the fact that, but along with the fact that: a man of blazing energies was set loose on a fiery path; his urge for warmth and stability warred with his urge for glory and eventually brought his career to earth; where the warmth he sought, like the blazing trail he wanted to leave in the sky, proved to be a dream.

There are other patterns of energy that suggest the work of magnetic and propulsive wave-forces. During Napoleon's comet-like trajection, his "suasive power" is often shown displaying its capacity to attract and energize followers, to set "iron filings" in arrangements of his own willing.

We saw his enthusiastic men at Austerlitz snatch up torches and follow him on his progress along the battle line, as though they were the comet's burning tail. This electric magnetizing power energized men even from a great distance: a nucleus-center was removed when Napoleon's men in Russia learned that he had broken trust with them and deserted, and the atoms went spinning off wildly. It was as though a charge had suddenly been switched off when the French in the Pyrenees received the news of the decisive defeat of Napoleon at Leipzig: "they had the stiffness taken out of them" and surrendered their grand position (III,III,vi,393).

This electricity could do its transforming work under the most adverse circumstances: Napoleon's approach to the troops at Grenoble, unarmed, coat open to show his medals, is like the introduction of an electro-magnet into a "hostile" field: the current is suddenly switched on, the field reversed and realigned. This magnetic force, in the ascending days of his career in the drama, rearranged men (as we see him after Ulm, telling the conquered Generals where to stand,

93

I,IV,V,75) and nations, set up puppets on thrones, and changed the map with the mass force at his command.

And we discern his downward path also in terms of the displacement or loss of that energy: losing his hold upon his officers after Borodino; losing his own center at Fountainebleu and at Avignon, so that his will (deserted, like the troops in Russia) went spinning off its track in wilder and wilder circles, while another part of his mind slumped into weary indifference and his body sank into sleep.

In the drama then, because he is so much more highly charged with turbulent energies than any other man on the stage, Napoleon convinces us that he is indeed one of those epochal men

> . . . who wade across the world
> To make an epoch, bless, confuse, appal. . . .
> (III,VII,ix,521)

We can get some sense of the appalling impact that force made on its entry, when we realize that all the images of energy that run through the action after Moscow trace a downward course: they depict, after all, a bearer of a finite —though abnormally great—supply of power, and by the end this supply has burnt out and left an inert mass.

To get a sense of the full curve we must turn to Hardy's little myth of Napoleon's "birth": not his first appearance in history, and not his first appearance in the drama, but the moment in which his unprecedented force was revealed to the human imagination. For Hardy it was at the island of Lobau that the son of nature and war was born.

> The July afternoon turns to evening, the evening to twilight. A species of simmer which pervades the living spectacle raises expectation till the very air itself seems strained with suspense. A huge event of some kind is awaiting birth. (II,IV,ii,233)

94

At two o'clock in the morning the thousands of cooped soldiers begin to cross the bridges, producing a scene which, on such a scale, was never before witnessed in the history of war. . . .

The night has been obscure for summer-time, and there is no moon. The storm now breaks in a tempestuous downpour, with lightning and thunder. The tumult of nature mingles so fantastically with the tumult of projectiles that flaming bombs and forked flashes cut the air in company, and the noise from the mortars alternates with the noise from the clouds.

From bridge to bridge and back again a gloomy-eyed figure stalks, as it has stalked the whole night long, with the restlessness of a wild animal. Plastered with mud, and dribbling with rain-water, it bears no resemblance to anything dignified or official. The figure is that of NAPOLEON, urging his multitudes over.

. . . A hum of amazement rises from the Austrian hosts. . . . (II,IV,ii,234)

We appreciate now the disruptive, unprecedented shock that Napoleon made when he entered human history. Hardy's view of the "birth" of the epoch called Napoleonic is remarkably close to D. H. Lawrence's imaginative vision of history.[23] Lawrence takes the round earth as his subject, and sees the fire of life within it as erupting, periodically but unpredictably, to set loose energies that destroy old forms of life and in turn create new ones. These irresistible shocks set the character of each new era—unlike any other ever seen in history. Although the study does not mention *The Dynasts*, Hardy's Napoleon could have been a stark example of Lawrence's imaginative thesis: a "mutative" force cast up by the heaving earth, destroying old order, flinging forth his own.

But, as Hardy shows, Napoleon is not the only elemental

[23] D. H. Lawrence, *Movements in European History.*

force to be displayed. He comes face to face at Moscow with a new "sport" of nature: a "monstrous" (III,I,vii,348) breaking of the rules of war, even as changed by him. Hardy depicts the encounter in wave imagery as if to tell us that here, in bare phenomenal terms, we are witnessing two pulses of the Will, an old one impacting upon a new one and being driven back.

VOICES OF ADVANCE GUARD

Moscow! Moscow!
This, this is Moscow city. Rest at last!

The words are caught up in the rear by veterans who have entered every capital in Europe except London, and are echoed from rank to rank. There is a far-extended clapping of hands, like the babble of waves, and companies of foot run in disorder towards high ground to behold the spectacle, waving their shakos on their bayonets.

The army now marches on, and NAPOLEON and his suite disappear citywards from the Hill of Salutation.

The day wanes ere the host has passed and dusk begins to prevail, when tidings reach the rear-guard that cause dismay. They have been sent back lip by lip from the front.

(III,I,vii,347–348)

This new uncanny manifestation of the Will also enters upon the stage through an image of birth. In dumb-show we are shown the preparations to abandon Moscow and prime it for burning, directed by Rostopchin:

Whose emissaries knock at every door
In rhythmal rote, and groan the great events
The hour is pregnant with. . . .

(III,I,vi,346)

96

The waves that met Napoleon at Moscow and swept him back to France next converge with the tide of resistance welling up in other nations, and these close in upon France: "They glide on as if by gravitation, in fluid figures, dictated by the conformation of the country, like water from a burst reservoir . . ." (III,IV,i,398).

One great force of nature has been lifted up to overthrow another. And the human terms of the analogy, the drama suggests, make for just as prodigious an "exception" of nature.

SPIRIT IRONIC

Yea, the dull peoples and the Dynasts both,
Those counter-castes not oft adjustable,
Interests antagonistic, proud and poor,
Have for the nonce been bonded by a wish
To overthrow thee.

(III,VII,ix,520–521)

As if to demonstrate not only its independence of its own projections (Napoleon, the bonded nations), but also its independence of any consistency with itself, the Will then raises up again that which it had cast down. The Ironic Spirits relate the new turn of events in impersonal language:

In Paris there is discontent;
Medals are wrought that represent
One now unnamed.

(III,v,i,429)

The new phenomenon is welling up in a new part of the reservoir; it is not understood by the Parisians or by Napoleon, both of whom will be carried upon it for one last tidal surge of the wave. Then there will be a new epoch, with new displays of light and sound and energy, showing the Will demonstrating both the "laws" of matter and motion, and its own lawlessness.

4. IMAGES OF UNFREEDOM

There are certain visual details in the drama that take the form of brief miniature copies of the determinism behind the stage; or that serve as elaborate looking-glasses mirroring the fact that the drama is all a show, a "play," a spectacle, a dream.

Some images figure forth the vanity of man's supposition that he is free, that initiative or passionate involvement are anything but mechanical or that they have power to change the course of things.[24] One hilarious illustration of this kind is the man standing in the crowd cheering Pitt at Cheapside: "a blade opening and shutting his mouth like the rest, but never a sound does he raise!" (I,v,v,102.) The man's defense, when his fellows see him "gape in dumbshow," is that it is not niggardly of him to begrudge the government his breath, but rather ". . . it's economy; a very necessary instinct in these days of ghastly taxations to pay half the armies in Europe!" (I,v,v,102.) Besides, "If ye was ten yards off y'd think I was shouting as loud as any."

The scene is a perfect foil to those heated debates in Parliament in which the members pretend to amass Yeas and Nays by persuasive arguments "As though a power lay in their oraclings," when in fact (according to the anatomizing light) each decision works unconsciously,

> And would be operant though unloosened were
> A single lip!
>
> (I,I,iii,26)

Hardy does make his three Parliamentary scenes seem to be mere expenditures of breath, with little correlation between the vote, which dutifully follows party lines, and the

---

[24] Other passages that sound ironic themes are: Napoleon on "Georgy," II,III,ii,212; Metternich on Maria Louisa's "freedom" from parental constraint, II,v,iii,269; Meneval and Maria Carolina on Marie Louise's windblown will, III,v,iv,441 and 443; Madame Metternich on Napoleon's just-announced marriage plans: "as good as wrought," II, v,i,258; comparisons of words to bubbles, II,III,v,225 and II,v,iii,271.

verbal direction of the debates. In the third debate, for example, feeling oscillates from one side (groans of "Oh, oh," III,v,v,449) to the other (two lines later: "Cheers"). The final overwhelming vote to support the government's position, closely following upon the exclamations in the passage quoted above, seems as though precast, operating independently of the words mouthed. Given this powerlessness of words to change action, the economy of the citizen at Cheapside going through motions only, saving his breath, seems quite rational.

The musical box that is knocked to the floor in the palace of the prince of Godoy is an instantaneous picture of all that seems mechanical about the pulses that move men: set off by accident, it sends off melody and rhythm into vacancy until, we may suppose, the mechanism winds down. It could be an emblem for the café scene at Vienna, where citizens rise and sit, peruse their papers and clink their glasses, the young ones up and animated, the old ones sedately down, as though they were toy figures moving to a tune on a music box.

Two brief pictures serve as emblems of the force that plays with the world. One is the ship, "l'Inconstant," which bears Napoleon away from Elba as does the fickle Will. The other is the "portrait of the young King of Rome playing at cup-and-ball, the ball being represented as the globe" (III,ı,iv,342). The presumptuous humanism of the allegory is mocked, of course, in that neither the boy nor his father can cup the world. But the irony beyond that is more frightening: that the world is indeed in the rough hands of an infant.

The images we have been considering focus on the unreality of human enterprise in the face of overpowering determinism, and portray it as an ironic joke. But the images we shall consider next look from another angle at the same fundamental incongruity, and see the joke as tragic. One image represents the suffering of individuals: this is the picture of George the Third in his madness, kept

under "restraint," the miserable days of his old age protracted by his physicians and resented by his son. He becomes an emblem, no less universal because an extreme case,
of all the dynasts,

> a suffering soul,
> Mocked with the forms and feints of royalty
> While scarified by briery Circumstance . . .
>
> (II,vi,v,304)

Napoleon, who seems constitutionally to suffer less, shares
with the English king the common human predicament, for
both "monarchs" are trapped in their lives. Once, at Fontainebleu, the Spirits seem to speak of Napoleon as an
emblem of the "fall of kings":

SPIRIT OF THE YEARS

> Herein behold
> How heavily grinds the Will upon his brain,
> His halting hand, and his unlighted eye.

SPIRIT IRONIC

> A picture this for kings and subjects too!
>
> (III,iv,iv,414)

Their motto applies to the companion picture of the suffering English king, just as the description above of George
III applies to the predicament all people find themselves
in: seen from without as free and powerful, feeling within
as though imprisoned in their lives, thicketed all around,
waiting out existence.

The mass suffering that is such an important fact in the
drama is caught in three pictures that are perhaps three
versions of the same picture: the drowning of two thousand
Russians on the Satschan lake in Austerlitz, a deliberate
calamity triggered by Napoleon's "vulpine" order; the destruction of some eighteen thousand wretched French fugitives cannonaded as they pressed over the bridge of the
Beresina, an act of literal and symbolic retribution by the

Russian officers; and the explosion of the Lindenau bridge "ginning" twenty thousand Frenchmen seeking to retreat from Leipzig, an accident of Napoleon's increasingly "Feeble foresight" (III,III,v,391). We can make one picture-sequence out of all three catastrophes. An "innocent" waterway (in time of peace never thought of as a strategic crossing) is located next to a scene of war in which one side loses and flees for life, the other pusues for death (almost every scene in the war is located in relation to a river, stream, or brook). Fugitives seek to cross the water; their crossing is deliberately fired upon. Men die, not with hand raised against an enemy but in the "innocent" act of fleeing from hostilities. They roll into the waterway, and the water is choked with them until they are submerged into the current and carried away. Then the river continues as it was before man came into the scene; and the screams of human anguish are succeeded by "the purl of the river and the clickings of floating ice" (III,I,x,357).

The disaster of the Beresina bridge adds one detail more to the composite image:

CHORUS (OF THE PITIES)

Then women are seen in the waterflow—limply bearing
their infants between wizened white arms
stretching above;
Yea, motherhood, sheerly sublime in her last despairing,
and lighting her darkest declension with limitless
love. (III,I,x,356)

This instinctive self-sacrifice, of desperate delivery to the future at the very moment of apocalypse, is, like most human efforts in the poem, to no avail; but it lightens the darkness and somehow lifts species-love above the "declension" of the whole.

THE thematic images discussed above provide emblems of meanings important in the drama. The next images convey an elaborate set of imitative details that parody, rather than emblemize, the whole.

The first example of an image-parody occurs at the Prince Regent's fête at Carlton House soon after the "victory" of Albuera. The decorations of the party are fat imitations of points of that murderous battle. On the dais the Regent swelters in the gorgeous uniform of a Field Marshal; the state table is decorated by a picturesque brook; the whole scene is lighted, and warmed, by innumerable wax candle chandeliers that, "owing to the heat," dribble wax upon the "uniform" white satin of the ladies. A function of the elaborate mirror image, it seems to me, is to demonstrate, by the easy, banal imitation in this exhibit, how the "real" show (actual firsthand experience in the present) is to be distinguished from the cheap sham show (pretending easy knowledge of another's struggle). The "real" show is marked by the presence of suffering, and by those in it being unable to break off the make-believe, "go out,/ And find some fresher air upon the lawn" (II,vi,vii,318).

The next parody holds a mirror to that very electrical "method" by which the Will is presented in the drama. In this passage from the stage directions introducing the scene entitled "A Fête at Vauxhall Gardens," I shall use italics to mark the imitative details.

> It is the Vitoria *festival* at Vauxhall. The orchestra of the renowned gardens *exhibits* a *blaze of lamps and candles* arranged in the shape of a temple, *a great artificial sun* glowing at the top, and under it *in illuminated* characters the words *"Vitoria"* and *"Wellington."* The band is playing the *new air,* "The Plains of Vitoria."

> All round the colonnade of the rotunda are to be read *in like illumination* the names of Peninsular *victories,* underneath them *figuring the names* of the British and Spanish generals who led at those battles, surmounted by wreaths of laurel. The avenues stretch-

ing away from the rotunda into the gardens *charm the eyes with their mild multitudinous lights,* while festoons of lamps hang *from the trees elsewhere,* and *transparencies* representing scenes from the war. (III, II,iv,372)

Every clause in these two paragraphs imitates the way that materialism is visualized in *The Dynasts.* Life is an "exhibit," as, here, a festive display. Overall arches the great mechanical source of heat and light; underneath are other lights arranged in shapes of things that men call the things themselves; people move to the strains of the air of the moment; illuminated figures display the names, to the edification of onlookers, of places and participants of events in which the Universal Energy was prominently manifest; transparencies reveal some of the scenes behind those mere names; and the eyes of the onlookers are "charmed" by long vistas of space and dissolving lights, and pleased also by effects of light in the foreground.

It is almost as though through these three elaborate "instant points" Hardy were taking the reader step by step through a developing statement about the experience of his characters and about our own experience as readers of *The Dynasts.* The viewer is warned in the first image that vicarious experience (even when most extensively sympathetic and imaginative) is limited. In the second he is given a view of the imaginative technique itself and of some of its rewards. And in the third detailed "show" image, the Tableaux-scene at Vienna, he is given a glimpse of what it might be like if consciousness should have broken its spellbound engagement in the show and should end its "willing suspension of disbelief." The details that build up this suggestive image are first presented in the stage directions but are then scattered through the conversation of several characters; the quotations from the text (III,v,ii,431–433), therefore, will necessarily be somewhat out of context.

The image is introduced with details somewhat like the

first two "shows": the perspective is from a "bird's-eye view" of a grand saloon lighted by the blaze of a thousand candles and highly decorated. There is a stage arranged at one end on which historical "Tableaux Vivants" are in progress. Distinguished ladies and statesmen are spectators—and simultaneously, to the view of the spirit-watchers, part of the spectacle (even as those spirits, in turn, are to us).

Then, "something happens," some "strange news" arrives that breaks the spell of the pageant upon the viewers and the actors. They "heed" it no longer; "all/ Turn murmuring together"; they stare, they blink, they are "thunderstruck." The "sovereigns," those with a great role in the show of things, show "By far the gravest mien"; those with an "English" sense for comedy and mutability are amused at the sudden reversal.

This is, of course, a scene telling what happened when the news of Napoleon's escape from Elba reached the ears of the Allies—a dramatic moment in the Napoleon story. What it presents, a sequence of straightforward events, it means. But it also reaches beyond itself for meaning. We can point outside *The Dynasts* to the *Life* for evidence that Hardy himself, as an architect and a poet, liked to see objects as poetic constructs that required the addition of something more, from outside the physical limits of their own borders, for aesthetic wholeness. Of course there is his constant recognition, discussed in the Introduction to this study, that: "The poetry of a scene varies with the mind of the perceivers. Indeed, it does not lie in the scene at all." But sometimes the poetic construct took in an "ordinate" that was another object: "Venice requires *heat* to complete the picture of her. Heat is an artistic part of the portrait of all southern towns" (*Life*, p. 194). Once Hardy noted that the architecture of a certain house was "incomplete without sunlight and warmth. Hence the dripping wintry afternoon without mocked his marble basin . . . and silver apse" (*Life*, p. 207). When he visited Tintern Abbey, he observed that "silence is part of the pile. Destroy that, and you take a limb from the organism . . ." (*Life*, p. 93).

We have read *The Dynasts* itself in this way, as describing in its arc the image of a mind that is completed only when readers put themselves as "ordinates" in its circle. This smaller picture-box also, like the larger diorama, shows its full curve of significance when it is seen to reflect objects outside the pageant itself, out in the drama, on out to the poem as a whole, and even beyond. So seen, it reflects all the poem's statements that history only seems to be "vivant" but is no more than a series of tableaux, pre-staged and pre-cast, and reflects one of the poem's central metaphors, that life is a dream. Finally, there is a "curiously hypnotizing impressiveness" in the intense prose that describes this scene. We may remember that Hardy in the Preface (p. xi) recommended that this very quality, the eerie effect achieved in the mummers' plays he witnessed in his youth, be aimed for in any production attempting to transfer *The Dynasts* from a mental theatre onto an actual stage. So viewed, with all these ordinates beyond itself to complete it, the scene with its interruped tableaux achieves greater poetic suggestiveness. It may be an image of death, which interrupts the "life-like" Tableaux Vivants men are gripped by, which wakes them from their dreams of life, and releases them into sleep at last. Or is it our own dream that is pierced as we read *The Dynasts*, our belief that life's masquerade and play are real? Are the people in Vienna figures for ourselves; are our minds as we read tranced with "mighty cogitations," "riddled through/ With strange surmises and more strange alarms"? If we see them so, the rays of the anatomizing vision will have done their piercing, dissolving work.

DURING the course of the drama the images of unfreedom set before our eyes are reinforced in our ears. Often the human characters have occasion to make some remark about their free-will, or to comment on the meaninglessness of life.

Because the theme of the drama is stated so emphatically by the Spirits, when words are spoken by human beings on these subjects, even though they may be addressed to a specific given situation, they echo in the reaches of space where the Spirits sit and where we watch and listen. The fact that the human beings do not perceive the impotency and automatic nature of their wills, nor realize that they are speaking truth in their disclaimers about their futility and inability, is ironic testimony to that truth. The unconscious wit in the speech of these human beings acts as a clever refrain, reminding us of themes without demanding that we look at them and ponder as we do with the concentrated prose of the Spirits or with the concentrated prose in the stage directions.

Sometimes we hear punning remarks on the compulsion of the human will:

NAPOLEON

And this much likewise you must promise me,
To act in the formalities thereof
As if you shaped them of your own free will.

JOSEPHINE

How can I—when no free will's left in me?

NAPOLEON

You are a willing party—do you hear?

(II,v,ii,261–62)

. . . she submits herself
With chastened duty to circumstance . . .
(Hortense *re* Josephine, II,v,ii,266—
there being an extra irony in the fact
that what Napoleon requires in his first
wife, he will get too much of in his second)
I shall do what I say! . . . I don't know what—
What *shall* I do!

(Marie Louise, III,IV,iii,404)

Other remarks testify to the futility of will and effort, in the face of predestination:

We shall have marched for nothing, O!
(English soldiers, I,i,i,9)
—Oh well: it was all learnt beforehand, of course.
(Member of Parliament on Peel's first speech, II,v,iv,275)
... a debate and a division that are only like the Liturgy on a Sunday—known beforehand to all the congregation. (Sheridan on the disparity between Parliamentary speech and action, II,v,iv,277)

All of these examples of thematic wit reinforce the drama's visual meanings and add to its resonance: they become mocking echoes, reverberating through the round universe and making it seem, not infinite in expanse but infinitely restricting, holding tightly in their bindings all creatures who are born into "sentience."

5. INFORMING SPEECH:
THE EXCHANGE BETWEEN CONSCIOUS AND UNCONSCIOUS

Up to now in examining Hardy's metaphysical perspective, we have considered particular features. Matters such as the key "scene" or metaphor governing the world in this light of the diorama; the angles at which other scenes were presented; details running throughout the drama and details that seemed to stand still for a moment and catch the many-layered meaning of the whole: these are formal, physical matters that can be handled and argued.

But in considering the metaphysical view as a poetic whole, and in attempting to demonstrate the way every aspect seems to fill out further the poem's central imaginative concept, I have found that other anomalies in the poem—ideas and odd features that have no demonstrable formal connection with each other—seem somehow also to fit into the whole we have been considering. The case that can be made for their imaginative unity is perhaps debatable; thus it is offered here as a speculation only, though one which, if convincing to the reader, could contribute further to our sense that in *The Dynasts* Hardy's imagination finds its full and rounded expression.

There are two kinds of speech in *The Dynasts*. One is of language; we have it set down, in the words, tones, and attitudes of the Phantom Intelligences and of those human persons who are not, following Hardy's interesting designation of the cast for each act, "mute figures." And there is also mute speech, speech that is not uttered in words but that consists of shifts of feelings and consciousness that are nonetheless present for going unnoted. To some extent this is the speech of all human beings, even of a Napoleon who in *The Dynasts* always has something to say, for no man can see around the whole that he would speak. But it is the fate of some human beings, either by chance of temperament or position or some other accidents of life, to be inarticulate about the inner things that matter most.

Hardy in his lyrics and stories and novels had demonstrated a unique sensitivity for people who could not or would not speak for themselves, defend themselves. In the tradition of the "Elegy Written in a Country Churchyard" and Wordsworth's poems about simple people, he too could point out and do justice to the immensities—of aspirations, intentions, dreams—unspoken beneath the narrow or hard facts of a person's life. He furthered this tradition by extending our sympathy to an unlikeable character like Henchard in *The Mayor of Casterbridge*: a man who is the harder to endorse the more we know him, while we do endorse those who ultimately condemn and reject him; a man who dislikes and ultimately condemns and rejects himself. Gray and Wordsworth made us pity and respect their characters; Hardy extends our sympathy for this man into love.

This power of sympathetic advocacy can translate mute, unspoken speech into words. In *The Dynasts* the characters who might remind us most of the luckless and inarticulate temperament of Henchard are "Ill-omened Moore" and the King of Prussia with his "mien of reserve." They are given brief sympathetic focus in *The Dynasts*, but share the camera with hundreds of other mute figures whom Hardy must speak for. It is a long list. There are the dying— Nelson, Villeneuve, Pitt, Moore, Josephine, and those many brave individuals (one example: Ruchel, II,i,iv,158) who are named in passing because they stood forth to face the enemy alone and were instantly shot dead for their effort. All of these had no time to express some last word before they died. (Hamlet spoke for them when he said to those who stood audience to his last act:

"Had I but time, as this fell sergeant Death
Is strict in his arrest, O I could tell you. . . ."

Hardy reports them and their cause aright to the satisfied.) There are the thousands of young soldiers, too many to name, who died for nothing on the battlefields of the war. The list includes those still more luckless soldiers denied even the vainglory of dying heroic deaths in battle, because they dropped out of memory in the marshes of Walcheren and the wastes of Russia and left no brave "tale of how we fell" (II,iv,viii,252). It includes noncombatants—civilians and camp-followers, women and babies—who were slaughtered in masses and became only unfortunate statistics in destruction, "Giving in one brief cry their last wild word on that mock life through which they have harlequined!" (III,i,x,356.) Even Napoleon, the master-rhetorician, earns a place here, when he perceives that Marie Louise has taken a lover and does not mean to return to him, and the feelings that the drama has made us expect to see at play go unspoken. The sympathetic roster of mutes extends even to the small, low-lying creatures of the field who are the forgotten victims of a battle. Earth is mute but the crushing of animals and insects and plants is to her as much a pain and premature loss as the cutting-down of a soldier-boy is to a mother:

> So the season's intent, ere its fruit unfold,
> Is frustrate, and mangled, and made succumb,
> Like a youth of promise struck stark and cold!
>
> (III,VI,viii,483)

In the terms of the key-image of the brain, all of the above are examples of the way that inarticulate stirrings from the unconscious, non-verbal parts of the brain are translated into words by the conscious part of the brain.

Sensory expression, in auditory and visual pantomimes without words, are given to other silent actions. In this category belong the remarkable and eloquent Dumb Shows, which are full of highly charged mute speech. Here too we may put the silent connections to be read among juxtaposed scenes whose thematic threads are the more suggestive for being unstated. The contrast of an immense aerial perspective, like the view of the Russian plains, followed closely by a narrow within-doors perspective, such as the scene in Marie Louise's chambers when Napoleon came home from Russia without an army, makes a wordless but clear judgment on the narrowness of Napoleon's mind. Another juxtaposition makes the opposite point: the last view of him before Elba, on the Avignon highway, and the scene in which he escapes Elba. His listless, haggard, indifferent weariness in the first scene, and the melancholy, flaccid, weary details of the second, suggest that a weary burden is being shouldered again with an unconscious sadness that could be expressed only in the monotonic language of the body. The list of speeches delivered is long, and the means of delivering them, verbal or subliminal, is varied.

Let us suppose that all silent phenomena exhibit, in the waves pulsed out by their life-energies, a "will" or "motive" to make some impact on the rest of matter, some impression on the great body of the Will, a wave pattern that does not simply rise and fall but that travels out to consciousness and is registered there. Let us assume that in *The Dynasts* the examples we have considered succeed. But the conveying of information in the drama is not a one-way affair only, from the sleeping depths of the brain to the spirit intelligences. The consciousness, too, "informs" the unconscious even when its information cannot change the actions the characters make. Surely this is how we should read the many disguised spirit appearances in the drama, with their early news and wide prophetic forecasts, and how we should understand the many parapsychological premonitions, strange warnings, apprehensions, ghostly visions, and bodiless voices in a writing ostensibly committed to science's monistic view of the universe. The phantoms of consciousness pass over the physical limitations of time and the impenetrability of matter to inform the fleshly characters. The characters continue on as though they had not heard it, because the pull, the momentum, the pressures which urge them on their courses are too great. But the information from the Intelligence is true and the characters perceive it as such, in passing, with that part of their minds which *is* detached and objective.[25]

True, the spirit visitations to the earthly level are taken by most critics to be more than mere voices of presentiment, heard but ignored. The more usual interpretation is that they have the power to effect definite and immediate changes in the human drama, not that they may only ("may") bring about future gradual changes in human tendencies over the long course of time, "When far-ranged aions past all fathoming/ Shall have swung by, and stand as backward years" (After Scene, 522). Two lines of criticism

[25] Napoleon's analysis (III,IV,ii,401) of this contradiction between man's perception of the unconscious drives and desires that "doom" him and his inability, notwithstanding, to disobey those drives, is true to the poem here. The drama, however, rejects the untroubled, "unconscious" attitude that Napoleon assumes as a result of this contradiction. This point will be discussed in Chapter Two's analysis of the "old hero."

take their start from this premise, and in so doing both take on, in my opinion, special problems.

One, approving of the Spirits as Hardy's *dei ex machina* and looking for occasions in which they advance on the human level the poem's melioristic design, resorts to unconvincing explication about the degrees of change effected in particular cases by individual Spirits,[26] and as a whole presumes an optimism about the powers of patient reason that I think is foreign to Hardy. The second line of criticism disapproves of the fact that the Spirits intervene, protests that their interference on the human stage, their speech with Villeneuve, Napoleon, and others, contradicts the materialism of *The Dynasts*,[27] and concludes that through them Hardy has introduced a dualism of spirit and matter into his supposedly "monistic" work. The line taken by this study differs from the second argument by interpreting the Phantom Intelligences as mental, not spiritual, phenomena; and differs from the first argument by interpreting them as

[26] I disagree with the position taken by J. O. Bailey, *Thomas Hardy and the Cosmic Mind*, pp. 33–151, which explains the Intelligences, citing specific instances, as "Channels of Causation" able to affect the material world. He claims, pp. 130 ff., that Villeneuve's suicide is prompted by the Spirits and is then forced to explain, unconvincingly, why their interference was in the interests of Universal Enlightenment. Unlike Bailey, I consider Villeneuve's suicide to be something he would have effected with or without the prompting of the Spirits. The Spirit of the Years only removed a delaying inhibition held by one part of his mind; the rest of his mind was set upon obliteration. Despite the premonitory misgivings felt by Marie Louise on taking final leave of Napoleon, and by her son on departing from Paris, those gloomy partings took place. I find myself in agreement with Bailey when he sees the Cosmic Mind undergirding *The Dynasts*, although not with the details in which he works the concept out—as in this point on the role of the Spirit.

[27] See Irving Howe, *Thomas Hardy*, p. 151. See also a critic from 1912, Lascelles Abercrombie, *Thomas Hardy*, p. 217. Despite disagreeing with Abercrombie on the question of Hardy's inconsistency, I consider his appreciation of the poem's faithfulness to science, and his spirited entry into the debate between the Years and the Pities, to be a remarkably perceptive early reading.

aspects of mind that have observing powers only and that are able to touch experience only as it is "out of touch," in the past or in the future.

The question of the materialism or non-materialism of mind is one that can be discussed in relation to Hardy and *The Dynasts* if care is taken to confine it to those points of reference.[28] It is safe for us to say that Hardy certainly did find "mind" a necessary and meaningful term, and that at the same time he rejected any theory of order that would introduce "an inconsistent rupture" in the physical law of the universe—as we see in his criticism of Bergson's doctrine of consciousness: "I fear his theory is . . . only our old friend Dualism in a new suit of clothes" (*Life*, p. 369). Within *The Dynasts*, then, "mind" is a function of matter (an impulse of nervous energy, highly specialized and evolved, let us say); and is in keeping with the physical universe that the poem assumes.

But it is understandable that readers of Hardy should fear (or hope) that his monism, too, even more than Bergson's, is only everyone's old friend dualism in old-fashioned clothes. For there surely is a glaring contradiction in the fact that a man who believed the world was open to explanation by human science alone should have written so much poetry—the lyrics and *The Dynasts*—in which ghosts and spirit phenomena speak to human beings. How is that contradiction resolved? In the passage on Bergson quoted above, Hardy goes on to say: "Half my time—particularly when writing verse—I 'believe' (in the modern sense of the word) not only in the things Bergson believes in, but in spectres, mysterious voices, intuitions, omens, dreams, haunted places, etc. etc. But I do not believe in them in the old sense of the word anymore for that" (*Life*, 370). "Par-

[28] For example, I think that Jacques Barzun, "Truth and Poetry in Thomas Hardy," p. 189, interrupts his excellent discussion of the high place of consciousness in Hardy's vision by slipping into an attack on scientific materialism that seems to represent his own (perhaps dualistic) view but not Hardy's.

ticularly when writing verse," he uses them—imaginatively, as part of his conscious interest in the strange and subtle gropings of the mind. This statement can be held up against the various speculations critics have made as to ghosts, beliefs, and belief in Hardy: imaginatively, not naively (contra F. R. Leavis: a poet of "pre-critical innocence");[29] not nostalgically (contra the critics who cite poems like "God's Funeral" and "The Oxen" to argue that for all his conscious skepticism Hardy cherished images of a past world before folk belief was eroded, to compensate for that lost period of faith in his own life);[30] not even scientifically and rationally, like Aldous Huxley studying psychic phenomena to find evidence of personal immortality.[31]

All of these critical speculations are partially true; but none of them accounts sufficiently for the aesthetic awareness, detached and fully conscious, in Hardy's statement. For Hardy uses "Spirits" as a fully conscious artist: one who knows that the human mind with all its ways constitutes a great subject for the poet; and who also knows that the incorporeal "impressions" of persons and places and incidents preserved in the mind to be summoned up like ghosts from the dark reaches of memory,[32] constitute an everfresh well of inspiration.

> I believe it would be said by people who know me well that I have a faculty (possibly not uncommon) for burying an emotion in my heart or brain for forty years, and exhuming it at the end of that time as fresh as when interred. (*Life*, p. 378)

[29] F. R. Leavis, *New Bearings in English Poetry*, pp. 57–58.

[30] Delmore Schwartz, "Poetry and Belief in Thomas Hardy," is one of the better-known critics who have made this claim.

[31] Bailey, *Cosmic Mind*, pp. 121–36, considers it likely that psychic phenomena are depicted as sober plausibilities in *The Dynasts*.

[32] My explanation of this aspect of the ghosts, as intense images preserved in Hardy's memory, owes much to the remarks of Elliott, "Ghostly," p. 289. The same point is made by Edmund Gosse, "Mr. Hardy's Lyrical Poems," p. 292.

Relativity. That things and events always were, are, and will be (e.g. Emma, Mother and Father are living still in the past). (*Life*, p. 419)

In *The Dynasts*, then, and throughout the poetry, Hardy's Phantoms are, literally, Shades and Shadows: adumbrations of the possibility of communication between past, future, and present, and of the mind's capacity to sense beyond the boundaries of the five senses. They are not arguments against the laws of matter, nor intimations of more-than-relative immortality, for they exist only in the mind, and live on, as do memory and dream, only so long as the mind which contains them lives.

Beyond this explanation, however, lies still another,[33] in the distanced point of vision habitually taken by the viewer of action in Hardy. This habit, found throughout Hardy's narratives and poems, surely comes to strongest expression in *The Dynasts* with the phantom remoteness of the Spirits and their disembodied hauntings of the human scene. Again, Hardy's *Life* helps to bring us closer to an imaginative motive that may have gone into shaping *The Dynasts*:

For my part, if there is any way of getting a melancholy satisfaction out of life it lies in dying, so to speak, before one is out of the flesh; by which I mean putting on the manners of ghosts, wandering in their haunts, and taking their views of surrounding things. To think of life as passing away is a sadness; to think of it as past is at least tolerable. Hence even when I enter into a room to pay a simple morning call I have unconsciously the habit of regarding the scene as if I were a spectre not solid enough to influence my environment; only fit to

[33] Guerard, *Thomas Hardy*, pp. 114–22, is, to my knowledge, the first critic (1964) to comment at length on this phenomenon. His commentary stimulated much of my own thinking, which in turn was confirmed by the 1970 work by J. Hillis Miller, *Thomas Hardy: Distance and Desire*, a work to be set alongside Guerard's as *the* study of Hardy's disengaged observer.

behold and say, as another spectre said: "Peace be unto you!" (*Life*, pp. 209–10)

This remarkable statement throws light on the many passages in the *Life* that speak of seeing souls outside of bodies, of seeing people as though they were ghosts, even on occasion of *being* a ghost. But for our particular purpose it helps us to complete our explanation of the Overworld Spirits by connecting them, finally, to the truths that the anatomizing perspective has revealed to us. Life is insubstantial; flesh is spectral; meaning is phantasmal; the course of action cannot be changed or even grasped by one's understanding. Therefore the mind that would view the scene of human life must climb to an Overworld, must distance itself willingly even as it is distanced unwillingly, and remember that it is as restricted by life as though it were in its body but effectively out of it.

There are certain satisfactions for the viewer of life who consciously takes on these limitations in his mind, a certain very limited sphere of "influence." His conscious will have recognized the unconscious, which is the beginning of a kind of wisdom. And the salutation it returns to the unconscious —"Peace!"—is a significant exchange. The "environment" has not been changed, but a certain harmony, a conversation of mutual recognition, has taken place. And for us readers, within and for whose minds these exchanges and conversations have been enacted, there is a paradoxical result: as de la Mare puts it, "When the last page is turned . . . how curiously quiet a sense of responsibility has edged into our minds."[34] The mind's image of the powerlessness of thought and of its own helplessness has made us more thoughtful, more responsible.

All these arguments can now be concluded and our circle closed. We turn back, carrying the knowledge we have gained from the drama, to the brain-image pictured in the first transparency. Now we can realize what we were shown

[34] De la Mare, "*The Dynasts*," in *Private View*, p. 26.

moving there before our eyes: the conscious and the unconscious establishing new aerial and underground connections between each other, and the whole vibrating as new
impulses make themselves felt alongside the old.

The hope at the end of *The Dynasts* is based upon three
things in the poem. The first is the "silent speech" that I
have read as an imaginative extension of the key brain
image, believing it to be implied or at least allowed in terms
of the anatomizing perspective. The second, is the fact,
acknowledged by the Spirits throughout the poem, that in
the course of time they themselves have evolved as phantom
intelligences from the brain, and thus that the fundamental
force of life *has* developed and may yet again. And the third
is the argument on which the Pities end their last hymn
and conclude their "case":

> We hold that Thy unscanted scope
> Affords a food for final Hope. . . .
> (After Scene, 523)

Once again consciousness is informed by the Will, informed this time that creation itself is too great, too mutative, too fecund, for the mind of man to set limits of possibility to it, or for his imagination, even with "exhaustive
strain and effort," to encompass it in an image. These three
evidences of present, past, and future stirrings in the brain,
all held in potentiality, are why, in the poem's final chorus,
the Spirits of the Pities hope that they sense, just beyond the
reach of their vision,

> Consciousness the Will informing, till It fashion all
> things fair!
> (After Scene, 525)

TWO

HUMAN OUTSHAPINGS OF THE WILL

1. PRELIMINARY REFLECTIONS

HARDY's poem takes into its optical exhibit many different lives, human and non-human, seeing them all as so many different forms of the Will's "outshapings." (The term is borrowed from a comment of the Spirit of the Years, who says that Napoleon's actions "do but outshape Its governing"; I,ı,vi,36.) But human beings in *The Dynasts* do not see themselves as mere shapes of equal importance with other shapes, not any more than they could accept the radically deterministic views, discussed in the previous chapter, that showed them to be tissues in a vast biological organism, or as atoms coalescing for a brief moment in time. They do not feel like tissues or atoms, but like persons, free in time though shaped by time. So, this second perspective sets up a point of view that is an opposite pole to the first, bringing its focus up close to human beings to delineate them as they see themselves. Unique individuals of a unique species; separate; self-directed; differing significantly from one another; and counting for more in the universe than the amount of energy that animates them into "sentience": that is how they see themselves, moving under an illusion perhaps necessary to life.

Their choices and actions, they think, are of central importance. Accordingly, this perspective sets human beings at the front and center of the stage and focuses upon them so intimately that it notes their private speech to themselves and even small changes of facial expression. Under such close scrutiny, individual differences emerge as large and significant, and these individual differences in turn lend themselves as data for the viewer to make moral distinctions and discriminations between one character and another.

"Moral," in this discussion, will be used in a descriptive sense as the "mores" or characterizing "ways" of a person or people. But we cannot do away with the prescriptive sense entirely: in discriminating among different mores it is presumed that some ways are better suited than others for the fundamental needs of life, and that experience validates some ways of meeting life and invalidates others.

Reflections on the making of moral judgments come in here because this perspective of *The Dynasts* not only allows us to make such judgments, it requires us to do so. Quite early in the poem, in the Fore Scene, a major precedent is established for making moral discriminations upon the leading human characters. The Spirit of the Pities announces what is to be the verdict of Pity, from beginning to end of the poem, on the drama's central character. Napoleon is about to assume the crown of emperor as the drama begins, putting on himself the weight of dynastic titles and trappings and tyrannies that he was to have removed from France forever. The Spirit of the Pities has no interest in watching this "rare spectacle":

> 'twere better far
> Such deeds were nulled, and this strange man's career
> Wound up, as making inharmonious jars
> In her creation whose meek wraith we know.
> The more that he, turned man of mere traditions,
> Now profits naught. For the large potencies
> Instilled into his idiosyncrasy—
> To throne fair Liberty in Privilege' room—
> Are taking taint, and sink to common plots
> For his own gain.
>
> (Fore Scene, 3)

What the Pities cannot understand or forgive in Napoleon is that such a man, so highly placed and empowered by nature to free mankind from its history of privilege and servitude, should choose instead the obvious, time-worn, lesser course, the conventional way of aggrandizement ("mere traditions," "common plots/ For his own gain"). Because he has turned willfully against the harmony of creation, they pronounce that he should be dismissed and removed from the human stage: he "now profits naught," his career should be "wound up," his deeds "nulled."

"Nulled" and "naught": these are strong words of condemnation to come from the poem's voice of Love. The Spirit of the Pities will hold to this conviction throughout the drama; and at the drama's close the Spirit of the Years, Pity's opposite partner in the poem's dialectic, will voice words of dismissal like them—"worthless," "gone," "meanest"—upon Napoleon in the wood of Bossu, the last scene in the earthly drama.

> Worthless these kneadings of thy narrow thought,
> Napoleon; gone thy opportunity!
> Such men as thou, who wade across the world
> To make an epoch, bless, confuse, appal,
> Are in the elemental ages' chart
> Like meanest insects on obscurest leaves
> But incidents and grooves of Earth's unfolding. . . .
>
> (III,vii,ix,521)

With the two leading Phantom Intelligences thus concurring in dismissal of Napoleon, their view shapes and influences our reading of the poem.

At the same time, also figuring importantly in our reading of the poem as it did in historical fact, is the slowly emergent and eventually triumphant opposition to Napoleon. Hardy sets up an interpretation of the struggle as a moral one by having the Pities immediately follow up their disapproving view of Napoleon with a lyric counterview of what a hero of men should be:

SHADE OF THE EARTH

> And who, then, Cordial One,
> Wouldst substitute for this Intractable?

CHORUS OF THE PITIES (aerial music)
We would establish those of kindlier build,
    In fair compassions skilled,
Men of deep art in life-development;
Watchers and warders of thy varied lands,
Men surfeited of laying heavy hands
    Upon the innocent,
The mild, the fragile, the obscure content
Among the myriads of thy family.
Those, too, who love the true, the excellent,
And make their daily moves a melody.
                                        (Fore Scene, 3)

The field for our discriminations has been drawn. On
the one side stands a single individual, a man who already
at the drama's opening is giving his name to the era and
remaking Europe in his image (with "heavy hands"). On the
other side is projected not one person but a composite
"those," unnamed because they are relatively new and un-
recognized on the human scene. (The shade of the Earth
remarks that "They *may* come . . . ," and the Spirit of the
Years adds that for such men to be leaders would mark a
departure from "accustomed lines"; Fore Scene, 3.) The
new men will be recognized by certain attributes that the
Pities delineate in their visionary song: an appreciation of
the value of life in all its ordinary daily manifestations; a
motivating sense that all living things share a common
need to enjoy daily life without annoy; and a readiness to
act upon this sense, to give their own strengths and lives
to protect weaker ones from being overridden and crushed.
These attributes are all aspects of consciousness; they are
summed up in the phrase, "Men of deep art in life-development," taking the word "art" in one of its senses,
"knowledge."
This description by the Pities of the attitudes of "those"
whom they would prefer to see in Napoleon's place shapes

our reading of the drama in two ways. First, Hardy has given us certain marks by which to identify Napoleon's moral opposites: we will measure all the characters against those standards and will recognize those whose individual outlines are in spiritual harmony with the ideal delineated here. And, second, as we recognize the successive "outshapings" of the new hero, they in turn will shape our judgment of Napoleon. Their attitudes and ways gradually sensitize us to the difference in attitudes and ways of the one man who is the common opponent of them all.

We may find somewhat familiar the imaginative polarity set up for the drama by the Spirit of the Pities. Hardy dramatizes the same contrast in attitudes—between setting value on impressive, combatative acts of exploit and preferring homely, kindly commonplace actions—in his much-anthologized lyric, "The Souls of the Slain."[1] And he has used similar type-casting in the many stories and novels where the characters, male and female, seem to fall into two broad types. Into the one type fall most of the Hardy protagonists, individuals who have in common, for differing reasons, the fact that they seem fated to occupy the position of observers unwilling or unable to engage in strenuous action or in normal human relationships; they are introspective in temperament, inhibited by a refined consciousness, long-suffering in character, and, in the eyes of the world, colorless and unsuccessful. This group of characters is faced with another group of people who are their constitutional opposites: temperamentally extroverted and uninhibited by complex thoughts, aggressive, successful, and attractive as the world judges such matters.[2]

[1] Thomas Hardy, *Collected Poems* (London: Macmillan, 1930), pp. 84–87. Hereafter page references to the *Collected Poems* will be cited in the body of this study, as follows: CP, pp. 84–87.

[2] The observer-actor division is provisional only, brought in to provide an approximate sense of lines that Hardy has used before. Examples of the first group might be: John Loveday, Giles Winterbourne, Gabriel Oak, Donald Farfrae, Clym Yeobright, Diggory Venn, Angel Clare, and Jude Fawley. In the second, smaller group would be: Robert

Critics, remarking on this double typology, have used it as the basis for much stimulating conjecture about the psychological springs of Hardy's imagination.[3] But we are interested here in the different shaping that Hardy gives to the typology in *The Dynasts*. The main difference we have already noted: the unusually exemplary, prescriptive moral that is explicitly drawn into the first statement of the two types of humanity. Another change is that his usual distinction between observer and participant does not hold in the drama: both types, the less conscious and the more conscious characters, are actors, and highly effective actors too. The reason for this departure in Hardy's use of the types lies, I think, in his subject matter, in the fact that for once he is working with a body of "given," objective, historical material, and not with matter created out of himself, so that he had to alter his established preoccupations and formulae. Given his subject, England's role in the war with Napoleon, the men of vision in it could not be disengaged and unsuccessful when for once, in historical fact, they were successful, and were so because they engaged themselves totally.

There is one other change of emphasis in the types in *The Dynasts*. In his presentation of some of the thoughtful characters in his novels—Farfrae and Clym, Angel and Jude, for example—Hardy works into their characterization the fact that they held "modern" views that gave them an advantage (or disadvantage) over rivals clinging to old ways of power and that set them apart from the ordinary people of their time. But "modernity," with the connotations of rationality and deracination that the term holds for Hardy, does not fit the turbulent years of 1805–1815. In this context the better word for saying larger vision, then, is "new":

Loveday, Edred Fitzpiers, Francis Troy, Michael Henchard, Damon Wildeve, and Alec d'Urberville.

[3] Some critics who have speculated on the psychological polarity in Hardy's actors and observers are: Guerard, *Thomas Hardy*; J. Hillis Miller, *Thomas Hardy*; and J. I. M. Stewart, *Thomas Hardy*.

"new" in representing an advancement over old, shallow assumptions about the uses of power. The newness need not be exclusively "modern"; it is as old as Christ and older.[4] Rather it is "new" in the sense of not-yet-established, not-yet-recognized or grasped by most minds.

A final difference lies in the elemental nature of the characters and the opposition. In the novels the introspective heroes sometimes come into direct competition with their anti-types over a mutually prized love; but, except for the tense period of the competition (in which the one whose merit was superficial usually carries the day), they live and let live. In the drama the state of war and emergency polarizes everything, and, in Hardy's imaginative alignment, opposites become opponents in real battles of war. The historical qualities of these men are simplified and purified to make the contest a poetic morality play.

Hardy has taken a well-known subject of demonstrated magnitude and representativeness in which, at the close of a long career of writing and thought, to shape what he has to say about life. It is part of the purpose of his design that we should begin our reading by looking at the characters—who in his other writings, as in life, elude labels—prescriptively, as exemplars as well as examples.

2. New Heroes and Old: A "Moral" View

Left to themselves, the men who are to become the future models of leadership would be in an unequal contest for our regard, for they are several where Napoleon is one, they are not-yet-established, where he is famous, and they do not possess his magnetic gifts for commanding attention. Hardy helps us to notice them by bringing their side into the drama first, introducing the earliest representative in the sequence, Pitt, before bringing Napoleon onstage. When the

---

[4] Milton presents the prototype of this "new" heroism in Jesus' inward, spiritual victory, decisively renouncing the "old" outward accoutrements of power and glory, in *Paradise Regained*.

prime minister first appears (Parliamentary Scene, I,i,iii), Hardy guides our attention further by using Overworld commentary to make clear to us that Pitt, despite personal ill-health and exhaustion, is giving himself totally to his country's need, and working to organize its forces according to his "dream of good guardianship." All leaders, indeed all men, are necessarily "watchers and warders," but the phrase used by the Pities in the Fore Scene is explicitly attached in the drama to Pitt: "his dream of good guardianship" (I,i,iii,17)—"guard" being a cognate form of "ward"; ". . . I, of all men, slight our safeguarding?" (I,i,iii,20); "in this vital point of watch and ward" (I,i,iii,21); "He wills the wardenry of his affairs . . ." (I,vi,viii,135). Pitt is one of the few who recognizes the danger Napoleon represents to order and peace in Europe; Pitt is the architect and builder of the defensive strategy that will eventually overcome Napoleon, although he himself will not live to see its purpose brought about. That accomplishment will be left to Lord Wellesley (Wellington), who is a visitor to Pitt's deathbed, as we are told in a brief aside (I,vi,viii,135) that marks the moment when, as events in Hardy's drama will show, the two principal instruments of history meet and a historic responsibility is transferred from the older man to the younger.

In the almost ten years intervening, the drama follows the struggle as it ranges over Europe and depicts it as kept alive by three men: Nelson, whose victory at Trafalgar put an end to the threat from the French navy; Moore, whose personal stoicism under adversity helped to inspirit the English in Spain into a disciplined, effective fighting force; and Kutuzof, who worked with the great Russian spaces to erase the French army in Russia.

These five are the men who make up the composite model we will watch in the emerging strand of Hardy's design. They will not be perfect, obvious heroes, but they are not supposed to be. Their "music," as the Spirit of the Pities has prepared us to expect, will be tuned to "daily" experiences, while the music of Napoleon's march across the stage is epochal, in the grand style. At times we may be hard put to see how the admiring dream-description of the Spirit of the Pities applies to these men with their various frailties: Pitt, according to the citizens on the London streets, is heavily in debt and is reputed to be fond of his glass of port; Nelson himself feels that his own private life has rendered "lustreless" his public service to his country; Moore, in his own eyes and in the eyes of the Overworld (II,II,v,198), is unlucky and "ill-omened"; Kutuzof, a sleepy old man, is looked down upon by fellow generals. Their "build" does not seem "heroic" and sometimes it does not even seem "kindlier": there is nothing gallant or humanitarian about Kutuzof's ruthless pursuit of French soldiers straggling in retreat from Moscow; and Wellington's sympathies, which extend on occasion to a disinterested, "sportsmanlike" admiration of brave fighting on both sides of the battle lines, are shown to be narrowly professional rather than broad and human.

Sometimes their claim to be the new hero hoped for by the Spirit of the Pities will seem to be accidental: they only happen to carry the fight against the man seen as the antithesis to those kindlier qualities. At other times it will appear to be a matter of tactics: their policies are less imposing than Napoleon's. But we will argue not only that through their policies and their achievements they put forth a concerted force that finally overcomes Napoleon, but that they also embody a different way (*mores*), a different approach to life, that is more in keeping with mankind's slowly developing consciousness.

This approach to life can be defined as one that does not lay heavy hands on the substance of reality, that respects it in all its manifestations, and that waits and watches for reality's inner design to emerge and declare itself. We can discern from a leader's mode of perception, his habits of speech, and his style of leadership whether he embodies this new approach or the one Hardy is contrasting to it.

Modes of Perception

Pitt states his own philosophy of perception early in the drama:

> Times they are fraught with peril, trouble, gloom;
> We have to mark their lourings, and to face them.
> Sir, reading thus the full significance
> Of these big days, large though my lackings be,
> Can any hold of those who know my past
> That I, of all men, slight our safeguarding?
>
> (I,ɪ,iii,20)

If the resolution in the first two lines sounds familiar, it is because it is very like Hardy's famous line, cited by himself and others as a statement of his realism, from "In Tenebris, II": "if way to the Better there be, it exacts a full look at the Worst" (CP, p. 154). All of the men we call new heroes respond to bad news and uncertainty with this ready, attentive concentration, aware of their own inner lackings, but subordinating that recognition to the extraordinary need to recognize and meet the dangers emerging from without. "I may as well be shot as not perceive/ What ills are raging here," Wellington snaps to the aide who urges him to retreat from the worst of the fighting at Waterloo (III,ᴠɪɪ,iii, 506). Pitt seeks out the bad news that comes from Ulm and Austerlitz. Nelson seeks out Collingwood to learn more details of his friend's disquieting theory that behind the distracting maneuvers of the French fleet lies a plan for the ships to whip around and attack the British coast. We see Kutuzof before Austerlitz and Wellington in all his battles in Spain listening intently to the sounds coming from the enemy lines, to discern the pulse of life and mood and momentum in them, and to read their "full significance." Even as they lie dying, Pitt strains to hear if his courier has returned with diplomatic news from Berlin, Nelson asks the specific names of men lost and ships taken, and Moore wishes to be lifted up to glimpse the direction of the fighting.

In the way that they face and respond to reality, these men instinctively model their actions on certain principles of life and of growth in nature. Pitt, in the statement quoted above, used the image of the man scanning the horizon for threatening weather; he goes on to use images of weathered, matured, solidly based growth to describe the army and the defensive alliance he would build for Britain. His Parliamentary Act in "Provision for England's Proper Guard":

> In process sure, if slow, will ratch the lines
> Of English regiments—seasoned, cool, resolved—
> To glorious length and firm prepotency.
>
> (I,i,iii,20)

He sees the same slowly matured, solid growth in his coalition:

> Thus now, sir, opens out this Great Alliance
> Of Russia, Austria, England, whereto I
> Have lent my earnest efforts through long months,
> And the realm gives her money, ships, and men.—
>
> (I,iv,i,66)

Wellington, later, in his defensive strategies on the field, acts upon the same instinctive principle of "prepotency"— that is, of moving or opening out only from a solid base of gravity, and having more substance behind and beneath than is put forward. That principle, I believe, is what is at work in the remarkable passage in the stage directions describing Wellington's fortifications at Torres Vedras, which we will analyze here:

> . . . It is perceived in a moment that the northern verge of this nearly coast-hemmed region is the only one through which access can be gained to it by land, and a close scrutiny of the boundary there reveals that means are being adopted to effectively prevent such access.
>
> From east to west along it runs a chain of defenses, dotted at intervals by dozens of circular and square re-

doubts, either made or in the making, two of the latter being of enormous size. Between these stretch unclimbable escarpments, stone walls, and other breastworks, and in front of all a double row of abattis, formed of the limbs of trees.

Within the outer line of defense is a second, constructed on the same principle, its course being bent to take advantage of natural features. This second rampart is finished, and appears to be impregnable.

The third defense is far off southward, girdling the very base point of the shield-shaped tract of country; and is not more than a twelfth of the length of the others. It is a continuous entrenchment of ditches and ramparts, and its object—that of covering a forced embarkation—is rendered apparent by some rocking English transports off the shore hard by. (II,IV,i,289–90)

The first sentence of this passage, in the space between the two uses of "access," captures in its indirect and heavy grammar the prosaic, methodical nature of the defense lines and of the man who arranged for them. The three paragraphs that describe each defense line put before us their bulk and impressiveness: "enormous," "unclimbable," "and in front of all," "impregnable," "continuous." The exactness of the terms for the things described—"redoubts," "escarpments," "breastworks," "abattis," "rampart," "entrenchment"—here, more than in other scenes where those words appear more casually, pile upon us a sense of the toil and effort, the cost in terms of sheer physical labor, required to raise them. Altogether, the viewing eye in the stage directions takes them seriously.

To the French officers who are viewing these fortifications, such heavy defenses typify Wellington:

> They are Lord Wellington's select device,
> And, like him, heavy, slow, laborious, sure.
>
> (II,VI,ii,291)

As Frenchmen they are temperamentally averse to such a solemn, deliberate, tasking method of procedure, and their amusement shows itself in their witty figures: the lines are bull-like, "burly, bossed disfigurements," "prim ponderosi-ties," they have "horns and tusks" and rear up "their fore-heads to the moon" (II,vi,ii,291). But as fellow-soldiers they respect the efficacy of this method: "Little strange/ Lord Wellington rode placid at Busaco/ With this behind his back!" "May he enjoy their sureness. He deserves to" (Massena, II,vi,ii,291 and 292).

Wellington uses the principle of prepotency with troops as well as with wood and earthworks. At each of his five battles in Spain, and at Waterloo, his procedure is to have his men take a stand and hold it, absorbing all enemy onslaughts; then, when he senses that the actual moment has arrived when the enemy's forces have unrolled to their full power, he signals for his men to open up and attack, putting into play the force they have held in reserve, and to follow through, pushing their advantage and momentum to a decisive end. In each of these battles, nature, reality, seems to confirm the principle borrowed from nature: it succeeds.

Wellington does not take the successes personally. It is less important for him, the agent, to be upheld than for the impersonal principle to be borne out. "I thought they looked as they'd be scurrying soon!" he exclaims after the turning-point at Salamanca (III,i,iii,337), and we sense an emphasis on the "thought" that is confirmed rather than the "I." At the battle of Nivelle he is more troubled than pleased by the sudden capitulation of the French from a "grand position" held long and stubbornly, until he learns that special factors were at work, and that his impersonal principle still holds true, a principle larger than the par-ticular individuals or nations who succeed for a time by using it.

As evidence that the principle is for Wellington a "select device" and consciously subscribed to, we have his speech at

Waterloo when he learns of Ponsonby's fatal charge upon the French lines:

> The Greys were bound to pay—'tis always so—
> Full dearly for their dash so far afield.
> Valour unballasted but lands its freight
> On the enemy's shore.
>
> (III,vii,iv,493)

The middle heroes—Nelson, Kutuzof, and Moore—make briefer appearances in the drama, and the principles they draw from reality are less explicit than those by which Pitt and Wellington see and act. But their principles, too, are living ones drawn from nature.

Nelson, sharing with Collingwood his hopes and fears for the coming sea-struggle, describes his sense of "dying fires" within (I,ii,i). He has wasted valuable time in his private love affair, and dissipated his limited store of vital force; his "effective hours," he recognizes at last, "are shortening here." That recognition makes it "ill-timed" to dwell for long on his remorse, or on his shadowed honor, or on his weariness with life; for such brooding would entail a further diversion of energy from the approaching battle. Thus the aim of effectiveness, of conserving and applying energy, motivates all his actions at Trafalgar. It explains the exposed position he takes on the deck of the *Victory*, where he can instantly see to damages and repairs and tactics, and, in his uniform and medals, be a conspicuous sign of encouragement to his men. And it explains his order that he be covered and borne quickly below when he is wounded, so that the men will not be distracted or demoralized by this different view of him. The French do not understand Nelson's motives, reading them as "eyeless bravery" (I,iii,i, 59) or as "dandyism raised to godlike pitch" (I,v,iii,90). But the English Admiral is more objective and clear-sighted, less preoccupied with his image and honor, and, above all, more effective than the French leader Villeneuve, whom

Hardy depicts as not only Nelson's opponent, but as also his mental opposite.

Moore, in his very brief appearance in the drama, is contrasted to Wellesley (Wellington) to show the different fortunes awaiting both men in Spain. Hardy's dumb-show descriptions of the passage of the fleet from England to the peninsula (II,II,v,197–99), establishes the image by which we are to understand Moore.

> Four groups of moth-like transport ships are discovered silently skimming this wide liquid plain. . . . A south-east wind is blowing strong, and, according to the part of their course reached, they either sail direct with the wind on their larboard quarter, or labour forward by tacking in zigzags. . . . (II,II,v,197)

> In the spacious scene visible the far-separated groups of transports, convoyed by battleships, float on before the wind almost imperceptibly. . . . The southernmost expedition, under SIR ARTHUR WELLESLEY, soon comes to anchor within the Bay of Mondego aforesaid, and the soldiery are indefinitely discernible landing upon the beach from boats. Simultaneously the division commanded by MOORE, as yet in the Chops of the Channel, is seen to be beaten back by contrary winds. It gallantly puts to sea again, and . . . labours round Ushant, and stands to the south in the track of WELLESLEY. (II,II,v,198–99)

Moore is like an unlucky ship singled out for misfortune, running into contrary winds where others glide along forward almost "imperceptibly," and doomed to play a minor role in history compared to Wellington's major one. But his response to adversity is to try again "gallantly" and to labor on forward.

This same image seems to figure in Moore's own view of himself, as he looks back over a course strewn with major frustrations and small victories:

—But it has never been my lot
To owe much to good luck; . . .
Good fortune has been mine, but (bitterly) mostly so
By the exhaustion of all shapes of bad! . . .

                                        (II,III,iii,220)

Moore acts upon the principle of the creature in the storm
who waits, intensely alert (the view on the road to Astorga,
II,III,i,209) to catch sight of gaps that need repairing against
the ill winds, and reinforces them strenuously; and who is
ready, when the ill winds exhaust themselves, to make the
most of opportunity and push forward with "notable"
energy (the view from Coruna, II,III,iii,216). It is the principle of endurance necessary to survival.

Moore is, of all the heroes in *The Dynasts*, the one who
most nearly approximates the ideal of patient effort that
Roy Morrell thinks is at the center of Hardy's moral vision.
He demonstrates, in Morrell's words, "the type of action to
which Hardy gives, perhaps, final emphasis: simple dogged
persistence, in which every individual is prepared to give
his last effort."[5] We turn to Edwin Muir, who supports
Morrell here, wth his explanation of why "dogged persistence" or endurance is so fundamental a virtue: "Their
[Hardy's men] highest virtue is uncomplaining endurance
of misfortune, a virtue which they share with women. In
describing endurance Hardy is best, for by enduring man
seems to rise above the malice of fate by a pure act of
magnanimity comprehensive only to himself."[6]

Our first view of Kutuzof, in the Russian headquarters on
the eve of Austerlitz, shows that he possesses an exceptional awareness that reality is unconditioned and unpredictable and will not conform to man's designs. He dozes
while the other generals debate strategy for the momentous
battle to come; and when he speaks at the conclusion of the
meeting, he recommends that the others sleep also. Alone,

[5] Roy Morrell, *Thomas Hardy: The Will and the Way*, p. 82.
[6] Edwin Muir, "The Novels of Thomas Hardy," p. 119.

he speaks in brief soliloquy: maps, plans, are so much paper; reality will disclose its own "true manoeuvre" when it arrives. We learn from this first appearance, then, how to view Kutuzof in subsequent appearances. His sleepiness is a metaphor for his passivity, and is analogous to the winter passivity of nature, which awaits, deeply attentive below the apparent unconsciousness and inactivity at its surface, the signal to act.

Pitt, Wellington, Nelson, Moore, Kutuzof: seen alone, each of these men has his moment in the drama in which he faces, and satisfies, destiny; seen together, with their various strengths, principles, and kinds of attention, they form a composite man of "deep art in life-development," whose approaches to reality follow and accord with reality's own rhythms.

THE first difference we see between the view these men take of the drama, and Napoleon's view, is in the Emperor's preoccupation with image, form, and design. Throughout the drama his mind is spinning out mental formulations (called, variously, "plans," "contrivance," "scheme," "project," "enterprise," "purposes," or, as the Spirit Ironic puts it in the last scene of the drama, "high-doctrined dreams," III,vii,ix,519) and projecting them in aggressive design upon the world outside. As we shall see, these plans often show little regard for the particularity and stubborn texture of reality. Rather, they show a mind concerned with form as an exercise and end in itself: a mind enjoying the wide range that these schemes encompass, the conjunctions they effect, the outlines that they shape, and, above all, the radiance rebounding into the eyes of beholders from the silhouette they make against the background of the ages. The high purpose inspiring each of his military projects is to "*carve* a triumph large in history" (II,iii,iii,215, italics mine). His plan to found a dynasty is an attempt to cast the silhouette into the future:

134

. . . I must send down shoots to future time.
Who'll plant my standard and my story there. . . .
(II,v,i,254)

Russia's great spaces are a dark background against which
his triumphant march can shine as the greatest and longest
the world has ever seen:

> Then let us forthwith stride the Niemen flood,
> Let us bear war into her great gaunt land,
> And spread our glory there as otherwhere. . . .
(III,i,i,328)

He is fond of referring to Alexander the Great (see "the
knot," I,II,iii,44; "namesake," I,VI,v,121; and "Eastern
scheme," III,I,i,330), because that young conqueror pushed
empire all the way to India, a highwater mark reached by
no other European. Alexander, the ancient world's epitome
of hero, has molded Napoleon's imagination even as Napoleon in turn will become a model of the same type of heroism for future impressionable minds.

At Waterloo it is still the question of a lofty, shining
image, and fear of darkening it, which absorbs Napoleon.
In the press of battle (III,VII,vi,502), his "star" requires
that the English squares be broken, and if Ney could be
helped to break them, " 'Twould write upon the sunset
'Victory!' " (III,VII,vi,504.) After the battle, when he rides
alone in the wood of Bossu, he still sees himself in his "lurid
loneliness" through the eyes of others, and worries about
the impression this last picture of himself in failure may
make on his heroic image. Had he been killed in Russia,
or killed himself at Fontainebleau, or been shot down on
the field at Waterloo, the shape of his life would have kept
its heroic outline through to the end.

He still sees only one possibility for nobility—that of
contending for glory, for which prize he thinks even Christ
is a contender—and still understands himself and all men
only as role-players and image-bearers.

> To shoulder Christ from out the topmost niche
> In human fame, as I once fondly felt,
> Was not for me. I came too late in time
> To assume the prophet or the demi-god,
> A part past playing now.
>
> (III,vii,ix,520)

In a world-view that downgrades fact and stresses its malleability to form, reality has no reality except as it makes "good showance" to the eyes and minds of others.

> My only course
> To make good showance to posterity
> Was to implant my line upon the throne.
> And how shape that, if now extinction nears?
>
> (III,vii,ix,520)

It follows, then, that with the collapse of the plans and the self-image he has been trying to project, Napoleon should speak of extinction and non-being.

> But for all this and this
> I shall be nothing . . .
>
> (III,vii,ix,520)

he says, earlier in the same speech, and the prospect of anonymity is a denial of his life's whole effort and more of a death than death itself. By the end of the speech he has found a consoling image to replace his former images for himself of star and planet—a meteor. It yokes his obscure present to his blazing past in a figure that still sets him apart from the rest of the earth for his greatness and condescension:

> Great men are meteors that consume themselves
> To light the earth. This is my burnt-out hour.
>
> (III,vii,ix,520)

Image, being all-important, more than compensates for the suffering that goes to sustain it. When Napoleon offers

136

this notion to persons who must suffer from his grand designs, he is not rationalizing; the comfort that to them is vain and substanceless is to him self-evident. He promises sincerely that Joesphine's grand sacrifice of her marriage will "gild" her "life's whole shape" (II,ii,vi,201). Accepting exile, he holds out to his staff as a solemn reward the chance to be included within the great image of Napoleon that will preserve himself and them from ordinariness:

> And I will give my hours to chronicling
> In stately words that stir futurity
> The might of our unmatched accomplishments;
> And in the tale immortalize your names
> By linking them with mine.
>
> (III,iv,iv,415)

Since he and persons close to him lack value and identity except as they provide the fuel of splendid fire-patterns, this definition holds all the more for those nameless thousands whose lot it is to be consumed in dynastic designs. He admires the English exploit at Walcheren, without blinking at the total and futile loss of life there, because it was

> well featured in design,
> Large in idea, and imaginative;
> I had not deemed the blinkered English folk
> So capable of view.
>
> (II,v,i,255)

When he returns to Paris from Russia, it is the failure of his conquering "enterprise" and not the loss of six hundred thousand men, its "stuff," that preoccupies him, since they are expendable: "Fishes as good/ Swim in the sea as have come out of it" (III,i,xii,364).

This kind of idealistic thinking, indifferent to particulars, to the reality of substance and feeling, to life itself, is a version of what the Spirit of the Pities called

> . . . laying heavy hands
> Upon the innocent,
> The mild, the fragile, the obscure content
> Among the myriads of thy [Earth's] family.
> (Fore Scene, 3)

For a while, Napoleon seems to succeed in making reality conform and submit to his designs. In his European victories against Austria and Prussia his projects are accomplished, and so completely that at Austerlitz he can exult, "Thus, as I sketched, they work!" (I,vi,iii,116.) In this happy moment, he seems to believe, as the syntax of his boast would suggest, that the events that follow his thinking are caused by his figuring. (Compare the remark Wellington makes when he has his expectations about a battle confirmed by reality: "I *thought* they looked as they'd be scurrying soon!"—III,i,iii,337. In Wellington's case, the figuring—"thought"—follows events, even when it precedes them in time.) The slip is easy, from seeing the current of action flow so markedly and uncannily with one's will and plans, to assuming that the confluence can be sustained by one's magnetic will and plans.

Yet events and men do not go according to plan in England, Spain, and Russia, where Napoleon's blindness to particularity makes him underestimate a people's will to resist. In private, he concedes that troubles and difficulties cannot be ignored. In this remark to Josephine he sounds almost like one of the watchful new heroes:

> Better quiz evils with too strained an eye
> Than have them leap from disregarded lairs.
> (II,ii,vi,199)

But a beautiful strategy should not be overcome by the specific difficulties of a situation; such particulars are not worthy of place in his own mind or in the minds of his lieutenants.

Villeneuve, for example, he considers a "moral coward"

for lacking the force of will to impose design upon substance:

> What shall be said of one who, at a breath,
> When a few casual sailors find them sick,
> When falls a broken boom or slitten sail,
> When rumor hints that Calder's tubs and Nelson's
> May join, and bob about in company,
> Is straightway paralyzed, and doubles back
> On all his ripened plans!
>
> (I,III,i,58)

In this speech the immediacies of the situation are treated
casually, and "plans" honorifically; the figurative plans are
described as though they had flesh ("ripened"), and material details—such as the two opposing fleets—are described
in insubstantial terms (bobbing tubs, slitten sails). Form
arrogates to itself the properties of substance.

Later in the drama, from the battle of Borodino and
after, he reacts to those aides and officers who bring him
ominous "particulars" (III,III,i,379) as though they were
disloyal. Those testing and stubborn underlying particulars
which are reality to the new heroes are to him undermining
and subversive of his idealistic reality. Since ills are treacher-
ies, so also the men who speak too much of them are trai-
tors, guilty of failing to keep the grand plan aloft by their
willed vision, as he has done.

There is an element of psychological truth in Napoleon's
subordination of material fact to mental preconception and
willed attitude. Positive, aggressive thinking and wishing
can go far to "make it so" and make up for disadvantages in
numbers. His soldiers' trust in him makes them believe
themselves invincible, which belief, in turn, helps them to
win. His enemies at Ulm and Austerlitz and Wagram are
overcome as much by surprise and dismay as by force of
arms. Psychology is at work throughout any battle: at
Waterloo, the drama's demonstration-contest, even cavalry
attacks are splendidly designed and "accoutred," the Spirit

of the Pities observes, "to terrorize/ The foe by aspect" (III,vii, iv, 496).

"Ceasing to bluff," said Gevrillière, his sworn enemy, of Napoleon, "then ceases he to be" (II,i,i,145). Because we know that Napoleon's constant purpose is the projection of an imposing front or bluff, we can see the unity between ends and means in Hardy's characterization, and understand why Napoleon's method also would naturally be a thing of imposing show and bluff. He is consistent with himself when at Leipzig he cheerfully plans to equalize the unfavorable odds and to fool the enemy with lines that are two-thirds their usual strength, to "look stronger by one-third" (III,iii,i,380); or when at Waterloo he cheers his disheartened troops with the knowingly false report that the auxiliaries descending toward them are friends instead of enemies.

His last speech to Marie Louise gives us our most penetrating insight into the way his looking and seeing is motivated by unconscious, wishful will and by the habitual choice to "bluff"; it also explains why he treats the factual world, and its reporters, as though they were wrong.

> Dismiss such fears. You may as well as not.
> As things are doomed to be they will be, dear.
> If shadows must come, let them come as though
> The sun were due and you were trusting to it:
> 'Twill teach the world it wrongs in bringing them.
>
> (III,iv,ii,401)

To sum up the two modes of looking at reality: it is not for some failure of will power or concentration that the old hero's attention is contrasted to that of his opponent and found weaker.[7] At Jena and Wagram, Ulm and Austerlitz, Napoleon is shown exerting the same degree of intent, self-

---

[7] This is another point at which I find inadequate Morrell's emphasis on human effort in his moralistic reading of Hardy's characters, as though accuracy, like success, were attainable merely by an extra exertion of will.

forgetful absorption in the action and the same successful sense of timing that Wellington displays in his battles. When Napoleon's vision loses its effectiveness, it is because his first loyalty is to external design. His plans proceed by impressing form from without,

> making inharmonious jars
> In her creation whose meek wraith we know. . . .
> (Fore Scene, 3)

Through him the Will, Creation, is laying heavy hands upon itself. But external form must either give up its rigidity, or be cast off, when the living substance that it is trying to contain begins to move.

The new heroes bring no grand plan to war or to life, except for the instinctual plan to live out one's life that is innate in Creation, innate in themselves and in the people they are leading and defending. Their plans work gradually and eductively, with the processes of nature, "outshaping," so that design emerges freely and willingly from within. When the Will works through them it is in compassion with its own substance.

Both modes, the imposing and the eductive, the self-destructive and the self-confirming, were shown in the transparencies (discussed in Chapter One) to be equally irresistible and equally unconscious: "Apprehending not how fare the sentient subjects of Its scheme" (After Scene, 525). But the view from up close to the human drama suggests that the victory of the one mode over the other is not accidental. By the very "nature of things," the properties of substance will eventually, in every pattern, reassert themselves against externally impressed form; and the regular, steady harmonies will in every pattern absorb the jarring, convulsive ones.

Modes of Speech and Leadership

The dichotomy noted above holds also for the ways the two types of heroes act as leaders. Napoleon's first speech in the drama—a communiqué—establishes an unmistakably dominating style and tone that cannot be confused with the language of any other character in the drama. It proceeds by long statements that sweep up the hearer or reader (here, Decrès) into its current:

> I am resolved that no wild dream of Ind,
> And what we there might win; or of the West,
> And bold reconquest there of Surinam
> And other Dutch retreats along those coasts,
> Or British islands nigh, shall draw me now
> From piercing into England through Boulogne
> As lined in my first plan.
>
> (I,i,ii,12–13)

The person addressed is not only put into a passive position by the sweep of the sentence; he is explicitly required to yield unquestioningly:

> —Now to the case:
> Our naval forces can be all assembled
> Without the foe's foreknowledge or surmise,
> By these rules following; to whose text I ask
> Your gravest application; and, when conned,
> That steadfastly you stand by word and word,
> Making no question of one jot therein.
>
> (I,i,ii,13)

Arresting inversions also put the hearer off-balance, since he must lean forward to catch the missing piece:

> If I do strike,
> I strike effectively; to forge which feat
> There's but one way. . . .
>
> (I,i,ii,13)

> Join him there
> Gravina, Missiessy, and Ganteaume. . . .
>
> (I,i,ii,13)

Napoleon sweeps up his meaning as well by making habitual use of verbal phrases that, because they hang in a main statement with relatively little indication of tense and number, avoid paying observance to the details of reality that affect and qualify action; phrases that thus seem to assert, in their effortless compassings, that a given order' is all but completed. In the following examples the packaging phrases are in italics:

> Next, *Venice, too, being taken,*
> *And Austria's other holdings down that way,*
> *The Bourbons also driven from Italy,*
> I strike at Russia—each in turn, you note,
> Ere they can act conjoined.
>
> > (I,II,iii,45)
>
> Where, *Austria settled,* I engage the Tsar,
> While Massena detains in Italy
> The Archduke Charles.
>
> > (I,III,ii,60)

Another example is his Berlin Edict forbidding commerce with England, in which the command, framed in unqualified infinitives ("to suffer . . . to cease forthwith. . . . To be detained. . . . To be good prize . . ."; II,I,vi,166), allows no restriction, and thus assumes an air of absoluteness.

The diction, also, in which his orders are expressed is domineering and assertive. See, for instance, the active and aggressive verbs in his plan for attacking England: "brave," "convulse," "hold," "cut" (I,II,iii,44); and those in his alternative plan for attacking Austria: "strike," "cross," "pause not," "strike" (I,II,iii,44-45). His later plan for the Austrian campaign actually enacts in its language the conquest he is formulating:

> Bernadotte *moves out* from Hanover . . .
>
> Marmont from Holland *bears* along the Rhine,
> And *joins* at Mainz and Würzburg Bernadotte . . .

While these prepare their routes the army here
Will turn its rump from Britain's tedious shore,
And . . .
Set out full force due eastward . . .
By the Black Forest *feign* a straight attack. . . .

Meet in Franconia Bernadotte and Marmont;
Transverse the Danube somewhat down from Ulm;
Entrap the Austrian columns by their rear;
Surround them, *cleave* them; *roll* upon Vienna. . . .
        So shall I *crush* the two gigantic sets
Upon the Empire, now grown imminent.
                                  (I,III,ii,60–61, italics mine)

Unlike the new heroes, who are regularly shown speaking face to face, Napoleon's speech often issues forth from a remove, through the written pronouncements of a "dictator," in the form of official addresses, directives, edicts, manifestoes, dispatches, and proclamations. The view of the French position on the eve of Austerlitz is an illustration of the procedure and the result of this type of communication from "on high." For most of the scene (I,VI,i) Napoleon is screened inside his tent, and only his voice emerges, dictating a speech to be read to the troops, in which he announces the layout and tactics of the coming battle. When someone interrupts, to question the wisdom of making public such secret matters, Napoleon explains his reason:

        The zest such knowledge will impart to all
        Is worth the risk of leakages.
                                  (I,VI,i,110)

The scene's end proves his point; the distance the Emperor keeps between himself and ordinary people gives a kind of divinity to his communications and makes his infrequent approaches in his own person among ordinary people seem like the gracious condescensions of a god, stirring in those "masses" deep emotion and outpourings of gratitude and devotion.

SOLDIERS

The Emperor! He's here! The Emperor's here!
(I,vi,i,112)

These cries are occasioned by the Emperor's coming forth
from his tent into the night air to survey the battle lines.
As the scene closes, his brief circuit along the field turns
into a triumphal procession lighted with torches improvised
by the cheering soldiers in spontaneous enthusiasm. The
onlooking Spirits comment upon this rare display of deception and need with its burden of irony and pathos:

CHORUS OF THE PITIES (aerial music)
Strange suasive pull of personality!

CHORUS OF IRONIC SPIRITS
His projects they unknow, his grin unsee!

CHORUS OF THE PITIES
Their loyal luckless hearts say blindly—He!
(I,vi,i,113)

The French are luckless, for Napoleon provides them
with only the semblance of communication. While still in
the tent he has ordered that the bad news of Trafalgar be
hushed and minimized. To "impart zest," information is
carefully dispensed and calculated—or "vamped up," as the
Spirit of Rumour puts it later in his interview with the
street-woman whose reactions speak for Paris after Austerlitz (I,vi,vii,132). Like most of her countrymen, she loyally
puts out of mind any doubts or misgivings about the truth-
fulness of Napoleon's perfect image ("Can revolution's
dregs so soil thy soul/ That thou shouldst doubt the eldest
son thereof?" I,vi,vii,131), and about the honesty of the
government's official explanation of Trafalgar ("But to
plain sense/ Things seems as stated"; I,vi,vii,132). And
Trafalgar, as we noted above, is but one piece of bad news
falsified to support an image.

The French are luckless also because Napoleon provides

145

them with only the mirage that he is with them, sharing their risks. Presence, like information, is a power carefully dispensed and calculated, balancing "zest imparted" with danger risked. His proclamation to the troops at Austerlitz promises, "Soldiers, your sections I myself shall lead" (I,vi,i, 110). But at the same time what is held forth is withdrawn: his "rashness" will not be "undue." Should there be "hot confusion" he will use "fit care," and he will risk himself only if the risk is for an instant, "wink-while":

> Nevertheless, should issues stand at pause
> But for wink-while, that time you will eye
> Your Emperor the foremost in the shock,
> Taking his risk with every ranksman here.
>
> (I,vi,i,110)

These words, spoken before this early battle, hold all too true in the drama that follows: Napoleon's identity with the men in the ranks is to be a thing of show only, lasting "but for wink-while," while issues are open or proceeding victoriously. At La Mure, when he must pull France behind him again, he symbolically asserts membership in the common body by sharing wine from a common glass. But he extricates his body from the common fate when that "one body" is pulled down at Russia, Leipzig, and Waterloo in mass collapses set in train by him.

We are not to take these nimble instances of "fit care" as proofs of cowardice. Napoleon's animating bravery at Wagram makes the Emperor Francis look like an ineffectual, pusillanimous leader by comparison, as Francis himself admits (II,iv,iii,242–243). Like his strategic presence at Wagram, Napoleon's desertions of his people in other scenes are to be understood as in keeping with his obsession with design. As the source of designs, the "head" is indispensable and irreplaceable. The "body" (the troops and citizens who are the material for designs) can be repaired and replaced. Napoleon could say in his own defense that other leaders—his "new hero" opponents, for example—work

146

with simple, elementary strategies obvious to the most ordinary common soldier; and, therefore, that such men can
afford to let themselves be lost, like the commonest, in their
causes. But the mind of a Napoleon, being the source of
brilliant designs not yet revealed and consummated, must
go on.

WHEN we consider the leadership exemplified by the opponents to Napoleon, we find significant differences in attitude that bear out our contrasting patterns of old and new
heroes. The ordinariness of their speech provides the most
noticeable difference. Rarely—only in moments of great
emotion—do they expand to the "high" style and noble,
poetic imagery that Napoleon employs in acting out his historic role.

Early in *The Dynasts,* in the Parliamentary debates, Pitt
makes some remarks about speech that have a subsequent
bearing on the way we read the drama. He is replying to a
clever address by Sheridan that had diverted attention to its
own gravity-defying wit and away from the grave subject
under consideration. Pitt in his address distinguishes his
own manner of speech from Sheridan's:

> Now vain indeed it were should I assay
> To match him in such sort. For, sir, alas,
> To use imagination as the ground
> Of chronicle, take myth and merry tale
> As texts for prophecy, is not my gift[,]
> Being but a person primed with simple fact,
> Unprinked by jewelled art.—But to the thing.
>
> (I,i,iii,19)

Pitt sets forth here, and demonstrates in his style elsewhere,
the following principles of rhetoric. There should be a
direct relationship of plain-dealing between a speaker, the
view he is trying to deliver, and his audience. Speech is a
means, information and elucidation the end. All the energies of language should go to delivering one's perception

("the thing") with maximum clarity and appropriate force, instead of being diverted to other "things," such as calling attention to the speaker and his art, away from the substance of the speech.[8]

Here in the field of rhetoric, just as above in the field of action, the same principles of "substance before image" (e.g., showing less than one keeps in reserve, and concentering one's energies for maximum power) make for effectiveness. The natural laws of matter govern throughout the monistic universe of this drama, unaffected by the varying degrees of "sentience" held by individual lives. But because individual lives are affected by those laws, their degree of "sentience" does make a difference to themselves. If they possess, as do these new heroes, a consciousness sensitive to the laws of nature, they can live in greater concord with the way things happen, can live without causing, or themselves suffering, needless "inharmonious jars."

The theory that there are three different levels of speech in *The Dynasts*, having to do with the position of the speakers relative to the strongest pulses of the Will, is by now accepted as a fundamental first step in understanding *The Dynasts*.[9] The theory has assumed, however, that there are no interesting variations inside the middle level, and that the speech of the dynasts who make up that level is

8 This view, that "jewelled art" should serve some serious communicative purpose, is one Hardy himself shared with Pitt. Writing of the young Hardy in the *Life,* he claims the principle as an ideal that he kept to in his writing: "Since coming into contact with Leslie Stephen about 1873 . . . Hardy had been much influenced by his philosophy, and also by his criticism. He quotes the following sentence from Stephen in his notebook under the date of July 1, 1879: 'The ultimate aim of the poet should be to touch our hearts by showing his own, and not to exhibit his learning, or his fine taste, or his skill in mimicking the notes of his predecessors.' That Hardy adhered pretty closely to this principle when he resumed the writing of poetry can hardly be denied" (*Life,* p. 128).

9 See Arthur McDowall, *Thomas Hardy,* pp. 174–75 and 183–89; Samuel L. Hynes, *The Pattern of Hardy's Poetry,* pp. 164–66; and F. R. Southerington, *Hardy's Vision of Man,* pp. 178–86.

uniformly undistinguishable. But certainly one basic distinction seems to be carried out through their speech, indicating whether a dynastic character possesses the "old" or the "new" sensibility: the simple distinction of whether the speaker channels his finite store of energy through his speech or lavishes a large part of that energy upon the instrument itself. The drama shows one line of leaders who speak in highly figured language (Sheridan, Napoleon, Villeneuve, the French officers commenting upon Torres Vedras), and suggests that they share a somewhat dashing "Cavalier" preference for form and image over prosaic substance. Against them the drama sets another line of leaders, each of whom in his particular way speaks like Pitt, "as a serious man on serious things" (I,i,iii,20), and shows that they share a more prosaic "Protestant" concern that energy and substance effect its own form.

With Pitt we see this concern demonstrated by the proof of a gift held in reserve, not used. The prime minister who claims to be "unpricked by jewelled art" can, when it accords with the occasion, release rhetorical powers of balanced form (his comments on painting, I,vi,vi,126) and felt argument (his Guildhall speech, I,v,v,103) that quite match those of any other orator in the drama. Except for these occasions, his speech is "daily," though effective, employing practical, workaday images (ale brewing, storms, seasoned growth) in a sober tone.

The speech of the three soldiers is laconic. Kutuzof's utterances are few and brief and gruff. The following examples are typical: "Ay, ay, Weirother; that's the question— eh?" (I,vi,ii,114); "Well, well. Now this being ordered, set it going./ . . . We now disperse,/ And luck attend us all. Good-night. Good-night" (I,vi,ii,115); " 'Tis well. So perish Russia's enemies!" (III,i,xi,359).

Wellington appears in more scenes than do the other new heroes, and Hardy shows him in some informal moments away from battle when he is relaxed (speaking sympathetically of the English wives at Salamanca, permitting the men to loot after Vitoria, and entertaining the French officers at Nivelle), before the long and close study of him under pressure at Waterloo. But Wellington's speech, in those relaxed scenes as well as in the ones under fire, is one-dimensional, not connotative or resonant, its flatness of timbre and colloquialism of style deliberately maintained to keep himself an impersonal and ready instrument. In fact, the more pressured the situation, the more deflating and relaxed grows his speech, almost drawling in its coolness. Before Waterloo he uses abbreviations (e.g., "Let 'em," III,ii,iii, 371), but they become progressively noticeable in the tension building up at Brussels and after.

> Blücher, I think, and I can make shift
> To do the business without troubling 'em!
> > (III,vi,ii,457)

> Now I must also go
> And snatch a little snooze ere harnessing.
> > (III,vi,ii,462)

> 'Tis pretty clear old Blücher had to take
> A damned good drubbing yesterday at Ligny. . . .
> > (III,vi,viii,481)

> Not yet. They shall have at 'em later on.
> > (III,vii,iv,498)

This kind of affected indifference is a personal braking device that preserves that attentiveness and deliberateness which we have seen is Wellington's special strength. But through him it affects his army also, as we shall see, transmitting the quality of coolness and level-headedness needed when men ". . . writhe to charge—or anything but stand!" Then it is that a placid, unexcited response like this one, "Not yet. They shall have at 'em later on . . . ," is efficacious, for even while it denies the specific relief requested, it relieves by example.

Moore's reserve seems to differ from that of the other leaders in being not a "select device" or an innate strength but an unwilling and regretted weakness, one more example of the ill-fortune under which he stoically labors. In his dying conversation, the only time he talks in the drama, Moore speaks of objective matters such as the battle, but breaks down, from diffidence or extreme reticence, when he tries to express the human loneliness and affections he carries within him. When he does manage to speak of those things, the words of emphasis are flat, unresonant, impersonal terms: "This suits . . ." (II,III,iii,221), "satisfied" and "justice" (II,III,iii,219), and "remembrance" (II,III,iii,221), as though Moore did not trust his own speech or his listener's reception of it.

The characters in Vienna who comment upon Moore after his death predict that his story will be remembered for combining "tender charm" with "strenuous feats" (II,III,v, 224). We may assume that part of the appeal which this briefly sketched character held for Hardy was his unreadiness to give form to substance, and his inability to express the vast reality that he feels. With this inability he takes his place in the long gallery of Hardy characters who suffer from constitutional wordlessness, and who need an informed sympathy to intercede and speak well for them. Here it is a weakness (which to Hardy is a "tender charm" and a virtue) that Moore contributes to the ideal new hero we put together from these historical approximations of it.

In his ineloquence, Moore stands in contrast to Nelson, who surely is the leader whose speech most realizes the word "melody." Informality and colloquialism are a part of its music, as they were in Wellington's: "tough work awhile for you and me!" (I,II,i,39); "Warm work this, Hardy" (I, v,ii,86); "done for me at last!" (I,v,ii,88); "Doctor, I'm gone. I am waste o' time to you" (I,v,ii,88). Nelson's metaphors are the good-humored ones of a sea salt: "But here I am— stove in—/ Broken—all logged and done for!" (I,v,iv,96); "—too late—/ My anchoring's elsewhere ordered!" (I,v,iv, 98). Its only literary allusion ("Ah, yes; like David you would see the battle!" I,v,ii,85) is familiar, kindly, and comes appropriately from Nelson, for in this drama he is like young David. There is sweetness and bonhommie in all its references to men and officers: "Thank'ee, good friend"; "poor youngsters," "that noble fellow Collingwood," "I know, I know, good Beatty!" "Bear me along, good fellows." Even its references to the enemy are good-humored, almost folksy: "villains"; "foreign boasters"; "those giants over here . . . swelling up so pompously"; "these braggarts."

Formalities are lowered in Nelson's bonhommie because what he sees is the common element of goodwill in each man, and so he addresses everyone in the drama informally, like a friend. In contrast to the image-minded old heroes, who speak often of "honour" and "dignity," "Fortune" and "Fate," abstractions do not have a place in his speech—until the end, when "duty," his signal-motto for Trafalgar, is the last word he speaks, as though he can finally feel he has met it. But "Necessity," though unspoken, is a word that suggests itself on the *Victory*. On the deck and in the cockpit, so quick is Nelson, so forthcoming with his goodwill and fellow feeling in tight situations, that it is as though he were a friend to Necessity as well as to everyone else. We can find a special meaning in Villeneuve's wistful tribute to his opponent's good fortune just before his own suicide (I,v,vi,104): for understandably, a man who lives and dies in such harmony with necessity would seem, to the outside view of someone less happily natured, to be the charmed recipient of necessity's favors, "blest and over blest."

The poem has a pragmatic interest in what heroes do with their powers of speech and whether they use them to educate and guide or to mystify and dominate. A world in which millions perish from the selfish impulses and sightless decisions of dynasts, cries for the kind of leadership of vision and compassion that the Spirit of the Pities sang of in the Fore Scene.

> Each for himself, his family, his heirs;
> For the wan weltering nations who concerns, who cares?
>
> (I,VI,V,125)

sings the Chorus of Pities after we are shown a scene sequence in which, first, at the command of one man, two
thousand perish beneath the ice of the Satschan Lake at
Austerlitz, and, next, two emperors engage in a diplomatic
minuet over the political ground that has been won and lost.
Clearly, they do not care for the peoples of the world; who
does, then? In silent answer, the next scene sequence shows
us Pitt receiving the news of Austerlitz, reeling from the
news as from a physical blow, and dying soon after. So much
does Pitt concern and identify himself with the suffering of
the European nations, that this identification becomes established in an image. He "dies" not near Bath nor at Putney
but at Austerlitz:

PITT

—Where's Austerlitz?
—But what avails it where the place is now;
What corpse is curious on the longitude
And situation of his cemetery!

(I,vi,vi,127–128)

And when he is shown on his deathbed, a month later:

TOMLINE

. . . The name of his disease is—Austerlitz!
His brow's inscription has been Austerlitz
From that dire morning in the month just past . . .

(I,vi,viii,134)

He has taken on, through his care and pity, the vast outlines
of that opening image of Europe as "a prone and emaciated
figure." Austerlitz, one of the inscriptions on the helpless
body of the Continent, is traced upon his brow also. In size
it is an apotheosis such as Napoleon would have envied,
though not have understood.

In his Parliamentary speech Pitt used the words "under
Providence" (I,i,iii,21), and Moore at his death alluded to
"Him who holds us in His hollowed hand" (II,iii,iii,220).

153

But to us, who share the Overworld vision and who have seen by the light of the diorama that there is no consciousness guiding the hollowed hand, it is urgently clear that the function of Providence must be supplied by human beings leading themselves.

The new heroes, counter-examples to Napoleon, stand in true, rather than feigned, solidarity with their followers. Moore at Coruna personally leads fresh troops to fill a sudden gap in the front lines, calling out "Forty-second, remember Egypt!" (II,III,iii,217.) The words, invoking the name of a difficult trial borne together in the past, inspire an enthusiasm that is unillusioned and realistic, yet strong enough to convert two stragglers into soldiers. Unlike Napoleon's surprising designs, Moore's simple strategy is plain to these two ordinary men ("As Sir David was wounded, Sir John was anxious that the right should not give way, and went forward to keep it firm"; II,III,iii,217). They are not misled as to the danger of the action Moore calls them to, for they joke to one another that it has felled Moore himself. But the image of Moore's selflessness, and the proud memory of their shared trials, is enough to draw them in full consciousness to share the struggle with him again.

The drama suggests that it is Moore's own stoic example that has transformed, and in this scene continues to transform, his men from "military objects" seen earlier in retreat into the "alert soldiers" represented by these two individuals. The suggestion is made through a resemblance established in a previous dumb-show description, in which a miscellany of stragglers is "preternaturally" disciplined and energized into good order by a stoical sergeant on the road near Astorga (II,III,i,207), and the later dumb-show description of Moore's little army before Coruna, which is said to be "harrassed" but "stiffened and grown amenable to discipline by the satisfaction of standing to the enemy at last" (II,III,iii,215).

Hardy includes in the drama two "death" stories, dealing

with Moore and with Nelson, which show that in the end what the followers of these two men love in them is that, though warriors, they value life and living over dead forms and causes.

Moore's burial, hastily performed in darkness under gunfire from the French, is presented from first to last as a series of formalities that have to go unobserved or abbreviated. But the officers present justify the hastiness of the observance by citing Moore's own basic attitude, which they understand and share.

HOPE

In mercy to the living who are thrust
Upon our care for our deliverance,
And run much hazard till they are embarked,
We must abridge these duties to the dead,
Who will not mind be they abridged or no.

HARDINGE

And could he mind, would be the man to bid it. . . .

HOPE

We shall do well, then, curtly to conclude
These mutilated prayers—our hurried best!—
And what's left unsaid, feel.

(II,III,iv,223)

The other story, which Hardy did not find in Southey or Beatty, his primary sources on Nelson, but in popular tradition, concerns the crew's tapping of the alcohol from Nelson's casket on the *Victory*'s journey homeward.[10] Here too, as with Moore above, the incident is made to sum up Nelson's basic attitude.

FIRST BOATMAN

. . . What was the men to do? Broke down by the battle, and hardly able to keep afloat, 'twas a most defendable

10 Walter F. Wright, *The Shaping of "The Dynasts,"* p. 137, provides this fact about the origin of the casket-tapping story.

thing, and it fairly saved their lives. So he [Nelson] was their salvation after death as he had been in the fight. If he could have knowed it, 'twould have pleased him down to the ground! How 'a would have laughed through the spigot-hole: "Draw on, my hearties! Better I shrivel than you famish." Ha-ha! (I,v,vii,107)

The earthy anecdote, coming after the sublimity of Nelson's death scene in the *Victory* and the loneliness of Villeneuve's suicide, enacts the grounding impulse we look for in twentieth-century poetry, the impulse to incorporate the totality, recalcitrance, and anti-poeticness of experience.[11] But of course, what at first sight depoeticizes Nelson's death and demythologizes his ideal heroism, ends by adding to his myth and strengthening the ideal with its antinomy.

In the case of Moore, also, the train of dignities omitted only adds to his genuine dignity and to the poetry of his end. Even the casual, prosaic remarks of his gravediggers become noble praise of the leader who felt more than he said and whose feelings were "true" to their depths:

> There is no time. Just make the bottom true.
>
> . . . He'll couch as calmly in this scrabbled hole
> As in a royal vault!
>
> (II,III,iv,222)

But our discussion of the virtues exemplified by the new heroes is not complete until we mention the habit of sober truth-telling, for on that aspect of leadership ultimately depends the world's hope of not only preserving itself but slowly improving itself. The old hero leads himself and others deeper into the age-old glamorous illusion that "war has beauty in it" (III,VII,iv,495). Pitt disabuses his countrymen of that romanticism:

[11] Robert Penn Warren, "Pure and Impure Poetry," in *Selected Essays*, pp. 3–31.

Tasking and toilsome war's details must be . . .
Not in a moment's stroke extemporized.

(I,ı,iii,20)

The response of his countrymen to his unillusioned policies
is shown in the conversation of the Londoners outside the
Guildhall after Trafalgar (I,v,v). They know that Pitt is
fallible, that his European policy, a failure at Ulm, is lifted
up by Trafalgar "for the moment"; but their affection is the
stronger for such knowledge—they speak as fellow-citizens,
not as subjects: "Well, whatever William's faults, it is a
triumph for his virtues tonight!" (I,v,v,103.) We are meant
to remember their jocular, realistic support when we come
to the Parisian prostitute's very different response to Napoleon (I,vı,vii): to her he is a hero on a pedestal, whose
power allows no question or insinuation.

Wellington, sued by his men for reinforcements and
relief at Waterloo and, that failing, for some hopeful encouragement or inspiring command, answers with only
bleak, bare truth: they must "Fight till they fall, like others
in the field"; "hold out unto the last,/ As long as one man
stands on one lame leg/ With one ball in his pouch! —then
end as I"; "he, I, every Englishman afield,/ Must fall upon
the spot we occupy,/ Our wounds in front" (III,vıı,vii,506–
507). Such harsh realism, far from sapping his men's confidence, makes it more firm:

AIDE

It is enough, your Grace.
I answer for't that he, those under him,
And I withal, will bear us as you say.

(III,vıı,vii,507)

Their confidence is more lasting than the enthusiasm of the
French troops at Austerlitz, because it is not based on illusion. If the worst happens and every Englishman does have
to fall on the field, Wellington does not ask them to undergo
anything that he is not plainly undergoing first; and, what-

157

ever happens, they will not have to cry out, as the French do in their final disillusionment, "We are betrayed!" (III, VII,viii,514.) Wellington can be sure, they can be sure, that even without reinforcements, "We'll still stand" (III,VII,vii, 509). The English have been educated by their leadership into mature, realistic, self-reliant men. There is no separation, with them, between leader and led, "head" and "trunk": they stand together in the action at Waterloo, one body.

Hardy gives us one other model of educative leadership to put beside the figures of the new heroes. It is a brief scene featuring the mayor and the citizens of Brussels, set in the night between the battles of Quatre-Bras and Waterloo. As I read it, the scene, which does not advance the dramatic plot, does contribute to the poem's theme of consciousness. When he inserted it as a little drama in the drama, Hardy probably had in mind Thackeray's mocking account in *Vanity Fair* of the panicked scramble of civilians to get out of Brussels. Hardy's own Brussels scene has a different tone and purpose and ending: his reader is shown that panic and selfishness can be transformed into humanitarianism by the influence of a good leader.

When the scene opens with the arrival of the mayor and his advisors at the Place Royale, "consternation" has reached a "crisis." He listens to the dismaying rumors that have frightened the crowd, then quietly calls their attention to some material facts on which they can base their own more sober judgments. He goes on to call upon an instinct other than self-preservation, and the people respond.

MAYOR

. . . Meanwhile, who is to attend to the wounded that are being brought in faster and faster? Fellow-citizens, do your duty by these unfortunates, and believe me that when engaged in such an act of mercy no enemy will hurt you.

CITIZENS

What can we do?

MAYOR

I invite all those who have such, to bring mattresses, sheets, and coverlets to the Hôtel de Ville, also old linen and lint from the houses of the curés.

Many set out on this errand. . . .

(III,vi,vii,479)

Their calm is twice tested by news of death and defeat in the scene, but the mood of sobriety prevails. An impulse that was blinding and constricting, even brutalizing, has been willingly put aside for one that is more far- and wide-visioned. Unconsciousness has given way in one part of the poem to consciousness. People elsewhere in the drama—the rioting Spanish at Aranjuez, for example—have in them the capacity to respond to the cause of fellow-feeling and to follow sober and honest leaders in the direction of responsibility. But this scene is an all-too-rare exception in *The Dynasts*, a paradigm of how it should be and must be before man can hope to awaken from his red nightmare of blood. It is not that way yet: Kings, Princes-of-"Peace," Prince-Regents, Emperors, and Tsars are themselves bound to old dreams and images, and do not yet lead the human family to the consciousness that disenthralls.

Vision and Images of Light

The difference in leadership can be summed up as a difference in vision. The old hero comes out of a dispensation that upholds transcendence, whether or not he still believes literally in a transcendent god. This pattern molds the way he sees and acts. He speaks from above, assigning others their parts in his play—as, here, to Queen Louisa:

NAPOLEON (with sudden frigidity)

It is for you to take what I can give. And I give this—no more.

(II,i,viii,178)

and here, to his men at Jena:

159

Nay, caution, men! 'Tis mine to time your deeds
By light of long experience: yours to do them.

(II,i,iv,157)

He is simply expressing the venerable classic view, in which the head imposes its hegemony over the other members of the body.

Just as Napoleon rules his people from above, like children (for example, his plan to distract the Parisians with the newly gilded dome to the Invalides, III,i,xii,364), so, he believes, Fate rules him, its agent, from high in the heavens. Throughout the drama Napoleon carries a special sense, not possessed by the other actors, of being an instrument of the unconscious force that is weaving history. But according to his statements of the relationship he has with the Will (see his apology to Louisa, II,i,viii,179; the disclaimer to Josephine, II,ii,vi,204; the soliloquy at the Niemen, III,i,i,330; his thoughts at Bossu, III,vii,ix,519), he is a totally unwilling and helpless party, while the Will's commands are overriding, thrusting, and inexorable. When he pleads it to others, this line of reasoning strikes us as only hypocritical, no more than a means of denying that Napoleon's own nature is "a willing partner" (see his words of command to Josephine, II,v,ii,262) with the stars and winds and laws of heaven whom he freely blames for the orders he gives. It is a rationalization, an evasion of what is in fact his active, as well as passive, share in responsibility; but on the conscious level the reasoning is sincere. The Spirit of the Pities himself, no pleader for Napoleon, grants as much when he says of the Emperor at Borodino,

So he fulfils the human antickings
He *thinks* imposed upon him. . . .

(III,i,v,344, italics mine)

Because his conscious logic allows no room for Napoleon to listen to the pleadings of others and stop the destructive course of his "star," the pleadings and misgivings must

emerge in the unconscious—his dream-visions at Charleroi
(III,vi,iii,467) and Waterloo (III,vii,vi,501) of all the corpses
and blood lost in his enterprises. Even then the fixed part
of his mind contends with the more sensitive:

NAPOLEON (in his sleep)
Why, why should this reproach be dealt me now?
Why hold me my own master, if I be
Ruled by the pitiless Planet of Destiny?
(III,vi,iii,468)

The results of Napoleon's partial comprehension of the
Will are—as exhibited in this drama—devastating. As the
Spirit of the Pities commented at Tilsit, "Better for Europe
lacked he such discerning!" (II,i,viii,179.) But for the purpose of our understanding of alternative heroic attitudes,
the result of Napoleon's one-sided perception is that he
misses the possibility that the Will may operate in harmony
with human nature, and the possibility ("gone thy opportunity!" Spirit of the Years—III,vii,ix,521) that he, Napoleon, may cooperate, actively and consciously as well as
passively, to lend his eyes to the Will's blind power.

The other heroes spoke, with perhaps less discernment, of
God and of Providence, yet they seemed to wait more actively upon him and to study the direction of his hand in
events, so that they could collaborate in bringing forth his
designs. In a dispensation that no longer subscribes emo-
tionally to transcendence and that accordingly respects life
for the not-yet-known immanent within it, man not only
obeys life's patterns but obeys in some creative way that
transforms present limitations and enlarges future possibilities.

We can better appreciate these distinctions if we look at
them in the images of light the poem leaves with us. Our
final view of Napoleon is of the burnt-out comet who has
consumed himself to light the earth. He is deadweight, an
insentient mass, passively dragged across the heavens; he
made quite an impressive fiery arc in the sky, but the sum

total of what he illumined with that fire was himself and his own outline as a mark to aim for.

Compare to him the smaller lights cast in the drama by the new heroes. There is Pitt in his Guildhall speech, turning the occasion from the glorification of the past deeds of any one individual (himself or Nelson) to a vision of an entire people's power and responsibility: a vision that, the Spirit of the Years tells us, somehow transcends the Will's laws of time, leaves the temporal frame of the diorama, and enters immortality, leading, educating the mind of man beyond its present limits.

There is the dying Nelson, sincerely grieving the death of his assailant, seeing straight into that stranger's world—the man's good intentions, his wife and friends and children— and mourning that the center of that whole world should have been removed unnecessarily through "the sorrow brought by me" (I,v,iv,95). The Spirit of the Pities is the articulate voice of the sympathetic imagination; the poem as a whole enacts that mode of perception in its method of presenting scenes, and makes it the basis for its melioristic hope; but Nelson actually embodies the warmth of human sympathy, and demonstrates, in this example of imaginative compassion, the power of sympathy to pierce the walls and create a new world of love.

There is the picture by which Moore is remembered:

> His was a spirit baffled but not quelled,
> And in his death there shone a stoicism
> That lent retreat the rays of victory.
>
> (II,III,v,224)

The metaphor of muted light irradiating the enfolding darkness seems to gather up all the gloomy scenes in which we saw Moore—the evening mire of Astorga, the grey sky after Coruna, the shades of the January evening in which he lay dying, the pre-dawn blackness over the hillside where he was buried—and to show Moore outlasting this external and internal gloom.

There is Kutuzof at the close of the council-scene at Austerlitz, putting out the little human lights, stepping forth
ino the open air, gazing into the darkness at the lights and
the sounds of the French. These are exactly the right movements for a character at the frame of a diorama, disengaging
himself momentarily from the dramatic conflict and looking
up and around and behind at the environing whole. Kutuzof alone shows an awareness of the poem's vast spaces
and darknesses existing beyond the drama. In this appearance he communes with that whole as a presence and sets
his consciousness to its vast spatial measure, so that when
later scenes are laid in a wider, more open and bare theatre
of war, he will move in harmony with its wider promptings.

There is Wellington, who so well provides for his troops
with supporting fortifications behind them and reserves
laid by for the end. Even in the moment of triumph and
release and expansion, as he "rides at a gallop to the most
salient point of the English position, halts, and waves his hat
as a signal to all the army" (III,vii,viii,514), he calls to his
men the counsel of deliberation, not to lose themselves in
their enthusiasm, but to make full use of the light:

> No cheering yet, my lads; but bear ahead,
> Before the inflamed face of the west out there
> Dons blackness. So you'll round your victory!
>   (III,vii,viii,514)

The images by which we remember these five leaders are
all ones of enlightenment: their sets of mind illuminate, to
minds who come after them, attitudes for meeting crisis, for
standing up to despair, for rounding one's efforts, for keeping a larger-than-human perspective on human struggles,
and for redeeming "necessitated" acts of destruction.

The Moral Value of Consciousness

We can appreciate how the human drama, understood in
this way as a struggle between enlightenment and obscu-
rantism, fits in with the high valuation placed on conscious-

163

ness at other parts of the diorama. It accords especially with the view through to the rear of the stage that made visible the "world's body" extended in space in a state of trance, unconsciously creating and rending itself, in some original center numbly inflicting the suffering and in its sensitive extensions suffering from the pain of its inflictions. The only means of breaking the destructive trance, in that view, is a move one way or the other, into total unconsciousness or total consciousness; and the move to consciousness was given a slight preference as the more creative way.

The value of consciousness was likewise underscored by the large formative devices of the poem; both the visual method of the diorama and the key image of the brain have vision and consciousness as their chief purpose. These devices tended to give prominence to qualities that promote consciousness: substance over form is a positive value in the dissolving technique of the diorama; solidarity and the free exchange of informed intelligence promote the living mind-body intercourse in the brain. The hope placed in consciousness, substance, solidarity, and education: these are politically liberal, democratic virtues also, at the heart of what the Spirit of the Years called "the naive and liberal creed/ Of our great-hearted young Compassionates . . ." (Fore Scene, 6), and they are in accord with Hardy's own faith, qualified but persistent, in evolutionary meliorism.

But the Overworld debate provides the strongest endorsement of a reading that finds a moral theme of consciousness in the human drama. There, above the stage, the question absorbing the conversing Intelligences in the Fore Scene and After Scene is whether the unconscious force creating and energizing the universe will remain forever unconscious. In the Fore Scene we saw the Spirit of the Pities put forth another version of that question, an experiment: a scanning of human history to see whether or not an attitude of compassion and sensitivity is emerging among men to replace the long-prevailing one of aggressive selfishness, with the two sets of mind, the old and the emergent, being repre-

sented by Napoleon and by certain "kindlier" men opposing
him. Pity's proposition would seem to have been confirmed
and accepted by the end of the drama, for in the After
Scene, when the Intelligences resume their debate—will the
Unconscious forever be unconscious?—it is as though nothing had changed, except that they speak without any reference to the drama that presumably was to have been evidence for one side or the other of the debate.

But tacit change has taken place between the two Overworld scenes, and it springs out of the human drama that
has been enacted in the interval. While the same views and
positions are maintained by the various Spirits to the end,
the tone and movement of the debate has shifted, most
critics agree, from an opening in which authority was in-
vested in the Spirit of the Years, to a closing in which the
Spirit of the Pities has assumed the dominant voice. The
transfer of authority is achieved in the following speech:

SPIRIT OF THE PITIES

Thou arguest still the Inadvertent Mind.—
But, even so, shall blankness be for aye?
Men gained cognition with the flux of time,
And wherefore not the Force informing them,
When far-ranged aions past all fathoming
Shall have swung by, and stand as backward years?

(After Scene, 522)

The key argument, which states now as a certainty what
in the Fore Scene was only a wish ("'*twere* better far";
"*Wouldst* substitute"; "We *would* establish . . ."—Fore
Scene, 3; italics mine), has emerged out of the drama: "Men
gained cognition with the flux of time. . . ." This triumphant
perception provides a basis for the possibility of communion
and exchange between the part and the whole. Because of it,
the Spirit of the Pities is able to point out with a new
superiority in his tone an inherent limitation in the Years'
vision, that it is reductive because it is past-bound: "Thou
arguest *still* the Inadvertent Mind . . ." (italics mine). His

own sympathetic desire and vision enable him to imagine the future from openings and gropings that elude the objective net of history that is the Years' final account of life. In his last speech the Spirit of the Years seems to acknowledge as much, that the Pities' intelligence possesses some sight—illusory or not—beyond the range of his own "strong-built thought":

SPIRIT OF THE YEARS

Something of difference animates your quiring,
O half-convinced Compassionates and fond,
From chords consistent with our spectacle!

(After Scene, 524)

Certainly the Pities' newly intimated confidence dominates the debate to the end, and wins for them the last choral speech in the poem. (I read the last stanza as voiced by the Pities in chorus and not by the Intelligences in concert. Even by this, the more restrictive of the two alternative readings, it is still a hopeful conclusion.) From that privileged position—the last reach, we may say, of consciousness—they look out from the edge of the known cosmos and sing out their hymn of awakening:

But—a stirring thrills the air
Like to sounds of joyance there
          That the rages
          Of the ages
Shall be cancelled, and deliverance offered from the
     darts that were,
Consciousness the Will informing, till it fashion all
     things fair!

(After Scene, 525)

So, then: when we view the human drama in respect to the poem as a whole, we are corroborated in reading it as an enactment of the cancellation of "rage" and the deliverance of consciousness. And when one individual, Napoleon, is viewed against the great whole, and is seen to constitute an obstruction, even a reversal, of the great slow cosmic process of light and healing, we can understand, assent to, we can even wish a swift and clean execution of, the Spirits' words of judgment: he "profits naught," his thoughts are "narrow" and "worthless," his career should be "wound up," his deeds "nulled."

3. COUNTER-REFLECTIONS

Having completed our "moral" reading, we can compare it now to works by critics of *The Dynasts* who have also made close studies of the human drama. At several specific points the interpretation above, detailing the successful efforts of the new heroes, comes close to Roy Morrell's. He, for example, notices as we have the effect that two individuals, the brave English sergeant on the road to Astorga and Moore at Coruna, have upon events.[12] But it is difficult to agree with the moral emphasis Morrell puts on individual initiative, prudence, and "will-power" (almost a moral athleticism) in Hardy, although the human "scope" Morrell points to is an element in Hardy's work, and part of the design of *The Dynasts*.

J.I.M. Stewart corrects Morrell's emphasis with his sensible comment on the temper of Hardy's meliorism. Stewart reminds us that while Hardy did not subscribe to the transcendent dogmas of Christianity, neither did he accept the invitation that came to him to join the Rationalist Press Association;[13] and that while Hardy probably did place a "limited but . . . realistic hope in man's ability, if he chooses,

12 Morrell, *Thomas Hardy*, pp. 77, 82.

13 We can add another observation to support Stewart's "neither-nor" here. Out of the apparently casual memoranda that Hardy made and saved over the years and that he carefully selected for inclusion in the *Life*, there are very few notes made of what Hardy did for Christmas, traditionally a time for affirming the past, but many notations of how he spent New Year's Eve, a time for affirming the future. But, and this seems appropriate to Hardy's temper: it was usually not "celebrated" but observed quietly. He "watched it in."

to play the evolutionary game and survive as an alert and wary and adaptable animal," we may "doubt whether this sort of evolutionary meliorism greatly moved Hardy or quickened his imagination."[14] We remember also Katherine Anne Porter's remark quoted in another chapter of this study: "He [Hardy] did believe with a great deal of commonsense that man could make the earth a more endurable place for himself if he would, but he also realized that human nature is not grounded in commonsense, that there is a deep place in it where the mind does not go, where the blind monsters sleep and wake, war among themselves, and feed upon death."[15] Morrell avoids such deep unconscious places, preferring not to see the "Will" as implicit in Hardy's work before *The Dynasts*, and even in this poem to see it as only mythological superstructure, not part of Hardy's vital meaning.[16]

But the poem itself seems to demand a larger approach, one that comes to terms with the deeps and the upper spaces. Here we find more adequate the general approach taken by those other critics of *The Dynasts*[17] who have looked for vital connections between the Overworld and the human world, connections that function in the poem's theme of the struggle between consciousness and unconsciousness.

Basically, the design we have set forth above is not importantly different from the interpretations of any of these

[14] Stewart, *Thomas Hardy*, pp. 43–44.

[15] Katherine Anne Porter, "Notes on a Criticism of Thomas Hardy," p. 157.

[16] Morrell, *Thomas Hardy*, p. 73.

[17] Amiya Chakravarty, *"The Dynasts" and the Post-War Age in Poetry*; J. O. Bailey, *Thomas Hardy and the Cosmic Mind*; Southerington, *Hardy's Vision of Man*; and Jean Brooks, *Thomas Hardy: The Poetic Structure*. Brooks's interpretation of the human drama touches the "moral reading" of this study at several points, as, for example, this statement on p. 285: "Napoleon is the man of heroic force and 'suasive pull of personality' who refuses the challenge to become this new kind of hero, falling back instead on an outmoded epic pattern. (There is some analogy with the Eustacia/Clym opposition.)"

other critics who try to draw together the same "worlds" in the poem; for we share many of the same general assumptions and we all use Hardy's *Life* as our secondary, supporting text. The one point of divergence is that in our study we do not see a direct, immediate, and causal link between the Overworld and the human world, where these others do. This study starts from the assumption that in Hardy's universe there is by nature a gap (we would call it a "time-lag") between vision and action; and that this gap may be bridged only in prospect and retrospect; and that, therefore, improvement, meliorism, enlightenment, must be very long-term and gradual.

Where other critics, then, assert with some positiveness that the various "moral" designs they see in the drama have a validity and application outside that specific ten-year period of history, this study would have to disagree. For, in fact, by the poem's own testimony, events right on earth invalidate that design. After all the hope that "Fair Liberty" would be established in the place of privilege, after all the pain and suffering and agony and waste, the whole chapter of history will prove to have led nowhere: "Europe's mouldy-minded oligarchs" will be propped up anew (Spirit of the Years, II,vi,vii,320); the mildewed and dingy Bourbon standard will be hoisted up again; and the prospect remains that many, many more hoodwinkings still lie between the "pale pathetic peoples" and the "light" (Spirit of the Pities, III,iv,iv,414). We must admit, then, of the design the poem shows in its picture of ten years of human history, in which are interwoven a long-dominant "old" strand and a gradually emergent "new" one, that this very design is blurred in the poem's long view ahead into time.

The poem blurs its own design when it looks back, past the truth of the importance of the "new" versus "old" consciousness, to suggest that consciousness itself is a product of accident and circumstance. We saw in our reading that the lines separating the "old" and the "new" consciousness follow cultural and national divisions. The same Continental culture, with its traditional values of "honor" and "image," unites, beneath all their individual differences, Napoleon, Ney, Villeneuve, the French officers shown reacting to Wellington's fortifications, the various Parisians, and the "loyal, luckless" French soldiers. The men in the drama who lead and think and act in accord with "substance" come from Russia and England, nations that have been cut off and "enisled," by historical circumstance, from being shaped by those prevailing "old" cultural assumptions and values. Can the people who are the result of these different shapings be isolated, brought up before our minds for judgment, and held responsible?

Hardy himself had only pity for the individuals who were the living victims of accidents of shaping. He shared Blake's understanding of the power of "mind-forg'd manacles," although his own reaction does not contain Blake's anger and impatience. There is an incident recorded in the *Life* of a visit he made to a training college for schoolmistresses that probably was molding the very minds that would someday reject Hardy and his views. Hardy commented:

> Their belief in circumstances, in convention, in the rightness of things, which you know to be not only wrong but damnably wrong, makes the heart ache, even when they are waspish and hard. . . . You feel how entirely the difference of their ideas from yours is of the nature of misunderstanding. . . . There is much that is pathetic about these girls, and I wouldn't have missed the visit for anything. (*Life*, p. 235)

If people cannot be isolated for criticism, the factors that went into shaping them are themselves just as difficult to isolate and mark for criticism and change. They are as enormous, and as unpurposive, and as hard to do anything to but accept, as the connection between weather and biology. The poem notes the "mercurial temperaments" (I,i,ii,

14), the love of change and brief span of attention (I,III,ii,61) of the French, and the phlegmatic reserve, the "slow, stolid style" (I,I,viii,180), enjoyment of irregularity (III,v,ii,432), and fundamental steadfastness (II,III,v,226 and 227) of the English; and ascribes these temperamental differences to differences in geography (III,v,ii,432).

These shaping factors are as subtle and fluid, as gentle and irresistible, as language. The epic roll-calls of the two armies poised against each other for their last decisive (and exemplary) struggle on the field of Waterloo reveal in tone and diction the same distinctions we found in our "moral" reading that separated the "old" and the "new" heroes.

> Discriminate these, and what they are
> Who stand so stalwartly to war.
>
> (III,vii,i,485)

asks the Spirit of the Pities, and the lists that Hardy assigns to the voice of the Spirit of Rumours proceeds to exploit fully the traditional tonal difference in the English language's two dictions, emphasizing with open-ended vowel sounds the smooth resonance of the Norman proper names and with closely placed consonants the rough bluntness of the Saxon (III,vii,i,485–486).

An index to the imaginative difference being set up between the two sounds and styles is the Château at Hougomont, which is mentioned in both roll-calls. The tongue shapes the eye, and the château is seen differently by each language. When the French lines are described it is referred to as "the peaceful panes of Hougomont" ("panes" is used in its extended, civilized sense of "surfaces"), while in the English description it appears as "dun Hougomont's old lichened sides," a house that is hedgey and mossy, close to earth, living and solid. Each time that this landmark is presented, it is surrounded with details that carry out the contrast: in the French description the details are shiny and metallic, stressing contrivance and artifice; in the English the surrounding items have to do with greenery and vegetation, contributing to the impression of natural substance.

The cultural, linguistic distinction brought out in this set-piece repeats the substance-image dichotomy—or, we should say, lies behind that dichotomy, renewing and perpetuating it. Not only Napoleon, the drama's leading "old" hero, but his nation and culture and mother-tongue are predisposed to value the bright-shining face that life presents, and to see being as means, a mere source of energy to put forth bright images. Not only the leaders of the two nations who overthrew Napoleon, but their cultures and languages were predisposed to appreciate the living substance of life in its many particular short-lived forms. Language, which reveals these preexistent differences in sensibilities and mentality, will continue to mold the minds and sensibilities of future heroes along these predetermined lines. It is two different cultures that are speaking, through the "lippings" of particular individuals, when at the close of Waterloo the English colonel appeals to the cause of life and calls on the head of the French Imperial Guard to "Surrender! And preserve those heroes' lives!" (III,vii,viii, 516), and the French general, with the grim approval of his countrymen, turns down the appeal:

> Mer-r-r-rde! . . . You've to deal with desperates, man, today:
> Life is a byword here!

> (III,vii,viii,517)

Hardy's love of England was not uncritical or narrowly patriotic. The national and cultural distinctions that in *The Dynasts* he drew into imaginative and moral ones are no more than historically convenient metaphors for the arbitrariness and accidents and vagaries of life's designing. Eustacia Vye, born the woman she was, "out of mode" with her time and place, is a conspicuous victim of such arbitrariness. But all are victims of arbitrary fortunes, for as soon as birth occurs the "mind-forg'd manacles" begin to shape each new instance of mind to some mold or other.

In discussing ways in which *The Dynasts* blurs its own moral design into the vast inclusiveness of its vision, we must mention the fact that, after all, it addresses the modern, mass phenomenon of a world war. Some readers have found this modern aspect of determinism one of the most powerful ways in which the poem speaks to us.[18] One sees a special modern pertinence to the question of moral responsibility in *The Dynasts*, where "if the hand that releases the bomb is not guilty of the death caused by the bomb"[19] (the example in the poem could be Napoleon's signal for the shelling of the ice-surface of the Satschan lake), then guilt, like motivation, lies beyond human reach, for responsibility is diffused to the point that it disappears. Here, too, we can say that the "modern" distance between the agent and the repercussions of his act is only an up-to-date metaphor for the age-old unconsciousness and irresponsibility of the universe that Hardy is deploring.

Morrell, too, acknowledges that in *The Dynasts* men must contend not only with a difficult world of nature but with society, that is, with a war that reflects the "man-made structure of convention and society" in which "common humanity, 'the Managed' (III,vii,viii,515), have pathetically less freedom than 'the Managers' for whom the war is plied. . . ."[20] Morrell seems to admit that there is something inherently unfair in this double burden, something that does not yield to his moral individualism, although he draws back from this conclusion. But we may state the contradiction for him: even if we grant that little individuals, components in the whole, may survive—may even succeed—by doing their utmost, they—"frenzied folks who profit nought/ [warring] For those who profit all!"

[18] Jacob Korg, "Hardy's *The Dynasts*: A Prophecy," pp. 31–32; Chakravarty, *"The Dynasts"*; Harold Orel, *Thomas Hardy's Epic-Drama*; Brooks, *Thomas Hardy*.

[19] Korg, pp. 31-32.   [20] Morrell, p. 86.

(III,vii,viii,515)—should not have to be toiling in the Managers' webs at all.

It is a measure of the power of *The Dynasts* that, by its large metaphysical speculations and its vast panoramic view and its sorrowing, brooding atmosphere, it makes us ponder such questions, and have second and third thoughts about our strongest-built interpretations. If we enter at all into the work, then we begin to share, despite our resistance, Hardy's sorrow, and to share the pity he has for all his characters. Albert Guerard, fearing the moral effect of this pity on Hardy's readers, makes a sharp and provocative analysis of what he calls Hardy's "incorrigible sympathy": "Hardy's last meaning . . . in retrospect appears to have been his central one: that no human being, in his doomed pursuit of happiness, deserves less than is given; that things not men are to blame; that *everybody* is good enough.[21] . . . which of Hardy's villains is irrevocably damned? And which—Sergeant Troy, Wildeve, Alec d'Urberville, even William Dare —does not benefit at least briefly from this universal sympathy?"[22]

I would agree with Guerard that "everybody is good enough" under the light of Hardy's "incorrigible sympathy." Certainly it is operating in *The Dynasts*, where generals and foot-soldiers are pitied in the stress of combat, and queens and regents far from the fields of battle are pitied for private conflicts in their domestic lives. Hardy does seem to say that stress and conflict are in themselves unfair: it is unjust to put such pressures on the weak walls of living creatures; they are not made to stand up to such strain. We can understand Guerard's misgiving, that if Hardy does not require his characters to be heroic, his readers will adopt that indulgent attitude toward themselves. Turning the mirror around, Walter de la Mare agrees that Hardy's men and women are no better than we are: ". . . intent on their all-

21 Guerard, *Thomas Hardy*, p. 156.
22 *Ibid.*, p. 158.

absorbing share in the egregious drama. . . . Entangled in
the webs of circumstance, the majority of them are the prey
of their desires, their aspirations or their folly, racked,
cheated by mischance, victims of age or affliction, or of a
tender and lively charm and innocence that is but a mockery
in its transitoriness."[23]

But when we speak of Hardy's pity we mean more than
his offering us sympathetic portraits of weakness under
stress in which we recognize and come to terms with the
fact of our own weakness. We mean also the sympathy in
the most minute details of pathos the author selects to report to us. The critic who, to my mind, best describes the
working of the "balance of sympathy" in Hardy's writing
is J. I. M. Stewart. Discussing the inconstant character of
the heroine of *A Pair of Blue Eyes*, Stewart relates how
our feelings change from condemning Elfride to defending
her against Knight, her unforgiving judge in the novel:

". . . Elfride appears booked for our severe disapproba-
tion.

"But it fails to work that way. . . . [Hardy] no more turns
down his thumb on Elfride than Chaucer does on Criseyde.
Progressively through her charm and the ineptitude of her
comical concealments we are afforded a view of her helplessness and pathos; and in the end it is upon Knight that
certain sufficiently grim words are spoken.

". . . these adjustments of vision or emphasis are greatly
to the advantage of the art of the book. We are not required to feel that we have simply assisted at an arraignment of feminine inconstancy. Rather our sympathies have
been called now here and now there, as must be so before
any actual spectacle of intervolved human fates."[24]

Stewart's reference to Chaucer and Criseyde is an inspired
one. Like the poem we are studying, *Troilus and Criseyde*

[23] Walter de la Mare, "Thomas Hardy's Lyrics," in *Private View*, pp.
100–101.
[24] Stewart, pp. 72–73.

also reached out to the stars and to philosophies of free will and determinism to explain the mystery of character. Chaucer's poem, too, is anything but an arraignment of its heroine, even as it attempts to come to some judgment upon her inconstancy. And, finally, it is part of Hardy's design in *The Dynasts,* as it was part of Chaucer's design in his poem, that we should experience, as we read, a shifting and a tension between judgment and compassion, so that we should realize, when we conclude our reading, that neither element can do without the other and that both elements are present, mutually requiring and qualifying each other.

That is why, therefore, the "moral" reading that we set forth above cannot be final. It tallies too closely with the judgment of the Spirit of the Pities in the Overworld, which is only one expression of Hardy's pity. Too closely woven a screen is formed by the very congruences and supporting connections we noted between this interpretation of the drama and other parts of the poem's structure: it prevents other counter-elements of pity, muted in the background of the poem's design, from coming to our notice. We must provide another reading that rights that imbalance by gathering up the evidence of that pity. The organizing image of the diorama is our model in this procedure. The veils that are lifted away in it only seem to be lifted away; they reappear, still bearing the same old designs, which still seem persuasive, on their surfaces; it is all the illusion-work of the dissolving light, whose logic is that each veil is "true" and each veil is partial.

4. The Differences Dissolve: A Counter-View

At issue is the point of view that, in the name of pity, would cleanly condemn Napoleon and his narrow thought for lack of pity. The Spirit of the Pities holds Napoleon's "soul" free and responsible for having chosen the outmoded track of power, "The thing it overthrew" (I,i,vi,33 and 34). The Spirit of the Years joins with Pity in blaming Napo-

176

leon for having missed a rare opening for responding to life
intelligently and creatively—as though life did, indeed,
provide openings for human intelligence and creativity.

SPIRIT OF THE YEARS

Worthless these kneadings of thy narrow thought,
Napoleon; gone thy opportunity!

(III,vii,ix,521)

SPIRIT OF THE PITIES

Yet is it but Napoleon who has failed.
The pale pathetic peoples still plod on
Through hoodwinkings to light!

(III,iv,iv,414)

The opportunity that the Spirits assume, we also found in
our reading above: Napoleon did have some "narrow scope"
for the exercise of consciousness, and he did, under the
poem's scrutiny, lose his historic chance to exercise it, failing
to leave "accustomed lines." But even granting his failure of
responsibility, and granting the need for destructive deeds
to be nulled, jarring careers wound up, and bad influences
counteracted, such sentences cannot be carried out cleanly.
Feelings and sorrow are involved with this kind of necessity
also, as they were in all the other exactions of "necessity"
that we witnessed in the poem.

The Overworld judgment that nullifies in the name of
Pity has its this-world counterpart in the Declaration of the
Allies, which proscribed "Bonaparte" as legally non-existent,
"without the pale of social relations," foe of the universe
and enemy of the world, and, for all these reasons, subject
to "public vengeance" (III,vi,i,454). But this dismissal of
the man's humanity does not hold everywhere in the poem.
Marie Louise, whose attachment to her husband is not
strong, nevertheless weeps for pity when she hears the edict,
feeling it vicious to outlaw a man "to be caught alive or
dead,/ Like any noisome beast!" (III,v,iv,442). Later the
stage directions give us a glimpse of Napoleon at the mo-

ment when he chances to read the proclamation on a half-defaced poster on a village wall: "His flesh quivers, and he turns with a start, as if fancying that some one may be about to stab him in the back. Then he rises, mounts, and rides on" (III,vi,i,454). The Spirit of the Pities has nothing to say here. But the instinctive reaction of the prudish girl, and the witness of the poem's observing eye as it compassionately records Napoleon's human reaction of horror, give us a wider outlook—a wider pity, as it were—than the viewpoint that condemns in the name of pity.

This outlook attaches significance to special details sympathetic to Napoleon that slipped through the net of the moral reading of the drama. For one thing, the worst accusations of his enemies make Napoleon out to be too thoroughgoing a villain. He does not eat babies (*contra* the woman in I,ii,v,52) and he does not take deliberate pleasure in making women suffer (*contra* First Member of Parliament, II,v,iv,274, and *contra* Alexander, II,v,vii,285): the drama shows him exhibiting sympathy for Louisa, concern for Josephine's welfare, anxiety for Marie Louise's life. An English officer calls him "our and all men's foe!" (II,iii,vi,397), but Napoleon is not the Anti-Christ that his enemies presume him to be, any more than he is the Christ whose "achievement" he presumes to exceed.

The drama sets before us an unbroken chain of examples of Napoleon's tendency to override individuals and peoples. This antisocial tendency makes peaceful life with him so impossible that he brings on himself the edict of the Allies, "beyond the pale of civil and social intercourse." True enough. But the drama shows too, in its penetrating spirit-views, that this Emperor who treats other men as if they were his puppets is himself but a chief puppet in the Will's hand, a device for manipulating the others.[25] He suffers all

[25] The Spirit of the Years promises in the Fore Scene (p. 6) that we will see Napoleon be twitched as a puppet and in turn set other puppets twitching. This promise is literally fulfilled in the scene after the victory at Ulm, when Napoleon directs the Austrian officers just where

men's plight of being moved by another will, but suffers it more directly and intensely. Thus our second perception of those scenes in which he is most overbearing and over-riding is that they are places where from within he is being overbourne and overridden. The conversation with Madame Metternich at Cambaceres' ball is a clear example: by fiat he would sweep established, far-reaching destinies aside and instantly establish new ones: "Now, here, tonight" (II, v,i,257). The heedless drive here as elsewhere is that of a man finally more compelled than compelling.

His insatiable drive for empire is likewise a compulsion: Europe, Russia, India—only the entire Universe will exhaust his urge, for his urge is the expression of the universal Will behind him. His declarations of weariness, while tinged with his usual self-deception, have to be taken seriously:

> Moscow was meant to be my rest,
> My refuge, and—it vanishes away!
> (III,ɪ,viii,352)

> Here the scene lingers still! Here linger I! . . .
> Things could not have gone on as they were going;
> I am amazed they kept their course so long.
> But long or short they have ended now—at last!
> (III,ɪv,iv,413)

He, too, like the other actors, is tired by the long Napoleonic drama.

That drama, in its outline, seems to follow the classic formula of *hubris—ate—nemesis*, pride—folly—fall. But at the high point of the arc, the height of Napoleon's "folly," when he takes the decisive step into Russia, elements of pathos are introduced along with the portents of just doom.

---

to stand on either side of his campfire and just where to approach and lay arms. Then he is seen against his fire, in the image of Years, as "a figure on a lantern-slide," dragged to the will of "the all-compelling crystal pane" (I,ɪv,v,76).

179

The fourth transparency of the brain is revealed (III,i,i,330), showing him as one of its offshoots; at the forestage he becomes suddenly despondent and begins to reflect on a sense he has long had of being moved by the force of history, "and oftentimes/ Against my better mind . . ." (*ibid.*). Those few musing words weigh more in his defense than all the assertions of blamelessness he makes elsewhere. They are followed by a self-deprecating verbal shrug: "Well, war's my trade . . ." (*ibid.*), as he lays aside reflection and takes up again his appointed course. The Spirit Sinister sings an ominous song about the death of Marlborough, and the scene ends with a last view of him riding across the swaying bridge over the Niemen, his figure "diminished to the aspect of a doll" (III,i,ii,331). The total effect of this series of sketches of human tininess overarched by determinism could have been to exhibit Napoleon's blind hubris under a harsh and scornful light. That is how Tolstoy would have handled the scene, but that is not the effect here. Hardy's overall view of Napoleon in *The Dynasts* is less angry than Tolstoy's, and more complex than the opening judgment of the Pities.

Elements of pathos—personal, peculiar to Napoleon, and also universal—continue to appear in the scenes that follow, softening their pictures of the operation of justice. The sighting of him on the Kremlin tower once more reduces him to tiny size, this time to "a small lone figure" (III,i,viii, 348) gazing down upon the deserted city, his hollow prize, and makes him resemble every frustrated being whose "hard-gained goal" proves empty or bitter. He is no longer the self-proclaimed exceptional man; misfortune brings him "within the pale." Below, inside the Kremlin, we see the Emperor in an unprecedented situation: for the first time his marshals presume openly to dispute his strategy and behind his back show signs of doubting his genius and even his good sense ("looks of incredulity," "shrugs"—stage direction, III,i,viii,351). For the first time he, like ordinary

men, is forced by pressure to grasp at some strategy or other
with no assurance that it or anything will extricate him
from the circumstances gripping him.

By the battle of Leipzig these unprecedented circumstances have worsened and the elements of pathos are more
emphatic. Napoleon's officers are disenchanted and murmur
together; his own mind has retreated from the pressures of
inimical facts such as numbers and battle odds until he has
lost mental contact and purchase on reality. His mood after
the lost battle is "lax," "inert," "idly singing." The language setting forth this situation suggests repeatedly a world
in which nature and man are conspiring toward one object,
to press him to death at last:

> . . . beneath October's clammy cope . . . (III,III,ii,383)
> . . . hemming hordes wax denser every hour. (*ibid.*)
> And now contracts the huge elastic ring. . . . (*ibid.*)

> The night gets thicker. . . . (III,III,ii,384)

> They have welded close the coop
> Wherein our luckless Frenchmen are enjailed
> With such compression that their front has shrunk
> From five miles' farness to but half as far.—
> (III,III,iii,385)

> . . . hemming in the north more thoroughly. (*ibid.*)
> . . . the unyielding circle shut around. (*ibid.*)

The Pities sum up how it must seem to a man squeezed
under all these lowering pressures—like a nightmare of a
narrowing, crushing pen:

SEMICHORUS I OF PITIES

> Now, as in the dream of one sick to death,
> There comes a narrowing room
> That pens him, body and limbs and breath,
> To wait a hideous doom.

SEMICHORUS II

So to Napoleon in the hush
That holds the town and towers
Through this dire night, a creeping crush
Seems inborne with the hours.

(III,III,iv,389)

Among those observers who, with us, are watching the
events at Leipzig, expressions begin to appear that for the
first time in the drama give the devil his due.

SEMICHORUS II [OF RUMOURS]

He knows, he knows that though in equal fight
He stands as heretofore the matched of none,
A feeble skill is propped by numbers' might,
And now three hosts close round to crush out one!

(III,III,ii,383)

sing the Rumours, and for once Napoleon's skill as a fighter
is presented positively, and not closely coupled with a warn-
ing that the skill is misplaced, abused, of nothing worth, etc.
It is presented positively a second time when the Rumours
give an account of the actual battle:

SEMICHORUS I OF RUMOURS (aerial music)

But for long whiles he [Schwarzenburg] fails to
win his will,
The chief himself being nigh—outmatching
might with skill.

(III,III,iii,386)

When the battle is over, the anxious citizens of Leipzig behold the state to which the French have been reduced and
take pity upon them:

In the darkness of the distance spread cries from the
maimed animals and the wounded men. Multitudes of
the latter contrive to crawl into the city, until the
streets are full of them. Their voices are heard calling.

182

SECOND CITIZEN

They cry for water! Let us now go down,
And do what mercy may.
[Exeunt citizens from the tower.
(III,iii,iii,387)]

Their pitying descent parallels the movement of the poem's sympathy to Napoleon, who cannot cry for water or mercy, and who, as we have read, can only voice occasional peevish rationalizations about his own blamelessness. In his inability to give true expression to his inner misery, which expression would win our support even after all the rage and outrage we have seen, he is like Michael Henchard, whose words also act against his own case to the very end.[26] The complex point of view of the author-poet, which can note the body's wordless speech in a detail like "A haggard shade crosses NAPOLEON'S face" (at Waterloo, III,vii,vi,502), speaks more movingly than these unsympathic heroes themselves in winning the reader to them.

If we are brought to see Napoleon as a fellow human in a situation of excruciating, inhuman pressures, sympathy may make us go on to wonder how he can bear up to them, and what may be his inarticulate feelings and thoughts. The natural next step is to imagine in such a character, as in anyone so placed, a natural weariness and desire to be free—not freed to start his enterprises up again elsewhere, anywhere, but freed from it all, released from his very self. And in the scenes after Leipzig and after the abdication it leads to, we find signs of such weariness. At Fontainebleau Napoleon's energy of mind is gone:

[26] Perhaps the curiously and uncharacteristically long goodby which Napoleon bids the rulers of Saxony at a time when there is need of haste (III,iii,v,389) is a lonely indirect reach for communication—corresponding to the moments in which Nelson (I,v,iv,97) and Moore (II,iii,iii,219) reach out for sympathetic contact and conversation when they realize the end is near.

Herein behold
How heavily grinds the Will upon his brain,
His halting hand, and his unlighted eye.
(III,iv,iv,414)

He has become "lax" to his own fate, falling asleep in debates about suicide or exile. He is indifferent to the shame of
putting on a Royalist white cockade—"What does it matter
if I do or don't?" (III,iv,iv,420.) A lot of life has been
packed into his brief career; now it is being drawn out too
long, and he is tired.

This weariness is, I believe, woven into the very texture of
the scene where he sails from Elba. The atmosphere at the
Palace, the quay, and the brigantine is, again, lax and
limp: the Bonaparte women sit for their farewells, the song
and the cheer of the sailors is "melancholy" and has an
automatic ring to it. What is missing is (figuratively) spirit
and (literally) wind:

> The night is warm and balmy for the season. Not a
> breeze is there to stir a sail, and the ships are motion-
> less.
>
> . . . The sails hang flaccidly. (III,v,i,430)

Napoleon is uncharacteristically still and silent as he waits
on deck for wind, and when the wind comes the ship is
silent too as it disappears in the moonlight. Contrasted with
the dispiritedness and passivity in this act of boldness and
independence are the "town lights, whose reflections bore
like augers into the waters of the bay" in the relentless
way that destiny is boring down once again on this man,
and the ironic over-enthusiasm in the recitative sung by
the Chorus of the Rumours.

The Force that brought Napoleon out of exile energizes
him, fitfully, for the next hundred days. He falls asleep
frequently but awakens to show something of his former
brilliance of strategy and speech. But by the end of the ef-

fort, as he slumps in the moonlight of the wood of Bossu upon his jaded horse, his mind still locked monotonously on questions of his own narrow destiny, even the Pities have pity and cease from holding their judgment over a man who is so tired and self-burdened:

SPIRIT OF THE PITIES

Peace. His loaded heart
Bears weight enough for one bruised, blistered while!

(III,VII,ix,521)

The moral view that Hardy takes of man in *The Dynasts* is a complex one. He does not assume that human intelligence can be given a moral imperative to sympathize, since an attitude of sympathy is, like everything else, a product of complex shaping. But neither does he assume, with Napoleon, that man is so totally the product of external forces that he cannot be held responsible for his sympathies, thoughts, and actions. Hardy's view weaves between these two positions. In *The Dynasts*, as in the novels and stories, he delineates the conscious and unconscious motives of his characters and represents the line of relative responsibility from character to action to consequences of action. But on the stage of *The Dynasts* he has an infinite field for tracing those lines on and on, out to where they at last dissolve in the mystery of their origins. This radical, anatomizing vision absolves his characters of ultimate (though not of practical) responsibility in a way that they cannot do for themselves, they who are so deep in their own lives and too single one way or another, assuming too much or too little responsibility, in their self-assessment.

How does Hardy express the doubleness of what he sees to be man's situation, blameless and responsible? Napoleon is his example, a man who is the agent of suffering across a world-wide stage, and who suffers also himself from the fact of Napoleon. Hardy wants to say that character is a finite vessel into which life is cast and that the life within suffers, and cannot overcome, the constraining mold of character. Determinism as propounded by both fatalistic and optimistic thinkers usually holds that environing circumstance is fate; in Hardy's view, also, determinism works in this external way. Another view of determinism, one naturally held by poets sensitive to the arbitrary power they possess to create a "cast" of human natures, holds that interior character is fate; Hardy's determinism, as we have just argued, includes that important insight. But to my knowledge Hardy is the only thinker and poet whose determinism puts the statements together: interior character *is* environing circumstance. His metaphor for this formula is that of dreaming, an extension of his central brain-image, and he uses dreaming to express a familiar human sensation of a spilling-over of consciousness beyond action, so that a human being is simultaneously in himself as he acts, and outside, watching himself act.

To appreciate all the freight that his dream metaphor is carrying, we should look at Hardy as part of a long tradition basic to Western thought. That tradition gives central attention to the sense of doubleness that is thought to be the result of human self-consciousness and that is held to be a trait that distinguishes man from other living things. If we may compress that involved tradition into reductive terms in order to get a cursory sense of background here, we can generalize and say that the sense of doubleness has given rise to opposing views of hope or of despair about man's capability to become good. For Socrates the spilling-over of consciousness was a proof of man's power for disinterested self-criticism, an encounter with conscience. Much later, for Whitman it was a power that guaranteed that man would always surprise, always elude, definition and quantification.[27] The orthodox Christian position, by contrast,

---

[27] Human consciousness in Whitman's romantic poetry shows two interesting similarities to human consciousness in *The Dynasts*. One feature found in both is its doubleness, as engaged actor and disengaged observer:

does not share the liberal hope that man possesses in and
of himself the means of attaining goodness and happiness.
For Paul, Augustine, Luther, and Kierkegaard, self-consciousness is precisely the problem, because it is a critical
faculty that is powerless to change the will and, worse, it is
an impurity that keeps every human impulse from being
wholehearted and uncalculating.

In *The Dynasts* Hardy takes an imaginative position
somewhere between these traditional alternatives. In his
dream-picture, self-consciousness is aware but powerless, as
in the tragic Christian view. But because it is powerless, it
is—as in the liberal view—*not* culpable, although com-

Apart from the pulling and hauling stands what I am,
Stands amused, complacent, compassionating, idle, unitary,
Looks down, is erect, or bends an arm on an impalpable certain
    rest,
Looking with side-curved head curious what will come next,
Both in and out of the game and watching and wondering at it.
                                    (*Song of Myself*, section 4)

The other is the image both poets draw of a dreaming soul wandering
dissociate from the body and looking forward expectantly to merging
with the Anima Mundi in the sleep of death:

Elements merge in the night, ships make tacks in the dreams,
The sailor sails, the exile returns home,
The fugitive returns unharm'd, the immigrant is back beyond
    months and years,
The poor Irishman lives in the simple house of his childhood
    with the well-known neighbors and faces. . . .

The homeward bound and the outward bound . . .
The consumptive, erysipalite, the idiot, he that is wrong'd,
The antipodes, and every one between this and them in the dark,
I swear they are averaged now—one is no better than the other,
The night and sleep have liken'd them and restored them.

I swear they are all beautiful,
Every one that sleeps is beautiful, every thing in the dim light is
    beautiful,
The wildest and bloodiest is over, and all is peace.
                                    (*The Sleepers*, section 7)

187

plicit in evil. Hardy's position results in an attitude toward man that is not one of pride, as in the usual rationalist view, nor of remorse, as in the tragic view, but of pity (sometimes self-pity) for man's bound condition.

Having located Hardy's view of human consciousness in relation to the main alternative views, we are in a position to consider the image that is his vehicle for that view.

THERE are three suggestive references to dream in Hardy's critical writings, references that indicate that dream held a special charge of meaning for him, and that can serve in quotation here to alert us to the special imaginative meaning he makes of it in the drama.

First, at his conclusion to his 1903 preface to *The Dynasts*, after he explains that the drama is intended primarily for mental performance, he goes on to characterize it as a play of "poesy and dream," saying:

> In respect of such plays of poesy and dream a practicable compromise may conceivably result, taking the shape of a monotonic delivery of speeches, with dreamy conventional gestures, something in the manner traditionally maintained by the old Christian mummers, the curiously hypnotizing impressiveness of whose automatic style—that of persons who spoke by no will of their own—may be remembered by all who ever experienced it. Gauzes or screens to blur outlines might still further shut off the actual . . .

> (Preface, xi)

We notice how Hardy associates hypnotic, sing-song speech and "dreamy" movement with a hypnotized, automatic, compelled state; the dreamy style that he suggests that the drama be enacted in is an expression of the play's determinism.

His suggestion has a wider reference than to *The Dynasts* alone. For he finds unsatisfactory other dramas that fail to see through the everyday waking world, that give too

188

much attention to the trappings of "the actual" or too much plausibility to conscious human control—in other words, that do not enough render the world as "dream." This is the criticism we find him voicing in the early 1890's, before he had worked out the dramatic form for visualizing compelled behavior that was to make *The Dynasts* such an arresting and strange contrast to anything that had been written by anyone before. In 1892 he wrote an essay called "Why I Don't Write Plays," explaining that he found the contemporary theatre had an emphasis on material properties and accessories that obstructed the attempt of a writer to present "the heart and meaning of things";[28] and that he, Hardy, found he could get nearer to them in the novel than in a drama. He expanded on this point in an earlier essay, "The Science of Fiction":

A sight for the finer qualities of existence, an ear for the "still, sad music of humanity," are not to be acquired by the outer senses alone, close as their powers in photography may be. What cannot be discerned by eye and ear, what may be apprehended only by the mental tactility that comes from a sympathetic appreciativeness of life in all of its manifestations, this is the gift which renders its possessor a more accurate delineator of human nature than many other with twice his powers and means of external observation, but without that sympathy. To see in half and quarter views the whole picture, to catch from a few bars the whole tune, is the intuitive power that supplies the would-be storywriter with the scientific bases for his pursuit. He may not count the dishes at a feast, or accurately estimate the value of the jewels in a lady's diadem; but through the smoke of those dishes, and the rays from these jewels, he sees written on the wall:—

[28] Thomas Hardy, "Why I Don't Write Plays," in *Personal Writings*, ed. Orel, p. 139. In 1892 the title of the essay was accurate.

> We are such stuff
> As dreams are made of, and our little life
> Is rounded with a sleep.[29]

The passage quoted at length clarifies much that is idiosyncratic with Hardy. It shows that he recognized that imaginative sympathy was his most important gift, outweighing any other powers of expression he lacked. And it explains his peculiar preference for mental over physical tactility, which preference helped to shape the incorporeal features of *The Dynasts* and helps to account for the mysterious incorporeality of many of the narratives, with their roads not taken, contacts not made, unions not consummated, weddings not legalized. But the passage's main value, for our purposes, is the way it comes to rest on dream. That we are dreaming our lives, or that our lives are the dream of some other mind, this, it is suggested, is to Hardy the secret truth lying "at the heart and meaning of things"—or is at least a metaphorical truth lying beyond the reach of material representation and more closely attained by the dioramic presentation he was to set up in *The Dynasts*.

If we follow this brief survey of Hardy's thought by an assemblage of his principal allusions to dream in *The Dynasts*, the sequence should persuade us that those allusions are not passing references merely but vehicles of deep meaning for the poem.

The metaphysical transparencies together constitute one such allusion, establishing in their six appearances the insubstantial, dream-like status of matter. But the sixth transparency is the one that explicitly equates human action and consciousness with dream:

> A transparency as in earlier scenes again pervades
> the spectacle, and the ubiquitous urging of the Im-

[29] Thomas Hardy, "The Science of Fiction," in *Personal Writings*, ed. Orel, p. 137.

manent Will becomes visualized. The web connecting all the apparently separate shapes includes WELLING-TON in its tissue with the rest, and shows him, like them, as acting while discovering his intention to act. By the lurid light the faces of every row, square, group, and column of men, French and English, wear the expression of a people in a dream.

(III,vii,vii,505)

"Acting while discovering his intention to act": this watching and wondering faculty, which Wellington and all the others have in common, looks on in rapt amazement at its own actions and intentions. It may be that we see here, in what is described of a sense of simultaneous experience, the imaginary origin of the Phantom Intelligences that Hardy gives being to and places as spectators above the human drama. They look on inquiringly and in them too discovery moves abreast with, but not ahead of, action. They too fall back upon "dream" to reconcile appearances on the front of the stage with "the heart and meaning of things."

Another allusion to dream takes place in an exchange between the Years and the Pities as they look down upon the field of Albuera and foresee the senseless waste of life that will soon take place there on "the sanguinary scene of the most murderous struggle of the whole war" (II,vi,iv,298). The Spirit of the Pities chants:

> I see red smears upon the sickly dawn,
> And seeming drops of gore. On earth below
> Are men—unnatured and mechanic-drawn—
> Mixt nationalities in row and row,
>   Wheeling them to and fro
> In moves dissociate from their souls' demand
> For dynasts' ends that few even understand!

(II,vi,iv,299)

The Pities are describing, with phrases like "mechanic-drawn" and "In moves dissociate from their souls' demand,"

191

an "automatic style" like that of the mummers that Hardy found so suggestive and impressive, because it brought out the hypnotic, dreamlike compulsion which he imagined was the true condition of human life. And how does the Years respond to this description of the Pities?

> Speak more materially, and less in dream.
>
> (II,vi,iv,299)

Many of the human actors in *The Dynasts* make casual remarks about dreaming, and even the most glancing of such remarks have a special eloquence against the backdrop of the dreaming brain. But since Napoleon is the drama's prime example of man's mysterious doubleness, all of the remarks made by him or about him—even those that seem to contain mere casual or plaintive reference to his sense of standing outside himself in a dream—must be of special interest to us. So looked at, many of these remarks stand out as unconscious gropings toward the mystery of the Unconscious, and more penetrating than his conscious attestations about destiny and irresponsibility.

Remarks describing Napoleon in terms of doubleness and dream do not appear in the drama until his fateful entry into Russia, at the same time that the other elements that enlist our sympathy begin to emerge. The first such statement is at the river Niemen, when he muses about the dissociation he has often felt between his own "better mind" (III,i,i,330) and the force that he senses, stronger than his own will, moving him. Soon after, at Borodino, the only occasion in the drama where Napoleon is shown to feel conscious revulsion against the bloodshed he has brought about, a metaphor of waking is used to describe his reaction to his own actions:

SPIRIT OF THE PITIES

> The ugly horror grossly regnant here
> Wakes even the drowsed half-drunken Dictator
> To all its vain uncouthness!
>
> (III,i,v,344)

By implication, the metaphor for those "uncouth" actions would be unconscious nightmare.

Later, at Leipzig, when he, his officers, his troops, even the horses, all, are exhausted by the losing struggle, Napoleon suddenly drops off into a deep sleep in the middle of dictating the next day's strategy. When he awakens some minutes later he "stares around him with astonishment" and seems not to know where he is or why.

NAPOLEON

Am I awake
Or is this all a dream?—Ah, no. Too real! . . .
And yet I have seen ere now a time like this.
(III,III,iv,388)

It is as though sleep were for him and all living things a release from the "too real" dream of life. The blankness of sleep temporarily reestablishes the blankness of non-existence on the other side of birth and death. In both sleep and death, consciousness is delivered from its isolation in separate bodies, disengaged from unreal, real-seeming dream. It is released to rest in peace, or freed to become completely spectral like the Phantom Intelligences, looking down over human life and human actions (as Napoleon did in his heavy sleep "ere now" before he awakened into the "time like this" that he was briefly distanced from), and seeing them dreamily as the illusions they are.

At this very point, as Napoleon pauses in astonishment before surfacing into consciousness and resuming his role, some of the strange, floating words uttered by another musing dreamer, the poet-speaker in "Wessex Heights" (CP, pp. 300–301), could have been written by Hardy for him:

Down there I seem to be false to myself, my simple self
   that was,
And is not now, and I see him watching, wondering
   what crass cause
Can have merged him into such a strange continuator
   as this,

193

Who yet has something in common with himself, my
   chrysalis.

Only when it floats into sleep or death does the intelligence
attain to the state of a completely free spirit, no longer
suffering in body the stress and pulse of the Will, no longer
held at one and the same time responsible and powerless, no
longer shackled to a line of trammeling consequences, no
longer sustaining a role in a drama pressed down from
without.

The Pities, for all their impatience to see Napoleon's
career wound up, cannot help remarking that his final
situation at Leipzig and afterwards is a nightmare of pressure and constriction: "Now, as in the dream of one sick to
death . . ." (III,III,iv,389, quoted above). In the protracted
nightmare he must endure all of the pain and fear, without
the relief, of death.

There is one last occasion in the drama when Napoleon
seems to return to himself and to his conscious life as
though from very far away, from the mental reaches of the
Overworld. It is at Fontainebleau, and once more he has
been sleeping in a break between two painful scenes, the
abdication just accomplished and the suicide he is about to
attempt. He wakes to find himself alone.

NAPOLEON

Here the scene lingers still! Here linger I! . . .
Things could not have gone on as they were going;
I am amazed they kept their course so long.
But long or short they are ended now—at last!

(III,IV,iv,413)

The speech expresses what we recognize by now as the sense
of standing outside the body, that strange continuator, and
watching one's life unfold. Napoleon's amazement in it is
like the wonder of the soldiers in the sixth transparency:
"discovering" what they are doing and intending; wearing
"the expression of . . . people in a dream"; amazed at their

194

enchantment even from within the spell. And lastly we note here Napoleon's (mistaken) sense of relief to be slipping off the weariness "at last!" The increasing sleepiness he exhibits here and from Borodino to Bossu have two motivations: the Unconscious Energy is withdrawing from him and some part of himself is also attempting to find release.

In his final weariness, too, Napoleon, Hardy's example, represents all living things. On whatever side of the great war, at whatever level, all are alike bound and exhausted. The Pities pray in benediction that the troubled soul of Villeneuve may "merge into nought/ Meekly and silently as a breeze at eve!" (I,v,vi,105), and they wish Pitt, in his dying, peace also, to "seek the silence unperturbedly" (I,vi,viii,137). In sleep the living can escape from time and join the great company of the dead. The dead tell them that "Better than waking is to sleep!" (Albuera, II,vi,iv,302) and protest that even their dissolving tissues "abhor/ The fevered feats of life" (Waterloo, III,vii,viii,515). And so, like the souls in Whitman's *The Sleepers*, they dream, Napoleon and every weary one, of going home, where all will be united, averaged, restored, infolded, and cleansed from fantasy.

And what of us, who read and mark these beings exhausted in their traces? For us to judge them, make exemplary models of them, discriminate too strictly and long between old and new, barbaric or enlightened, serves but to hold them longer in their molds, perpetuate their weary round. True pity would dissolve the mold and break the circle to end the weariness:

SEMICHORUS II OF THE PITIES

Should it never
Curb or cure
Aught whatever
Those endure
Whom It quickens, let them darkle to extinction
swift and sure.

(After Scene, 525)

195

5. THE VIEWS RECONCILED

Another viewing over, the diorama lights dim again, and gradually there reemerges to our gaze everything that was seen in the previous perspective, all given back, but now in this final radiance harmonized and reconciled with its counter-view. The moral perspective that emerges from the poem's dissolving pity is, as we might expect, one that on every side sheds light on ill and irradiates cure. It casts approving light on sensibilities "of kindlier build," such as those which this discussion described as new heroes; for these sensibilities help to relieve the present suffering condition of life and contribute themselves as examples, to become part of the future culture that will shape sensibilities and widen the groove of possibilities. And by making the sensibility of the old hero a primary object of consciousness, the poem enables the reader to objectify similar tendencies in his own mind, isolate them, distance them, perhaps even weaken their hold. This is the great tonic effect of the poem's moral vision.[30]

And for that faculty in the reader which recognizes kinship with the hasty, ardent Spirit of the Pities, the experience of the poem yields a judge/judge-not moral. We are to note evidence, discriminate, see causes and consequences, judge—and dissolve judgment. We are to have compassion for all in *The Dynasts*. "All" includes Napoleon and all who like him are unconsciously bound to power and force. "All" extends even to the dark energy of unconsciousness itself, source of pain but of beauty and joy too.[31] We may

[30] J. Hillis Miller makes this same point in *Thomas Hardy*: "In Hardy's writing the Will comes to consciousness and makes the models of itself or representations of itself which are works of literature . . ." (p. 265). "The poet's mind is the awakening to consciousness of this dreaming brain [the brain shown in the Fore Scene]. In the poet's extension into human language of the inscribing power of the Cause, the unconscious becomes conscious and Hardy's hope for a transformation of the cosmic energy, 'Consciousness the Will informing till it fashion all things fair!' is paradoxically fulfilled" (p. 267).

[31] Clearly, I disagree with the thesis of Southerington, in *Hardy's*

196

wish for it and them to awaken, or to sleep at last from tormented dreaming. But we should pause—the whole poem is such a pause—before we conclude that the whole or any part of the brain-web should be "nulled."

CHORUS OF THE YEARS (aerial music)

Nay, nay, nay;
Your hasty judgments stay,
Until the topmost cyme
Have crowned the last entablature of Time.
O heap not blame on that in-brooding Will;
O pause, till all things all their days fulfil!

(I,v,iv,100)

Vision of Man, pp. 211–14, that the Unconscious in *The Dynasts* is the embodiment of sickness and decay (as it is in Hardy's lyric, "The Sick Battle-God," which Southerington draws on extensively), against which conscious human morality must pit itself as a healing force. D. H. Lawrence's "Study of Thomas Hardy" has a truer perception of the unconscious universe in Hardy's vision. Lawrence sees that in Hardy the sphere of human effort is tiny in relation to the vast panorama of life, and that there is a vast mystery lying within the dark reaches of unconsciousness, holding yet-unfathomed possibilities of creation, as well as destruction, and larger-than-human meaning:

"This is the wonder of Hardy's novels and gives them their beauty. The vast unexplored morality of life itself, what we call the immorality of nature, surrounds us in its eternal incomprehensibility, and in its midst goes on the little human morality play, with its queer frame of morality and its mechanized movement. . . . [The] little drama falls to pieces, or becomes mere repetition, but the stupendous theatre outside goes on enacting its own incomprehensible drama, untouched" (p. 419).

INTERWEAVINGS OF THE WEB

HARDY sets the Napoleonic drama at the front and center of his stage. It makes a natural claim on the center of the viewer's focus, for like looks to like and a common human identity and interest is shared by the poet, dramatic personages, and viewers. But the poetry in which the drama is written links humankind to other natural phenomena through so many analogies that these linkings affect the dramatic focus, opening it and widening it out to the sides. The non-human lives that are brought into view play only minor parts in the dramatic events, but they perform an important service to the poem thematically. They constitute the focus of this perspective, which highlights, as though through a prearranged adjustment in the diorama's lighting, countless threads of interconnection drawing stars and water, earth and air, animals, birds and insects into the net with human beings.

1. A SAMPLE OF INTERWEAVING: BATTLE

To appreciate the pull of Hardy's net, let us look at how it works on a relatively small scale, when it pulls together opposites inside the lines of the human drama; for that will give us a sense of its characteristic direction and movement across the human lines. A key statement for us is that in which the Spanish citizens make common cause with Godoy's princess: "Common misfortune makes us more than kin" (II,II,ii,189).

The battles that run through the drama enact this truth again and again. The distinctions and differences that divide men and set them to fight each other are quite done away with in battle's even-handed and efficient processes of destruction. Trafalgar is the first of a series of demonstrations of the breaking down of division and the emergence of a strange unsought-for kinship. Two fleets were drawn to a decisive engagement at an arbitrary spot on the sea off Cape Trafalgar; the storm and waves that pounded the survivors did not recognize sides or victors or losers:

> Dead Nelson and his half-dead crew, his foes from
>   near and far,
> Were rolled together on the deep that night at
>   Trafalgár!
>   The deep,
>   The deep,
>   That night at Trafalgár!
>
>   (I,v,vii,108)

Sometimes the difference that the poem shows being broken down in battle is embodied in the individual leaders. In the Russian campaign, the opponents, Kutuzof and Ney, despite their differences in temperament and fortune and age, are seen as "twins":

> SPIRIT OF THE YEARS
> Kutuzof he:
> The ceaselessly-attacked one, Michael Ney;
> A pair as stout as thou, Earth, ever hast twinned!
>   (III,I,ix,354)

And at Waterloo two scenes are placed next to each other, to show Napoleon and Wellington in the same excruciating predicament, pressed to the breaking-point for reinforcements they do not have (Napoleon in III,vII,vi,503, and Wellington in III,vII,vii,506).

Just as he places views in tandem to call attention to what opposing leaders have in common, Hardy sets up parallel sights of opposing armies to illustrate their common nature. Before the battle of Borodino (III,I,iv,342) two juxtaposed views show the two hosts doing reverence to different objects, the Russians to a Christian icon and the French to a painting of Napoleon's son. The two groups, shaped so differently by their respective historical divisions —one still attached to medieval pieties, the other aggressively secular—are both urged by the same psychological need to reach for help, a need to which theism or atheism are only superficial, inadequate, and circumstantial answers.

Biological need unites opposites in the heat of Talavera.

SPIRIT OF THE PITIES

What do I see but thirsty, throbbing bands
From these inimic hosts defiling down
In homely need towards the little stream
That parts their enmities, and drinking there!
They get to grasping hands across the rill,
Sealing their sameness as earth's sojourners.

(II,IV,V,245)

Nature's elements corroborate the sameness there twice over: first, with a benign and soothing impartiality the setting sun shines on the exhausted soldiers, gilding the quick and the dead, French and English, "Till all around breathes drowsed hostility" (II,IV,V,246); then, with a terrible implacability fire breaks out, races across the charred field,

and hurt and slain[,]
Opposed, opposers, in a common plight
Are scorched together on the dusk champaign.

(II,IV,V,246)

At Quatre-Bras nature again testifies to the sameness of human enemies, using storm and nightfall to cover the different colors of the uniforms worn by the two forces.

CHORUS OF RUMOURS (aerial music)
Day's nether hours advance; storm supervenes
In heaviness unparalleled, that screens
With water-woven gauzes, vapour-bred,
The creeping clumps of half-obliterate red— . . .

Till Britishry and Bonapartists lose
Their clashing colours for the tawny hues
That twilight sets on all its stealing tinct imbues.

(III,vi,viii,482)

Hardy's recommendation for the staging of *The Dynasts* comes to mind again: "Gauzes or screens to blur outlines might still further shut off the actual . . ." (Preface, p. xi). Here the screen is rain and the blurring is done by night, but what is being performed is another version of the dissolving of conventional lines of human judgment that, in our previous chapter, we saw accomplished by the authorial pity that suffuses *The Dynasts*. There, lines of good and evil, credit and culpability, were dissolved. Here, lines of nationality and individuality are erased. Both kinds of lines, being merely "actual," are rubbed away to bring out what is "real," the common identity animating the core of the universe and the core of each of its extensions.[1]

"Common misfortune makes us more than kin." By this definition the horse is nearest kin to humanity in the

---

[1] It is this point in Hardy—the blurring of distinctions, and making the individual and the mass into one—that I think may have excited T. S. Eliot's animus against Hardy's genius. Writing in *After Strange Gods*, Eliot identified in Hardy an imaginative chain that he then criticized: landscape was a (mere) means of conveying life and people as vehicles of emotions; the fallacy in looking at people, not for their minds or beliefs but for their emotions and passions, was that in passion men are reduced to the same state (p. 55). Presumably, passion is to be resisted as morbid, for in literature it is not interesting or meaningful (or "edifying") unless it is depicted in strong men where there is moral resistance and conflict. Therefore, Hardy's "emotionalism" was a symptom of his decadence (p. 55).

drama, for it regularly undergoes with the soldier the horrors of the battles of the Napoleonic wars and is even more helpless and choiceless under battle-fire. Hardy seems ever mindful of these toilers and victims, including mention of them so often in his descriptions of difficult field conditions that they become a running image of the pain suffered without comprehension by brute nature.[2] Looking at them in quotation here, we realize the cumulative power of all of these allusions and of Hardy's indignation against the universe that lets such suffering go on.

The first mention that stands out occurs in the scene at Astorga.

> The Retreat continues . . . then enters a miscellaneous group of English cavalry soldiers, some on foot, some mounted, the rearmost of the latter bestriding a shoeless foundered creature whose neck is vertebrae and mane only. While passing it falls from exhaustion; the trooper extricates himself and pistols the animal through the head. He and the rest pass on. (II,III,i,207)

The horse is not the only one in this scene to go shoeless through the mire. It accompanies a procession of straggling humans who have been reduced to the status of "military objects," "some with fragments of shoes on, others barefooted, many of the latter's [sic] feet bleeding" (*ibid.*). The "shoeless foundered creature" and the mostly shoeless "military objects" have been moved from their usually distinct ranks on the great chain of being and dragged by misfortune to an intermediate ground of mutual misery where they are barely distinguishable from one another.

The fact that horses are tractable, can be trained to follow man's lead, brings them only punishment at Talavera:

> It so befalls that as their chargers near
> The inimical wall of flesh with its iron frise,

2 Cf. *Life*, p. 303, for Hardy's excerpt from his letter to W. T. Stead, voicing his concern for the suffering of horses in time of war.

A treacherous chasm uptrips them: zealous men
And docile horses roll to dismal death
And horrid mutilation.

(II,ɪv,v,245–246)

Again at Borodino horses and men are victims of the
same horror, begging together to be put out of their misery:

SPIRIT OF THE PITIES

But mark that roar—
A mash of men's crazed cries entreating mates
To run them through and end their agony;
Boys calling on their mothers, veterans
Blaspheming God and man. Those shady shapes
Are horses, maimed in myriads, tearing round
In maddening pangs, the harnessings they wear
Clanking discordant jingles as they tear!

(III,ɪ,v,345)

When Hardy describes the French army's retreat from
Moscow and paints the eerie hush hanging over it, he includes the horses in his account: ". . . we are struck by the
mournful taciturnity that prevails. Nature is mute. Save
for the incessant flogging of the wind-broken and lacerated
horses[,] there are no sounds" (III,ɪ,ix,354). The horses are
there both as themselves, a fact in the story, and also as an
example of how life at its cruelest works on its creatures,
raining down gratuitous punishment on beings who are
already punished beyond the reach of more.

At Leipzig they share exhaustion and pain with man:

Dusk draws around;
The marching remnants drowse amid their talk,
And worn and harrowed horses slumber as they walk.

In the darkness of the distance spread cries from the
maimed animals and the wounded men . . . (III,ɪɪɪ,iii,
387).

The Chorus of Rumours mentions horses once more when they describe the night march in the rain from Quatre-Bras to Waterloo. We saw here earlier the way that the weather and the darkness confounded the colors of the uniformed soldiers. As usual, what the men went through the horses went through as well:

> ——Cannon upon the foul and flooded road,
> Cavalry in the cornfields mire-bestrowed,
> With frothy horses floundering to their knees,
> Make wayfaring a moil of miseries!
>
> (III,vi,viii,482)

Finally, horses figure at Waterloo itself, where the cavalry attacks of Marshall Ney pour out the blood of both riders and steeds into what the Pities termed (III,vii,iv,497) "so barbarous a groove": "The glittering host [of Ney] again ascends the confronting slopes over the bodies of those previously left there, and [sic] amid horses wandering about without riders, or crying as they lie with entrails trailing or limbs broken" (III,vii,vi,501).

As Waterloo closes, the fighting of the French grows more and more crazed.

> Ney's charger drops—his fifth on this sore day—
> Its rider from the quivering body bounds
>   And forward foots his way.
>
> (III,vii,viii,512)

Ney's charger stands for all the other horses, and all of the horses stand here, as they have stood throughout, for creation's sentient flesh. The quivering body, with its registering senses and its sensitivity to pain, is taken leave of, numbed and deadened, as the presiding mind escapes from it into madness and suicide: it is left by Ney, who is last seen with broken sabre hurling himself "Once more into the carnage" (III,vii,viii,515), and by those desperate French soldiers who "blow out their own brains as they fly" (*ibid.*), and by the

Old Guard who laugh mirthlessly as they choose to be hacked and trampled to the ground.

Such is the patient service the horse renders to man in the battles here depicted and to Hardy in this interweaving, likeness-establishing perspective. It is an example of how flesh obeys designs bridled upon it, enduring suffering and exhaustion without comprehending the necessity for them, until it is discarded, released from further service, by death.

2. SIMILARITIES IN SHAPE AND MOVEMENT

We are now ready to consider as a group the analogies by which Hardy broadens his focus out to the edges of the universe, linking human beings to all the other phenomena of life. The point of conjunction is usually some similarity of physical movement. A sensitive scientific instrument, calibrated to register the kind of waves that we saw visualized in the poem's anatomy of the Will, would catch this likeness in movement; but a human viewer would have to have unusually keen and objective physical senses of hearing and sight to be able to notice it. These physical senses would have to be undulled by hereditary habits of attaching differences in value and kind to the human species and to species that appear "lower" than man on the medieval and Darwinian chains of being and "smaller" than man in size and lifespan and consequence. For a purely sensory way of perceiving different forms of life seems reductive when contrasted to the normally humanistic way of looking at the world; and, furthermore, is as difficult to sustain as was that radical view in the first anatomizing transparency, which, the Years told us, was achieved by "exhaustive strain and effort only" (Fore Scene, 6).

Again, we have to gather the analogies together, as we did the linkings of men and horses, to see that what at each separate encounter works to transmit a vivid and exact sensory impression, proves in the aggregate to have a com-

mon, coherent theme that makes a larger imaginative statement. Thus, at first when we encounter instances where the
noises of humanity seem to this poet's ear like the sounds of
animal nature, we are simply pleased with the vividness and
novelty of the comparisons. For Hardy to describe the noise
of crowd enthusiasm on a Paris street, heard from indoors,
as being like the thrilled hum in beehives "at evenfall/
When swarming pends" (I,i,ii,14), seems a fresh, and in its
context refreshing, comparison. (We do not notice that it is
the buried metaphor in *enthusiasmos* that Hardy has set
stirring.) In another sound-analogy, when the point of view
is distanced from the scene of a London party with its
"surging and babbling guests," we are arrested by the similarity that Hardy's ear catches when sound waves recede
from two usually different sources: "The confused tongues
of the assembly waste away into distance till they are heard
but as the babblings of the sea from a high cliff, the scene
becoming small and indistinct therewith. This passes into
silence, and the whole disappears" (I,i,v,32). Then we find
beauty and consolation in the sameness of the rhythmic
sound in the cries of men wounded at Leipzig and the cries
of birds: "there can be heard . . . the persistent cries from
the plain, rising and falling like those of a vast rookery far
away . . ." (III,III,iv,388). But when we put next to these
examples which allude to the sounds of insects, waters, and
birds, the great number of visual comparisons to these creatures, we realize that the analogies do more than provide
arresting or consoling refreshment to our senses.

The eye and ear that tries not to lose them becomes confused as to which side of these analogies to follow. When we
look down upon the world and the movement on it from
Hardy's characteristic aerial view, these images of men and
animals run in and out of each other. It is as though identities were exchanged between bodies in the moment they
touch and pass. Or, to use another optical image, the overall
effect of these running visual analogies is like the images

formed and broken in a kaleidoscope by jostling bits of colored glass against each other.

But let us look at them as they run through the design, the threads interwoven and their colors commingling. They start as early as the first transparency, where men are revealed vibrating like insects: "The point of view then sinks downward through space, and draws near to the surface of the perturbed countries, where the peoples, distressed by events which they did not cause, are seen writhing, crawling, heaving, and vibrating in their various cities and nationalities" (Fore Scene, p. 6). And they continue like an iridescence running in and out of Hardy's weave. Gleams are reflected from the accoutrements of the French cavalry in its maneuvers on the downs at Boulogne, gleams that flash in the sun like a school of mackerel (I,II,iii,43). Napoleon's boats seen from above "specked the water-shine" like "a flight of swallows" descending on a stream (I,II,v,55). The creep of the columns of the Austrian army, seen from mid-air, are called a "movement as of molluscs on a leaf" (I,III,ii,62), and again, a "silent insect-creep" (*ibid.*). The movement of columns of the French army is next traced until it gradually diminishes in the distance, also insect-like, into "a train of dust" (I,III,iii,63). Nelson's ships sailing toward Trafalgar are as "small as moths" to the aerial vision (I,v,i,81). Napoleon's soldiery, viewed from the upper air as they make their way over the Pyrenees into Spain "in a creeping progress" (II,II,i,181), resemble, first, serpents in the overall shape of their movement ("The thin long columns serpentine along the roads . . ."—*ibid.*), and, then, ants when the point of view advances near enough to see and hear their efforts, as they "laboriously" drag their heavy guns and baggage-waggons "up the incline to the watershed" (*ibid.*). The ships of the English fleet in their approach to Portugal float before the wind "almost imperceptibly, like preened duck-feathers across a pond" (II,II,v,198). The English soldiers abandoned at Walcheren fade "like the mist . . . silently!" (II,ɪv,viii,252). Marie Louise's vast marriage-procession, seen from above on the brown road out of Vienna, "looks no more than a file of ants crawling along a strip of garden-matting" (II,v,v,278). At Torres Vedras it is once again the concerted industrious movements of men that causes them to resemble a swarm of insects: "Innumerable human figures are busying themselves like cheese-mites all along the northernmost frontage . . ." (II,vɪ,i, Dumb Show, 290).

The same scene, still looked down on from "bird's-eye perspective," next shows "three reddish-grey streams of marching men"—the English army: "Looked down upon, their motion seems peristaltic and vermicular, like that of three caterpillars" (ibid.). The Russian army passes through Moscow in its retreat from Borodino, and again, seen from a broad perspective, the mass movement recalls the mass movements of other species: "all in melancholy procession one way, like autumnal birds of passage" (III,ɪ,vi,346). The French, climbing on each other to keep from drowning in the Beresina river, move as snakes would in the same desperate situation—both species driven by the same natural urge for self-preservation. The urge here results in the same actions and motions:

> To the other bridge the living heap betakes itself, the
>   weak pushed over by the strong;
> They loop together by their clutch like snakes; in knots
>   they are submerged and borne along.

(III,ɪ,x, 356)

On the morning of Waterloo the two armies are both compared to ants issuing forth from their ant hills, men and insects alike in their motions—the slow emergence from sleeping places, and quick shift into busy purposive movement (III,vɪɪ,i,484); alike even in bearing different-colored exteriors that declare that they both are born into different groups that will require them to pitch their loyalties and their life's blood into opposing grooves. The slow

movement on St. Lambert's hill, perceived only in its outlines by the anxious French, who peer from their place far
down in the field, is termed "a darkly crawling slug-like
shape," "the creeping shadow from a cloud," or only a wood
moving its new leaves (III,vii,ii,488–489). Looking again
into the distance from the same spot in the French lines,
the darting motion of Wellington's aides running with
orders from their chief to other English officers resembles
those "of house-flies dancing their quadrilles" (III,vii,ii,
489).

We spoke at the beginning of this section of a special
surrealistic effect achieved by all these sensory links. Perhaps presenting them here has repeated that effect, which
I believe is to reproduce "the phantasmagoria of experience" (a phrase that seems apt for this poem and that
Hardy uses in one of his essays).[3] "Phantasmagoria," a term
for a succession of optical effects presented or imagined, is
derived from the Greek verb *phainein,* to show or appear.
The more sober word *phenomena* has the same root. If
these analogies do in context, as they do in quotation, contribute a surrealistic, fantastic, dreamlike thread to the
poem, that would serve more than one purpose in Hardy's
design. We remember that in his poetic metaphor for life's
evanescence and insubstantiality and mere appearance of
reality, phenomena are the films of a dream.

WE can make certain generalizations about how these visual and auditory similes are made. First, the similarity on
which they all base their connections is in each case seen
or heard from a far distance. This remoteness has important
results: substance, texture, and characterizing uniqueness
are strained away, and only the outline comes through.
The pattern of rhythmic motion, the skeletal line, is what
shows, as in imagist poetry;[4] and, as in imagist poetry, tradi-

---

[3] Thomas Hardy, "The Science of Fiction," in *Personal Writings,* ed.
Orel, p. 135.

[4] George R. Elliott, "Hardy's Poetry and the Ghostly Moving-Pic-

tional emotional connotations have been filtered out to make for a moment a single physical aesthetic point. In the vast perspective of nature, the fall of men looks like the fall of "a swathe of grass/ Within a sickle's curve" (III,i,iii, 337), or like the crash of "trees at felling-time" (II,i,iv,159): no more than a movement in the natural process of life and death, and no more a reason for emotion than any other part of the process. In this perspective, the framing outlines are constant, and the substances that move through them are interchangeable.

Second, because of the far remove from which these analogies are made, they always refer to men in the mass.[5] We can understand why: it is from close range that individuality—and individual likenesses and differences—loom large. And Hardy is not interested in making each man vivid and unforgettable for his individuality and uniqueness. (We find ourselves back at the critical complaint that his characters are "curiously neutral,"[6] colorless, and unin-

---

ture," pp. 289–90, also notices that the skeletal outlines are what are most visible in Hardy's imaginative landscape (which he characterizes as memory's "region of shades," a "borderland between Being and No-Being"). Elliott goes on to note that since these patterns and silhouettes are abstract, there are universal correspondences for them: "His Wessex may be found anywhere, given the slightest trick of similarity, or fancied similarity, in the landscape. . . ."

Hardy's *Life* records another instance of the universality, and interchangeability, of basic "effects," once the accident of geography (here, Wessex vs. Venice) is screened out: "Yes: here to this visionary place I solidly bring in my own person Dorchester and Wessex life; and they may well ask why I do it. . . . Yet there is a connection. The bell of the Campanile of S. Marco strikes the hour, and its sound has exactly that tin-tray *timbre* given out by the bells of Longpuddle and Weatherbury, showing that they are of precisely the same-proportioned alloy" (*Life*, p. 193).

5 I noticed only three similes in which the comparison was between individuals: Napoleon at Wagram compared to a water rat (Dumb Show, II,iv,ii,234); Josephine cowering "like a frightened animal" (II,v,ii,259); and the Younger English Lady springing from her bed "like a hare from its form" (III,vi,iv,468).

6 Edwin Muir, "The Novels of Thomas Hardy," p. 118.

teresting. It is a matter, as we suggested in the last chapter, of what about man is of interest to the author, what he thought was "real" versus merely "actual," superficies.) Thus Hardy does not use imagery as Dickens does, to animate and bring out idiosyncrasy, but rather to point to the universal *anima*.

Hardy's metaphors and similes are not unique in having a bearing beyond the specific context in which they appear, reaching out to contribute their meanings to the whole world of the poem; but they are unusual in that the burden of their meaning is so much the same: all things are more than kin, by virtue of their interdependence, the condition of determinism that they have in common, and beneath all, the doom that awakens them together into life and sentience. Individuality is not only irrelevant next to this meaning; worse, it obscures and denies it, by emphasizing appearances, and by promoting the "dream" of independence and autonomy, when in fact life is dependent and interdependent. The truth cannot be seen in surface coloration and individual mannerism and personality; it requires a mass of phenomena, or at least a contrasting pair, to show its underlying unifying presence.[7]

The generalization can be made, then, of all of Hardy's interweavings of his threads, that they are best seen from a distant perspective, and that they assert together a relationship between men and other living phenomena that is more than a similarity—indeed, a fundamental identity.

[7] Early in his career Hardy doubted whether he could become a successful writer of novels "as usually understood—that is pictures of modern customs or observances," because these phenomena of the surface of life were not real to him. He would "have to look for material in manners—in ordinary social and fashionable life as other novelists did. Yet he took no interest in manners, but in the substance of life only" (*Life*, p. 104). Later in his career, when his kind of novel expressing "the substance of life" had found, or made, its own audience, he writes less diffidently: "The literary productions of men of rigidly good family and rigidly correct education, mostly treat social conventions and contrivances—the artificial forms of living—as if they were cardinal facts of life" (*Life*, p. 213).

Some of the particular points, refinements, of this generalization will be uncovered when we trace out the connections of these threads.

3. DISPARITIES EQUALIZED IN THE WEB

Hardy's central subject—the infinitely extended network
of forces that operate irresistibly and unconsciously on human beings, which he characterized in terms of the Will
versus human wills—is already a large one indeed. The
perspective we are considering, through the act of outreach
performed by each analogy, now expands that subject further by drawing the rest of life with mankind into its view.
Its diverse inclusions persuade us that Hardy's anatomizing
vision is as wide as it is deep, and create the illusion that his
poem has accounted for the totality of life, leaving out
nothing.

All the analogies we have mentioned so far began with
man and yoked other forms of life to him by some similarity in motion. But the linking can be effected from the
other side and in massive stillness, as when Hardy turns his
distancing, correspondence-noting gaze on great tracts of
land. In the old creation myths, earth is often the female
body or the mother fertility-principle; similarly in Hardy's
poem, it is a tissue very close to the innerlying Will, one of
its first outshapings, as it were. At the same time that it is
a body of the Will, it looks in shape like a human body, as
the passages below suggest.

> The nether sky opens, and Europe is disclosed as a
> prone and emaciated figure, the Alps shaping like a
> backbone, and the branching mountain-chains like
> ribs, the peninsular plateau of Spain forming a head.
> Broad and lengthy lowlands stretch from the north of
> France across Russia like a grey-green garment
> hemmed by the Ural mountains and the glistening
> Arctic Ocean. (Fore-Scene, 6)

> The beholder finds himself, as it were, caught up on high, and . . . he gazes southward towards Central Europe—the contorted and attenuated écorché of the Continent appearing as in an earlier scene, but now obscure under the summer stars. (III,ii,iv,376)

> Europe has now sunk netherward to its far-off position as in the Fore-Scene, and it is beheld again as a prone and emaciated figure of which the Alps form the vertebrae, and the branching mountain-chains the ribs, the Spanish Peninsula shaping the head of the écorché. The lowlands look like a grey-green garment half-thrown off, and the sea around like a disturbed bed on which the figure lies. (After-Scene, 521)

"Emaciated," "contorted," "attenuated," "prone," lying on "a disturbed bed": the words suggest that the continent resembles man not only in shape, but in "common misfortune," both suffering on the rack of existence, both choicelessly submitting to and enduring an ordeal imposed from elsewhere.

Bonamy Dobrée is particularly sensitive to the kinship between earth and man in Hardy:

"With Hardy the earth labours, suffers, and groans, is scarred with experience like any human being."[8]

"In Hardy's novels it may not be fate that is shown working through us, but it is certainly the earth working through us, both the earth and ourselves being part of the expression of the Immanent Will, or, if you prefer, the blind Creative Principle."[9]

That "working," as Dobrée views it, belies the "hammer-strokes" of Fate that E. M. Forster hears beating down upon the characters in Hardy's novels.[10] It comes not so much from circumstances without as from within, in a common rhythm, "something repeated and eternal, like the

8 Bonamy Dobrée, "Thomas Hardy," p. 28.
9 *Ibid.*, p. 32.
10 E. M. Forster, *Aspects of the Novel*, pp. 93–94.

flux and reflux of waves upon a beach"[11]—or, we may say, looking at *The Dynasts'* image of a massive human shape with smaller human bodies toiling upon it, like the rise and fall of bodies breathing together. And, further, Dobrée adds, "in contradistinction with resounding hammer strokes is a quality of silence, the silence of tragedy brooding over an accidented landscape."[12] But beneath the correspondence in the shapes of man and the land there lies a further, and central, meaning: what is true of the "outshapings" is true of the core, of the life-force itself. It too is choicelessly suffering the suffering it imposes. Although he himself rejects it, George Elliott discerns that meaning and its importance:

"Here is a *real* 'pathetic fallacy': the poet extends his pity to Necessity itself. This confusion is . . . at the very center of his vision. . . . His devotion to simple, inclusive, and sombre design brings him close to the notion of Fate. But what his architectural sense demands, his humanitarianism denies. Viewing the universe as a Single Being, he sympathizes with it too much to believe it capable of a really sinister policy. . . . Often, to be sure, Hardy takes on the peculiar attitude of blaming God for human troubles while denying God's existence. But generally he likes to imagine for deity a sort of lackadaisical existence which has none of the potency of Fate, and which deserves far more pity than blame—he pities God's incapacity for pity."[13]

Hardy's passages, then, present an explicit image of identity in the superimposed figures of man and earth, microcosm and macrocosm. In the stretches between these explicit images the identity submerges to allow the human drama its prominence; but as the drama proceeds we are given passing reminders of the special correspondence between earth and man. The heath, under a certain light, shows

[11] Dobrée, "Thomas Hardy," pp. 36–37.
[12] *Ibid.*, p. 36.
[13] George R. Elliott, "Spectral Etching in the Poetry of Thomas Hardy," p. 1,194. Elliott's remarks seem especially applicable to "the pathetic Me" in Hardy's "The Wind Blew Words," CP, p. 419.

dark pits "like the eye-sockets of a skull" and tumuli gleaming like bronze armaments (I,II,v,53). "The face of the
ocean is fringed on its eastern edge by the Cape [Trafalgar]
and the Spanish shore" (I,v,i,81). To Pitt looking at the
map after Austerlitz, Europe appears to be a dead body
under Napoleon's heel (I,VI,vi,128). A scene description
sets the Plain of Vitoria before the reader in a point-by-
point analogy to "the palm of a monstrous right hand"
(III,II,ii,367–68). The detailed simile does more than dia-
gram the battlefield: it makes the hand, with its thumb-
ball, "Mount of Wars," "Moon," its "Line of Life" dropping towards the wrist, its mounts at the finger bases, its
bent finger-tips, into a felt presence, more real and palpable
than the transitory events taking place on its surface. All
the above make a casual image like "earthquake thrills" in
an incidental remark by Berthier to Napoleon,

> Vaguely-voiced rumours, sire, but nothing more,
> Which travel countries quick as earthquake-thrills,
> No mortal knowing how.
>
> (II,vi,iii,297)

a phenomenon whose "how" *we* can know, since it is comparable to a shiver or some other autonomic sensation
running through the human body.

Humanity is magnified when it is linked with these
massive images of continents and earth. We encounter more
often the other kind of comparison, to the small and the
tiny, connecting armies and navies and vehicles of state to
insects and serpents and feathers and mist. As we look back
upon them we must observe that, while the eye that first
visualized them may have been entirely neutral, the result
in the reader's eye is not neutral. The human side of the
equation is inevitably reduced in stature and importance;
for the valleys to be exalted, the mountains and hills must
be made low. These equalizing analogies establish a prevailing "wide" view, wider than any one form of life alone,

just as it is more spacious, with its aerial perspective, than any one place.[14]

This wide perspective throws ironic light on the obsequious speech of the President of the French Senate to Napoleon, with his claim that the birth of one baby boy makes insignificant all other developments in Europe, that next to that news, "nothing" has happened:

> Nothing in Europe, sire, that can compare
> In magnitude therewith to more effect
> Than with an eagle some frail finch or wren.
>
> (II,vi,iii,297)

Although the man speaks them in folly, his words are true: in its relation to the Will, a frail finch is of as much—and of as little—effect as an eagle, a human, a defeat on the battlefield, or a national bankruptcy.

On occasion Hardy would seem to share the reader's partiality to human "magnitude," and to disapprove of the Will's equalizing indifference. Thus at the great reversal at Ulm, the reader's intelligence, and presumably the poet's, take a position close to the Ironic and the Pitying Spirits and at a critical distance from the Spirit of the Years when he voices his views as impassively as the Impassivity of the Will. The fate of humans at Ulm is of no interest to the Will, says the calm, objective Spirit:

> Ah, no: ah, no!
> It is impassible as glacial snow.—
> Within the Great Unshaken
> These painted shapes awaken
> A lesser thrill than doth the gentle lave
> Of yonder bank by Danube's wandering wave
> Within the Schwarzwald heights that give it flow!
>
> (I,iv,v,76–77)

---

[14] We are allowed to see a little joke in all those expressions in the drama in which human beings say to each other self-importantly: "All the world will be there" (Halford and Baillie, II,vi,v,309).

For in human eyes there is a difference between the waves set off down the Danube from the glacial waters on the Schwarzwald, and the train of events set off at Ulm by the neutral forces behind all things. Both may be, similarly, wave impulses, alike in shape and alike in registering no message back upon the force that set them in motion. But there is a difference in the feeling and suffering that attends on each; in magnitude Ulm sets off more painful reverberations than does the Danube's splash against the riverbank. The Spirit of the Pities, the reader, and presumably Hardy, the dramatist who in the very next scene sympathetically sets forth Pitt's reaction to Ulm, together feel this difference, and it is part of the poem's prayer that the entire universe should someday awake to this recognition of the measure of pain.

At either end of the drama the Spirit of the Years gives us statements that show a view of human struggle and human agony that is characteristically impassive, unmoved by the slightest subjective bias toward humanity over other forms of life or by any subjective experience of suffering. The countless human lives that are convulsed in the mass upheavals brought about by Napoleon are termed

> frail ones that his flings
> Have made gyrate like animalcula
> In tepid pools.
> (Fore Scene, 6)

This jarring and reductive simile is spoken by the Years to the younger Intelligences at the beginning of the drama. At the drama's end, when the same Spirit addresses its final word to Napoleon, type of pathetic-man as well as type of old-hero for the drama, the Spirit does so with a simile which again flattens mankind's valuation of itself:

> Such men as thou, who wade across the world
> To make an epoch, bless, confuse, appal,

217

Are in the elemental ages' chart
Like meanest insects on obscurest leaves
But incidents and grooves of Earth's unfolding. . . .
(III,vii,ix,521)

But this is the levelling view—or rather, viewlessness—of the Will, expressed in the levelling language of the Years. Surely it is not shared by this poet.

But even as we make the claim we must withdraw it. Such is the force of Hardy's similes—those we have seen already in this chapter and those that we have yet to see—that we feel he is at once peculiarly aware of the pain that human beings undergo in existing, and at the same time just as sensitive to the reality, need, and vulnerability of all other creatures in existence. Statements that a man is of no more consequence than microscopic life in a tepid pool or than the meanest insects on obscurest leaves, can be read, at least theoretically, not only as ironic equations levelled against humanity's self-valuation, but also as sober and positive truths, declarations of the tragic value of every existence. All occupy central spots in the immense universe as each senses it, all are worthy of poetic attention, all are included in Hardy's sympathy, as wide and deep as the universe.[15]

[15] Selected quotations from Hardy's notebook, which are preserved in his *Life*, demonstrate this artistic attention and sympathy:

"(1882) August.—An ample theme: the intense interests, passions, and strategy that throb through the commonest lives." (*Life*, p. 153.)

"(1882) May 13. The slow, meditative lives of people who live in habitual solitude. . . . Solitude renders every trivial act of a solitary full of interest, as showing thoughts that cannot be expressed for want of an interlocutor." (*ibid.*)

"(1877) May 30. Walking to Marnhull. The prime of bird-singing. The thrushes and blackbirds are the most prominent,—pleading earnestly rather than singing, and with such modulation that you seem to see their little tongues curl inside their bills in their emphasis. A bullfinch sings from a tree with a metallic sweetness piercing as a fife. Further on I come to a hideous carcase of a house in a green landscape, like a skull on a table of dessert." (*Life*, pp. 113–14.)

"Same date: I sometimes look on all things in inanimate Nature as pensive mutes." (*Life*, p. 114.)

218

So a transfer is made: in the scale of values, human life is somewhat lowered and animal life raised by the repeated linking of both in the poem's imagery. And other exchanges are accomplished also. One, a psychological transfer, is effected through the physical similarities that have been established to the viewer's eye and ear. The theory that action is the result of involuntary drives, of instincts below the level of consciousness, is generally accepted as accounting for animal behavior, but resisted as an explanation for human behavior. However, as the reader sees humans and non-humans associated in so many instances and pronounced similar in so many respects, his mind begins to become more and more open to the possibility that the similarity might hold for motivation also, and that the actions of men and of animals may be alike involuntary.

4. Antitheses Reconciled in the Web

Each thematic link established by the poem's similes, trafficking over the highways established by the sensory links, enables the poem to achieve a victory over whatever divides living things from each other. One such thematic link we saw at the conclusion of our last chapter, the weariness that all living things take on when they enter existence. This feeling, we saw, is an inherent condition of life; all who live, whatever their situation in a society that is unequal and a universe that is inequitable, experience exhaustion and revulsion at life's contrarieties. In scenes of battle we saw it in horses and men, and we see it also in domestic scenes, in ballrooms and boudoirs. All across the continent, in England, Spain, France, Austria, and Russia, royal apartments "become transparent" (as in II,vi,vi,310) to show us that affairs of state are inseparable from sexual affairs, as we watch statesmen driven in eagerness into entanglements and then driven in disgust and boredom from those same entanglements, all "But as the unweeting Urger may bestead" (II,vi,vi,312). These affairs and drives may seem frivolous, ("faint fancies," the Years calls them, in apology on this very point), instances of the kind of psychological suffering that the idle rich have the time to give themselves to, compared to the physical pain borne by the brutes whose bodies must do their work and take the front in their battles. But Hardy includes many of these scenes in his design, partly to show the varieties of threads that intermesh in the web, and partly to establish a contrast that will eventually be overcome.

George the Third and his son make up two threads that we shall take as our example. In the two appearances of the man who rules over England throughout the war, the drama shows a man whose gaze is blinkered in its view of means (refusing Pitt's request for a bipartisan ministry, supporting Chatham's Walcheren expedition) but fixed clearsightedly on ends the poem regards as true (the evil of lives wasted in bloody "victories," the urgent need for leaders to promote their people's welfare). The king rises above personal limitations and above class in his concern and in his suffering. The "great black gulfs" of depression that life drags him through make him an extreme example of all the "throbbing" "captive lives" racked on the loom's "mistimed fabric" (II,vi,v,304). The sequence of scenes after Albuera that conclude Part Two form a unity, starting with the genuine sufferings of the old king and moving to the comic tribulations of the prince regent; they carry us from the serious to the petty, but take us also to still another example of a being frustrated in his station and vexed by life's contrarieties. For a brief moment the Prince-Regent, like his father, rises above the limits of his nature and social position, and for a moment his cry against "the whole curst show" (II,vi,vii,318) is greater than itself and speaks for the poem and the poet. As the scene sequence ends, the Spirit of the Pities looks for relief out of the windows of the Regent's apartments and notes the break of day:

SPIRIT OF THE PITIES

Behold To-morrow riddles the curtains through,
And labouring life without shoulders its cross anew!

(II,vi,vii,321)

There is a double emphasis in the second line of this passage, I believe, on "labouring" and on "life." The line,
following upon the scene of the aristocratic fête at which
"all the world" was present, has a class reference, certainly,
but beyond that a human reference.[16] And beyond, there is
a reference to all that is mortal, as the Spirit of the Years
reminds the Pities, to steady him as he flinches at the king's
anguish:

Mild one, be not too touched with human fate.
Such is the Drama: such the Mortal state. . . .

(II,vi,v,304)

The divisions of class, then, are removed, along with the
breakdown in the divisions of species. Another distinction,
that between the destroyer and victim, is done away with
in the course of a snake-image that appears in a dumb
show depicting the allied invasion of France after Leipzig.
At the beginning of the scene the invading armies are
likened to snakes and the town of Mannheim to a human
victim:

DUMB SHOW

. . . anon certain strange dark patches in the landscape, flexuous and riband-shaped, are discerned to be
moving slowly. Only one moveable object on earth is
large enough to be conspicuous herefrom, and that is
an army. The moving shapes are armies.

The nearest, almost beneath us, is defiling across the
river by a bridge of boats, near the junction of the

16 "Some wear jewels and feathers, some wear rags. All are caged
birds; the only difference lies in the size of the cage. This too is part of
the tragedy." (*Life*, p. 171.)

221

Rhine and the Neckar, where the oval town of Mannheim, standing in the fork between the two rivers, has
from here the look of a human head in a cleft stick.
. . . The undulating columns twinkle as if they were
scaly serpents. (III,IV,i,398)

But the image will not hold still, any more than would an
actual snake. It is a reversal for the human to have his
head under the cleft stick; usually it is the snake who is
thus caught and the human being who holds the stick.
Which is which? As the Dumb Show continues, describing
first the Russian hosts, then the Prussian, then the Austrian,
then the English, we see several "ductile" masses converg-
ing in their "flexuous courses," moving without opposition
or discernible effort, as snakes glide, gracefully; the figures
are "mostly snake-shaped, but occasionally with batrachian
and saurian outlines" (ibid.). We realize that the worm has
indeed turned, that it is Napoleon who is the human prey
of these imagined snakes, that it is he who, like Mannheim
in its cleft stick, is about to be isolated and pinned down.

The image is brought again to our minds during Napoleon's removal to Elba, when an angry mob is assured that
he is no longer a threat to France:

> . . . His fangs being drawn, he gnashes powerless now
> To do you further harm.
>
> (III,IV,vi,419)

But the osmosis-like process that we have claimed is at
work at other points in the poem—in the diffusion of
meaning between the cosmic and the human brain, between
one protagonist and another, and now between human
beings and other forms of life—is at work between the versions of this image also. The metaphor of Napoleon as a
captured and impotent snake pours its meaning back into
other instances of the snake figure: to Mannheim, to the
serpentine armies. As in all these analogies and similes, the
different contents and the different proportions of corre-

sponding figures are not the variables that count. What matters, because it is the basis for correspondence and sympathetic identification, is the common relativity all share, and that common relativity is guaranteed, always there to be found, because of the unconditioned presence of the Absolute at the back of the stage. And so all who are related in serpent imagery here are equalized: the Emperor who will be pronounced "disturber of the tranquility of the world" (III,vi,i,454), the tranquil town, and the armies that hunt him down in order to restore the old order and peace. The roles of hunter and hunted, captor and captive, active and passive, are superficial; at the core, all are passive, all are victims.

Another simile, in the act of spanning the division between human and insect life, lowers the bar between life and death. We have discussed it in our first chapter, where we considered the material base that Hardy points to in all phenomena: the French army seen from the air as a monstrous dun-piled caterpillar laboring and heaving across the winter landscape of Russia (III,i,ix,353–54). As usual, Hardy links two kinds of life by shape and movement. The elongated object, like an insect creature mutely trying to follow a mastering impulse "urged by That within it," wanders "Israel-like" across the wilderness. Hardy's mind makes the same connection as does the imagination of D. H. Lawrence in *Movements in European History*, where mass human phenomena, such as the "Israel-like" wanderings of the crusaders, are similarly described as "urged by That within it": like the swarming behavior of insects, wonders of nature beyond understanding. Here, the "object's" hesitant probing attempts to find passage at Tarutino, then Jaroslawitz, then back at Borodino, then Smolensko, correspond to the bobbing and looping motions that a caterpillar makes with its sensitive head as it tests the ground before it. The army's "brabbling multitudes" of camp-followers are the legs that make it seem "not one but many"; the human arms and weaponry are its bristling "pile." When the snow begins to cover the ground, this army, like a caterpillar, is unequipped to survive. It continues its painful creep deathwards, peeling off parts of itself against the frozen ground until it comes to nothing, in a silent, uncomplaining process of disintegration and transmutation. The bodies falling to the wayside are absorbed into the snow, the land, the birds, the sky. Seen from afar, where the pain and loss and waste of individuality cannot register, this spectacle demonstrates the mysterious economy of nature. In the insect world the comings and goings of generations are too short-lived and myriad for man's eye to follow: nature is both prodigal in her pourings-out of lives, and thrifty; nothing is lost; the weak and the dead are consumed by the strong and the living; death and life are one process, a single unbroken thread.

Elsewhere the poem has made much of the difference between life and death. That difference is a crucial one to the living, whether they be those few who seek death or the majority who fear and resist it, because death severs their tie to unpurposed energy and cross-purposed impulses. But that difference is a subjective one that the aerial observation point of this scene quite leaves out, along with other subjective feelings like pain and injury, which are intense realities to those who live in casements of flesh. From the loftiest, most abstract viewpoint that the mind can attain, life and death can be seen to be the same, and so there is no mourning at the passing of a caterpillar or of an army. Nor is the opposite felt, celebration at death, or lamentation for the prolongation of existence, reactions appropriate at other vantage points of the poem; for those sentiments would preserve and emphasize the difference between life and death. The dissolving of that distinction is accomplished here by an observant sensory faculty, detached, at this level, even from sympathy, a pure and remote wonder.

Finally, we come to the most notable union of humans and non-humans in the poem, the detailed and modulated

lyric beginning, "The eyelids of eve fall together at last,"
which closes the scene on the field on the eve before Waterloo. Hardy himself remarked upon this passage:

> . . . the lyrical account of the fauna of Waterloo
> field on the eve of battle is, curiously enough, the page
> . . . that struck me, in looking back over the book, as
> being the most original in it. Though, of course, a
> thing may be original without being good. However, it
> does happen that (so far as I know) in the many treat-
> ments of Waterloo in literature, those particular per-
> sonages who were present have never been alluded to
> before. (Letter to Clodd, *Life*, p. 453)

As we shall see, the antitheses Hardy is able to compose
through this union of opposites will be harmonized at a
very different distance and in a very different mood of intelligence from the abstract view we have just considered.

First we need to place the lyric in its dramatic setting:
it follows an aerial song by the Chorus of Rumours, which
tells of the movement of the two armies through the pouring
rain and the falling darkness as they take their various positions at the field of Waterloo. Already in this chapter we
have referred to that song because it described how, in the
rain, the mire, and the nightfall, distinctions between
friend and foe, "creeping clumps" of men and "flounder-
ing" horses, became obliterated and all were imbued with
the same earthlike color that objects take on in the dark.
At this point, when a common resemblance among all the
newcomers to the field has been established, the choruses
of the Years and the Pities, alternating with each other, take
up the singing account:

CHORUS OF THE YEARS (aerial music)
The eyelids of eve fall together at last,
And the forms so foreign to field and tree
Lie down as though native, and slumber fast!

(III,VI,viii,483)

The first distinction is made in order that it may later be overcome: the various intruding "forms," which we saw become one body, now lie down in deep sleep as though they belonged on the scene; but, while they may be in agreement with the time of day—which, like them, closes its eyelids—they are quite foreign, and do not belong, to that place. This distinction is developed further by the Pities: unlike the intruders, the field, which normally would enjoy calm at this time, is kept awake and tensely vigilant by "proofs" of trouble descending upon it—a great and exceptional calamity like an earthquake or an eclipse, but less natural than these: contrived, suspicious, a needless "harlequinade." Then the Years recounts the "proofs": the "thud of hoofs," the press of heavy wheels and cut of wheel-rims, the digging of trenches, the tramp and tread of boots. These military "ponderosities" have already scattered or crushed the tiny field-creatures—the hare, the swallow, the mole, the lark, the hedgehog, the snail, the worm, the butterfly—and will do worse on the morrow, saturating the ground and soaking the very worms with blood. This is victimization of the innocent indeed, a deep injury and opposition that cannot be superficially coated over by the tinting shades of twilight or the muddy rains; this is, as the chorus of Years says, "a worse than the weather-foe" (*ibid.*). But in the very next stanza, while adding one more injury to the score of enmity and estrangement, the Spirit of the Years suggests a ground of kinship in "common misfortune":

> Trodden and bruised to a miry tomb
> Are ears that have greened but will never be gold,
> And flowers in the bud that will never bloom.
>
> (ibid.)

At the very point where the poem's eye comes so close that it can feel the bruisings of the grain and the buds—close enough, as the chorus of Pities tells us in the next stanza, to intuit the very "season's intent" and know just what it regrets—at that point what the eye comes upon is not a uniquely defining secret but a basic resemblance that unites the grain with the humankind who dealt it the alienating injury.

"Like a youth of promise struck stark and cold. . . ." The comparison releases many images in the reader's mind: gallant young officers dancing "The Prime of Life" in the ballroom at Brussels; a young Wessex sergeant singing in Spain about golden days back home with the "Budmouth Dears"; the men at Walcheren who "might have fought . . . and . . . died well" (II,iv,viii,252); the French boys who disappeared in the snows of Russia; the infants drowned in the Beresina river. The poem has set before the reader many versions of the "season's intent," "frustrate" and "mangled"; many versions of the "youth of promise" whose life is cut down "ere its fruit unfold." The early deaths of the human youths, and the loss of the grain while it is green, is a universal fact that transcends the circumstance of how, and by whose agency, the loss was dealt.

And then there are the older men, past their greenness, who have not been woven into this harmony; the Spirit of the Years in his last chorus brings them in too. Unlike the soundly sleeping young men, the old toss fitfully on the wet ground. They share a state of restlessness with the field itself, and share also the way that state comes upon them: "thrills of misgiving" pierce the "artless champaign"; rheumatic pains, stabs, aches, chills, and cramps pierce the old men. With a loop of the net they are brought into the harmony achieved in this passage.

In the concluding stanza the souls of the sleepers (I take "each soul" to refer specifically to the veterans, but also, generally, to all who have been designated in the choruses, men and animals) sigh in presentiment of the death that awaits on the morrow. Death, in this last mildly sardonic word sung by the Spirits Sinister, will settle all dispute about who is the holder of this field. It will not be those outsiders who take temporary positions upon it, "as though native"; not even those "natives" who live out their lives with it; but only those dead ones who become incorporated into it. Their lease materially supercedes all claims of youth, age, power, nationality, date of arrival, and species.

Thus death settles and reconciles. At the end of the lyric and the scene, the scene description seems to take us back to where we were when the passage began, before "The eyelids of eve": "The fires of the English go out, and silence prevails, save for the soft hiss of the rain that falls impartially on both the sleeping armies" (III,vi,viii,484). For it is raining again, on both armies. But a greater gulf than we could see before has been opened to the weather, the gulf that separates man from the field, his arts from nature, his actions from the world that lies all before him for him to act upon, and his tendency to inflict pain from the counter-capacity to absorb it. The impartiality of the poet has shown us that gulf and then washed it away under the impartial rains.

And what is the focus that reconciles these antinomies? Not what we have come to expect for this perspective, and what we saw operating dramatically upon the army's death-throes in Russia, the detached, pattern-seeing one of "pure" science or art. We meet here its opposite: the view of sympathetic identification that comes so close that it penetrates the body and enters the core and cracks the atom of individuality and releases—oneness of nature. As the colors at either end of the spectrum bend and turn into each other, so do these two views from either end of the pole of vision —the far and the near—deliver identical truths.

5. Meanings Reinforced by the Web

There remains for us to suggest the meanings that the interweaving perspective brings to support the great theme to which the poem builds: "Consciousness the Will informing, till it fashion all things fair!"

The first meaning that its similes bring into consciousness is the mutuality of all living things. That meaning derives, of course, from the view set at the opening of the poem and discussed in our first chapter, of the common—and continuous—origin of every phenomenon, every event, every aspect of life, in unconscious energy. Another dimension to that view was studied in the second chapter, the perspective from the experience of some of the beings infused by the unconscious energies: the sense of frustration, shock and wonder, lived in by creatures who *feel* like conscious subjects while actually living lives of puppet-objects strung and moved by unconsciousness. The view in this third perspective is from one particular (human) set of objects whose subjective feelings we have come to know and to pity, over to other creatures who also live and move upon the great unconscious, also are innocent of ever choosing to exist, and yet also are made to suffer, as though they were guilty of creation, the conditions of existence.

This view sees that these misfortunes which commonly define all creatures also connect them in a bond of fellow-suffering; indeed, since there are no facts more important than these defining facts, it sees that these facts make all creatures "more than kin," make them versions of each other, fellow-objects who will recognize each other as fellow-subjects. The view of mutuality, then, not only informs the reader's intellect with its consciousness of fair and unfair; it informs the reader's *will*, moving it to desire to mend an unfair, unjust universe with fairness, to treat all living things as one wishes oneself could be treated, to live—insofar as one has in one's control—as though life were already what it should be.

Hardy stated this idea in a letter he wrote to the Humanitarian League, congratulating it for its work in general and for its defense of animals in particular; he chose to include the following passage from it in his biography:

Few people seem to perceive fully as yet that the most far-reaching consequence of the establishment of the common origin of all species is ethical; that it logically involved a readjustment of altruistic morals by enlarging as a *necessity of rightness* the application of what has been called "The Golden Rule" beyond the area of mere mankind to that of the whole animal kingdom. Possibly Darwin himself did not wholly perceive it, though he alluded to it. While man was deemed to be a creation apart from other creations, a secondary or tertiary morality was considered good enough towards the "inferior" races; but no person who reasons nowadays can escape the trying conclusion that this is not maintainable. And though I myself do not at present see how the principle of equal justice all round is to be carried out in its entirety, I recognize that the League is grappling with the question. (*Life*, p. 349)

We see that Hardy meant for us to take seriously, as a corollary arising out of this perspective, *The Dynasts'* version of the golden rule and of what was soon to be expressed by Schweitzer as "reverence for life."

Two critics, Chakravarty and Pinto, comment upon the remarkable sensitivity to all forms of life that made Hardy "the first great European poet to treat animals with exactly the same respect as human beings."[17] Chakravarty explains it as a "conception of morality . . . [extending] to the entire world of conscious sentient beings" that is based upon Hardy's harmonization of the theory of evolution with an increase of sensibility.[18] Pinto adds: "Hardy's imaginative apprehension of the kinship of man to the lower animals is a contribution to the growth of human sensibility comparable with the concept of the brotherhood of man which was the great legacy of the romantic poets."[19]

But there is a danger in considering in isolation from the poems in which they appear such matters as a poet's

[17] Vivian de Sola Pinto, "Hardy and Housman," p. 47.
[18] Amiya Chakravarty, *"The Dynasts" and the Post-War Age in Poetry*, p. 23.
[19] Pinto, p. 48.

contribution to the growth of human sensibility or the concepts he may stand for, though they may be praiseworthy ones such as the Golden Rule or the brotherhood of sentient beings or even the brotherhood of man. For concepts and principles, in themselves, will rise and fall in critical favor as times and principles change. Chakravarty and Pinto, and probably most critics who have been drawn to make detailed studies of Hardy, admire his liberal ethic. But there are critics of other persuasions who, because they disapprove of Hardy's views ("sentimental liberalism" and "merely secularistic benevolence"),[20] make a negative example of him and dismiss or attack his poetry. And it is true that Hardy's views on the suffering of animals—and on all suffering—become no more than sentiments when removed from their context. The point is that the views and the poems require each other to be seen whole. Hardy eludes those who address the concept or sentiment or "ism" without studying how it is expressed. But, viewed in context and in this perspective as it follows from and leads to each of the others, it becomes instead a "necessity of rightness," true to, and within, the poem's vision and logic.

To conclude this discussion of Hardy's sensitivity to the "whole animal kingdom," we need add only the following: that it should be seen not only as a concept, a particular perception, but as a demonstration of the very movement of perception. That movement is the basic indispensable leap that imagination takes to transcend distance and otherness and to acquire living knowledge.[21] The movement is accomplished by way of sympathy, travelling hand to hand from the feeling and sentience within oneself to

[20] Hoxie Neale Fairchild, *Gods of a Changing Poetry: 1880–1920*, pp. 250 and 246. Elsewhere in this study I have noted other critics of Hardy's liberal social positions, especially Eliot and Blackmur, who would agree with Fairchild's views.

[21] Benedict McCormick, "Thomas Hardy: A Vision and a Prelude," pp. 155–56, considers that Hopkins and Hardy are alike in possessing and exercising this power of sympathetic imagination.

that within another body. In *The Dynasts* we can see these leaps of sympathy, this movement of imagination, carried out to the farthest reaches.

We can gather a second large meaning from Hardy's similes. By so often aligning man with the "lower" forms of life, he makes man shed some of what sets him off in uniqueness. This shedding has benefits as well as drawbacks. The autonomy of human reason is our example: reason is proved to be only half-free, a projection, like all the other projections, of the unconscious. But if man's unique claim to sovereignty over the rest of creation is jettisoned, so is man's unique guilt—the curse of human self-consciousness that so many have blamed for human unhappiness and even the world's unhappiness. The drama shows suffering going on quite unconnected to human reason. Human beings suffer painful deaths from "natural" causes—fire, sickness, accident; animals suffer—some through an act of man, like the horses on the battlefields and the flora and fauna bruised by man's battles; but still others suffer through no act of man: ant armies marching to war against each other, a caterpillar freezing in the snow, a clutch of snakes fallen into a river and drowning in a loop. True, the drama shows human reason, human consciousness, adding to the distress of individuals (the mental anguish of a Villeneuve or King George the Third, for example) and to the suffering of the world at large (the irrational decisions of leaders positioned to affect many lives). After all, by being part of the web, reason and consciousness share in the distortion resulting from the original misalignment of the loom. But not all of the strain and tearing in the weave can be laid to that, or any, thread. Removing threads from the frame—removing man from the field of Waterloo, or removing man's distressed intelligence from his body—would not end the general suffering. And even beyond those extremes: removing "sentience" from all creation, as the Pities are driven to recommend in anger, would not end the fact of distress and waste, but only the knowledge of it, and a testimony against it.

Hardy does, throughout his writings, profess to regret the evolution of human consciousness in all its aspects, often commenting that introspection, "too much reading," knowledge, education, science, experience, are what set apart for sadness a Clym or a Tess or a Jude, alienating them from the simpler, happier "folk" they were born into.[22] He wrote toward the end of his life to Alfred Noyes: "The Scheme of Things is, indeed, incomprehensible; and there I suppose we must leave it—perhaps for the best. Knowledge might be terrible" (*Life*, p. 410). And unawareness (as found among the uneducated laboring class in the country-side) makes for contentment, because it is a version of "in-sentience": "Indeed, it is among communities such as these [in Dorset] that happiness will find her last refuge on earth, since it is among them that a perfect insight into the con-ditions of existence will be longest postponed."[23] But state-ments such as these are, as we have been told by Hardy, impressions only. They are not as complete as that collec-tion of impressions, *The Dynasts*. In the poem they would be voiced by only one of the Spirit Intelligences. Hardy's sadness, and his despair about life, expresses only one side of his complex vision of man's mind. In its doubleness, part slave and part free, partly encased in creation and partly projected upward enough to get a perspective on that fact, consciousness—with all its imperfect attempts to exercise and enlarge itself—is man's, and life's, source of hope.

We can better see how this hope might work if we turn to the brain-model and translate into its terms the views of

[22] Dorothy van Ghent, "On *Tess of the d'Urbervilles*," pp. 205–209, applies this standard of deracination to Hardy's major characters, a standard that seems to me to be insufficiently relevant to most of them, and certainly extraneous to the tragedy of Tess.

[23] Thomas Hardy, "The Dorsetshire Labourer," in *Personal Writings*, ed. Orel, p. 169.

this perspective. If, as the anatomizing view declared, all living things originate and draw sustenance from the single source of being, then the Pities, articulators of the faith that consciousness shall, in time, inform the will, can claim that a part of the Will itself is tentatively expressing itself through their voice, their view of what is "fair," and their determined faith. And so they do claim:

> Yea, Great and Good, Thee, Thee we hail,
> Who shak'st the strong, Who shield'st the frail,
> Who hadst not shaped such souls as we
> If tendermercy lacked in Thee!
>
> (After Scene, 522)

Not only is their faith guaranteed by being ascribed to the only force that can accomplish it; but the means for that accomplishment are guaranteed also. The very interweaving of the threads and interpenetration of the tissues promise that the intelligence and feeling that is evolved in one part of the brain will gradually penetrate—like a thrill vibrating through a body or a solvent diffusing itself through permeable membranes—and inform and make fair the whole.

These are imaginative possibilities—even logical probabilities—within the physical system of the brain-model: waking to consciousness of fairness is one of the brain's impulses or thoughts or dreamed intentions; impulses at one part of a web, as we have seen, stir and shake the whole fabric. Do these tendencies hold good when transferred to the outer universe of *The Dynasts*, with its Over World, solar systems, planets, continents, histories, nations and opposing intelligences? The stirring that is sensed in the last chorus of the poem is "like to sounds of joyance": in its tact the poem puts up two screens against our certainty: "like to" and "sounds of." The microcosm and the macrocosm both remain models, "as ifs," turning on the edge between what is and what may be.

These are some of the large significances that Hardy has brought forth by introducing these other forms of life into

234

the poem's consciousness and yoking them metaphorically with the humans in the drama. In the next chapter we shall again meet on the sidelines creatures like these; but this time they will not be caught up in the dramatic action, nor will they be thematically hitched to the human actors to deliver some burden of poetic analogy—they will not be, that is, "supporting" actors in the service of this drama. Rather, they will be the principals in other dramas that even this great poem cannot go into. Where our consciousness comes to an end, the Will has only begun.

FOUR

THE PERIPHERY OF VISION

THE diorama includes on the border of its picture of life a whole realm of hitherto unperceived phenomena living their lives alongside the human story. These phenomena represent separate spinnings from the Web of Life; they brush glancingly against the drama's threads without being woven into the poem's major design. In *The Dynasts* they occupy the same position in the poem's regard as do the phenomena taken note of by the speaker in Hardy's poem "Afterwards"—they are "noticed."[1] In that lyric poem, the flap of delicate-winged green leaves of May; the soundless movement of the "dewfall hawk" as it alights upon the "wind-warped upland thorn"; the hedgehog's furtive passage over the lawn in the "mothy and warm" darkness; the mysterious full-starred heavens of winter; the "outrollings" of a bell's vibration, falling still and rising again as a breeze cuts across its path—all these manifestations of life in "Afterwards" are recollected by the poem's speaker, who wonders if in the future they will remind others that he was "a man who used to notice such things" (CP, p. 521).

There is a greater number and variety of "noticings" in *The Dynasts*, but they resemble the phenomena in "Afterwards"; for in both works they come into view as though they existed independently of the poet's attention and indifferent to his existence. This independence and indifference gives them, as regards the poet, an equality, a grave dignity, a purity (because they are untouched by the poet's human considerations); or, we may call it, a wildness. Their wildness, as we shall suggest at the end of this chapter, carries in itself certain empowering implications for the

[1] There are similar phenomena, "noticed" and registered without comment, all through the *Life*.

poet who merely takes note of them and leaves them in their "natural" state, unyoked. Thoreau's words apply here: "In wildness is the preservation of the world." And next to them we shall put some words that Hardy wrote in one of his prefaces, but that fit here as we picture him, like a naturalist, approaching a world of phenomena like Thoreau's wilderness: "Unadjusted impressions have their value, and the road to a true philosophy of life seems to lie in humbly recording diverse readings of its phenomena as they are forced upon us by chance and change."[2]

This chapter will take issue with a certain idea that seems to have been accepted in Hardy criticism: that Hardy employed his scenery (and other such natural phenomena) as though it were the footpedal of an organ, to enforce the emotion at work like music in his plots and themes. The statement is true when it is put straightforwardly, as in Bonamy Dobrée's appreciation of the way scenery operates in Hardy's best novels: it enters into the lives of his characters, they merge with it, it alters them; "Egdon Heath is itself a character, and acts on human beings just as other humans do."[3] But when the idea is put more restrictively, that Hardy used scenery *only* to give form to feeling, I disagree. The formulation of that idea I trace back to T. S. Eliot's remarks on Hardy in *After Strange Gods* (1934), because, if that occasion was not the first introduction of it into Hardy criticism, it was the most influential:[4] "He [Hardy] seems to me to have written as nearly for the sake of 'self-expression' as a man well can. . . . In consequence of his self-absorption, he makes a great deal of landscape; for landscape is a passive creature which lends itself to an author's mood."[5]

This idea, that Hardy forced landscape into a mold, was taken up by other Anglo-American form critics of Eliot's

---

[2] Thomas Hardy, Preface to "Poems of the Past and Present," in *Personal Writings*, ed. Orel, p. 39.

[3] Bonamy Dobrée, "Thomas Hardy," pp. 31 and 28–32.

[4] See Chapter Three, note 1, *supra*.

[5] T. S. Eliot, *After Strange Gods*, pp. 54–55.

day, as in this example from R. P. Blackmur. (In the following passage we can read "landscape" where Blackmur uses "experience"; both terms refer to the objective world of phenomena in which man is placed, which is what we are concerned with.)

"Pattern was the matrix of experience. If you could show experience as pattern, you showed all that could be shown; what would not fit, what could not be made to fit the pattern, did not count. Further, Hardy's idea-patterns were not heuristic, not designed to discover, spread, or multiply significance, but were held rather as rigid frames to limit experience so far as possible and to substitute for what they could not enclose."[6]

Then, as late as 1968, a critic sympathetic to Hardy, F. R. Pinion, echoed the earlier restrictive judgment: "Hardy rarely describes scenery for its own sake in his novels and poems. Rather it reflects or comments ironically on 'the human condition.' "[7]

The dioramic viewing-frame in *The Dynasts* is indeed a "rigid frame to enclose experience": the last three chapters have traced the three related perspectives that make up its unyielding pattern. But I hope in this chapter to demonstrate that there is more to say about Hardy: that he did show, and show "for its own sake," what "could not be made to fit the pattern," and that he showed it in a manner for which "heuristic" (from *heuriskein*, to discover, and related to "eureka") is in fact the best adjective—in a way that allows the reader the discovery—allows significance to spread and multiply and compose its unpredictable patterns in his own eyes.

1. Elements Seen in this Perspective

To make this case I mean to discuss four different elements in this perspective: the animals, human beings, de-

[6] R. P. Blackmur, "The Shorter Poems of Thomas Hardy," p. 22.
[7] F. R. Pinion, *A Hardy Companion*, p. 125.

tails of scenery, and other workings of nature that inhabit the periphery of Hardy's stage. To set against the critical opinions given above, and to set the tone of the following discussion, I propose as examples the following passages from *The Dynasts*:

> Such unbid sights obtrude
> On death's dyed stage!
> > (Burke on the *Victory*, I,v,iv,96)

> Ay, thus do little things
> Steal into my mind, too.
> > (Nelson, I,v,iv,97)

> —Hence to the precinct, then,
> And count as framework to the stagery
> Yon architraves of sunbeam-smitten cloud.
> > (Spirit of the Years, Fore Scene, 6)

Non-human Life, Indifferent to the Drama

The unadjusted impressions in *The Dynasts* are noticed partly because they are uninvolved in the main action. The poet's eye, like a painter's, seems to look for a piece of "still" life at the side of the most furious human scenes. Its calm perspective, by bringing a point of stillness to the midst of action, confers wholeness on the scene; provides a momentary contrast to the agitated and suffering emotions of the actors; inserts a local spot of resistance to the irresistible movement of sympathy that is Hardy's dominant mode of creation; and, finally, presents a note of skepticism to the solemn viewpoint often expressed in the scene-setting prose descriptions, that an impending event is of great significance for human and even for universal history.[8]

---

[8] "Historic" is shown in this perspective of the diorama to be only a narrow, human term. Nevertheless, in his having selected *this* war to dramatize, and in the closeness with which he enacts certain scenes, the dioramist implicitly shows that these events are, nonetheless, important and of epic magnitude. He explicitly invites us to see as "historic" Pitt's speech before Commons (I,I,iii,19–21) and at the Guildhall

An example of the quality of impassivity that we have been describing occurs in the allusion to the river Tagus as it edges along the scene of a riot outside the royal palace in Spain: the sound of its continuing flow implies its indifference to the fact that a mob of angry people are making history in Spain: "A mixed multitude of soldiery and populace fills the space in front of the King's Palace, and they shout and address each other vehemently. During a lull in their vociferations is heard the peaceful purl of the Tagus over a cascade in the Palace grounds" (II,II,ii,183). Similarly, the Maceira River is not disturbed or deflected from its regular courses by men's passionate sufferings at historic Vimiero: ". . . A dust is raised by this ado, and moans of men and shrieks of horses are heard. Close by the carnage the little Maceira stream continues to trickle unconcernedly to the sea" (II,II,vi,205). At Albuera, when rain comes after the "ghastly climax" to that battle, it is not, with the gentleness of its fall, making any comment, ironic or tender, upon the hideous result of violence lying beneath it; for it is totally unaware of what it is touching. "Hot corpses . . . accumulate on the slopes, increasing from twos and threes to half-dozens, and from half-dozens to heaps, which steam with their own warmth as the spring rain falls gently upon them" (II,VI,iv,301). If, as Pinion thinks, we can look for scenery in Hardy to be used to reflect or comment ironically on the human condition, then this place in the drama would have been an appropriate spot to expect it. The very fact of the rain's insentience could have further underscored the fact that destruction is dealt without percipience and is suffered without being perceived. Sometimes in Hardy that meaning is drawn (in this drama, Walcheren is a notable instance); but not always, for Hardy can also, as here, leave nature's neutrality neutral.

(I,v,v,103); the abandonment by the Russians of their capital (III,I,vi,346); and the battles of Ulm (I,IV,v,77), Wagram (II,IV,ii,233), Albuera (II,VI,iv,298), Leipzig, (III,III,ii,383), and, most of all, Waterloo (III,VII,vii,504 and 508; III,VII,viii,511).

Other instances can be cited in our counter-reading. At Borodino, in an interval of restfulness between two scenes of battle suspense, Hardy again shows life going on simultaneously in strands of the web that are separate and different and mutually unconscious of each other, though close by one another in space: "The two multitudes lie down to sleep, and all is quiet but for the sputtering of the green wood fires, which, now that the human tongues are still, seem to hold a conversation of their own" (III,I,iv,343).

At the end of the description of the calamity at the Beresina bridge—an incident that out of all the many scenes of mass death in the poem is the most charged with details of feeling—there appears one more glimpse of nature proceeding with life as usual, powerfully indifferent to the suffering of her creatures: "The flames of the burning bridge go out as it consumes to the water's edge, and darkness mantles all, nothing continuing but the purl of the river and the clickings of floating ice" (III,I,x,357).

The language used to present the phenomena in all these quick examples keeps very close to the sense-impressions they make on the observer's ear: "purl," "trickle," "steam," "sputtering," "purl," "clickings." The phenomena have not been filtered through the process of human valuation, and are free of the language of abstraction. Are the clickings or purls to be considered "good" or "bad" in relation to human events? We do not know; they are kept close to "raw," i.e., unfiltered, sensory fact. That is why, in this next example from the battle of Leipzig, the phenomenon of a striking clock seems so "unperturbed" by human history: "The Leipzig clocks imperturbably strike nine, and the battle which is to decide the fate of Europe and perhaps the world, begins . . ." (III,III,ii,383)—and why, in this view of the upper Rhine landscape as it is crossed by armies coming together to invade France and force Napoleon to abdicate, the effect conveyed is of a great body on which the events of human history make no impression: "In spite of the immensity of this human mechanism on its surface, the winter landscape wears an impassive look, as if nothing were happening" (III,iv,i,398).

Most of the phenomena we have cited so far can remain undisturbed on the sidelines because they are large entities —waterways, rain, fire, landscape—too amorphous to be held and harmed by man. And yet, look at the great phenomenon that crowns the "framework" over the last grand charge of the battle of Waterloo: "NEY and FRIANT now lead forward the last and most desperate assault of the day. . . . It is about a quarter past eight, and the midsummer evening is fine after the wet night and morning, the sun approaching its setting in a sky of gorgeous colours" (III, vii,viii,512). We would expect this display of sky, arching sublime and clear over the human turmoil and confusion with which it is contrasted below, to be beyond contamination. But we are told at the end of this same scene that man's destructiveness has stretched out to spoil the air itself: "The night grows clear and beautiful, and the moon shines musingly down. But instead of the sweet smell of green herbs and dewy rye as at her last beaming upon these fields, there is now the stench of gunpowder and a muddy stew of crushed crops and gore" (III,vii,viii,518).

This passage has serious implications: the concussive assault upon life and nature enacted at Waterloo makes the reader ponder what it signifies for humanity's capacity to destroy. How far is man's reach, and how permanent is his impress? It sullies the land and even the air, but it does not stretch as far as the moon, which remains unshaken in its high place over the heavens and undimmed in its spread of radiance over the show below. Man's grasp, then, can bring death to individual bodies—plants, animals, air and waters, but is not great enough to do permanent violence to the body of the whole. The mire of Waterloo dries, and the fumes of gunpowder are blown away. Even as Hardy notes this injury done by one part of creation to another, he lets us reflect that it will be absorbed and healed.

When there breaks out in *The Dynasts* a cry for uncreation,[9] there is a recognition—unstated but implied, in effect taken for granted—that creation is inexhaustible and cannot be brought to an end. This recognition, which is often the tacit assumption beneath the poem's many expressions of despair, is stated explicitly only once, and there turned into a ground for hope and thanksgiving:

SEMICHORUS II OF THE PITIES (aerial music)

We hold that Thy unscanted scope
Affords a food for final Hope. . . .

(After Scene, p. 523)

This perception of life's indestructibility, which Hardy holds in his particular, cross-grained, indirect way, puts him into imaginative kinship with two other poets. Hopkins and Lawrence each held a vision of freshness and power and beauty abiding at the core of each cell of life, beyond the reach of man, unaffected by custom, incomprehension, or destruction. Hopkins, in "God's Grandeur," sees life inexhaustibly renewing itself from within: springing up and firing forth like oil out of the ground; indeed, the more that it is pounded down and crushed by man's greed and insensitivity, the more it brims up. Lawrence throughout his lyrics and stories sees life-beneath-death in images of root and bulb and phoenix: there the flame lies, preserved from man's reason under cover of darkness to be born again; "kept," as Hopkins would have put it in "The Leaden Echo and the Golden Echo":

Far with fonder a care (and we, we should have lost it)
    finer, fonder
A care kept.

Each of these poets testifies with Hardy against the abuse by man of nature, one part of life against another, perceiv-

---

[9] See the following examples: Shade of the Earth and Spirit of the Pities, "But why any?" (I,I,ii,15); Pities, "'shame'" (I,v,iv,99); Semichorus II of the Pities, "extinction" (After Scene, 525).

ing it as a wasteful act of sacrilege and murder, an offense against the original anima, even a version of sinning against the Holy Spirit. But each of them sees this grave human offense as absorbed by the universe, deflected into something harmless, and ultimately made hopeful: providing over and over an opportunity for life to demonstrate how it abounds, above and through the injuries done to it. Thus we find we are granted, in these modern perceptions of old truths, versions of both original sin and *felix culpa*.

In *The Dynasts* Hardy's testimony to the unconditioned force of life is a backhanded one. He wishes it could be curbed or cured, either made purposive or extinguished. He also hopes that purpose will waken forth from within it, "genial" and "germing," at the poem's end. But he is sure only of the inexhaustibility of that force, containing all contrarieties, being subject to none. In Lawrence's critical appreciation of this very point, we can see the affinity between Lawrence and Hardy:

"This is the wonder of Hardy's novels, and gives them their beauty. The vast, unexplored morality of life itself, what we call the immorality of nature, surrounds us in its eternal incomprehensibility. . . . And this is the quality Hardy shares with the great writers, Shakespeare or Sophocles or Tolstoi, this setting behind the small action of his protagonists the terrific action of unfathomed nature; setting a smaller system of morality, the one grasped and formulated by the human consciousness, within the vast, uncomprehended and incomprehensible morality of nature or of life itself, surpassing human consciousness."[10]

Lawrence's statement accounts for the importance of the non-human creatures in *The Dynasts*. They are living proof of the independent existence of life beyond man's reach and of its continuance in "wildness"; and this wildness, this independence, this never-to-be-comprehended or exhausted mystery, is, in turn, man's best and "final Hope."

[10] D. H. Lawrence, "Study of Thomas Hardy," p. 419.

Human Life, on the Edges of the Drama

As we look at the sidelines, we meet humankind along with the other forms of nature living on the edge of the drama, human beings untouched by the large events of the war, or only marginally involved in them. They are not remarked upon by the leading actors, to whom they would seem part of the background merely, like the flora and fauna of a scene. But they do register to the eye of the poet, who positions and fills each scene for us in the prose descriptions. Although this poet has a larger vision than do his leading actors, he, too, as we noted in our last chapter, sees human beings as one with the flora and fauna that grow upon the back of earth and breathe to her rhythms. The emphasis in that view was on the mutual pain of that labored breathing. But there is more to be said about earth and her outgrowths. To the naturalist, the pleasure of the study of flora and fauna is to discover their mysterious attunement to their background, their subtle correspondence to locality and season, and the varieties they embody of "natural" beauty and "natural" virtues for species-survival: a collective, indigenous beauty and virtue, lying beneath individuality. The people in the margins of Hardy's drama make only brief imprints upon the record; but as we trace those different imprints, we shall find that they lead to a recognition that is like that which gives the naturalist his pleasure.

Persons whose historicity Hardy documents in a footnote are, literally, on the periphery. There is Mrs. Prescott, who followed her English officer husband from Ireland to Spain and found him dead on the field at Salamanca: about her we are told, in a footnote upon which Hardy enlarged with later information in 1909, "that she remarried, and lived and died in Venice; and that both her children grew up and did well" (III,i,iii, footnote p. 338). There is also the sergeant whom Hardy shows before the battle of Vitoria, reminiscing about his past in Wessex: "Thomas Young of Sturminster-Newton; served twenty-one years in the Fifteenth

(King's) Hussars; died 1853; fought at Vitoria, Toulouse, and Waterloo" (III,ii,i, footnote, p. 365). And at Waterloo, two "real" Englishmen on the edge of that climactic action survived to bring the tale back to Hardy. Hardy's notes introduce a bible-quoting officer's servant present at the English camp behind the lines at Mount Saint-Jean: "Samuel Clark, born 1779, died 1857. Buried at West Stafford, Dorset" (III,vii,v, footnote p. 500); and a soldier who experienced directly the ordeal on the field at Waterloo:

> One of the many Waterloo men known to the writer in his youth, John Bentley of the Fusileer Guards, used to declare that he lay down on the ground in such weariness that when food was brought him he could not eat it, and slept till next morning on an empty stomach. He died at Chelsea Hospital, 187—, aged eighty-six. (III,vii,viii, footnote p. 518)

These persons would be statistics only, nameless and forgotten in history, like the dead youth in Gray's country churchyard, but for the accident of their having been known to Hardy and thus having been named in the circumference of his imaginative design. For, of course, each of these footnotes also implies the presence of the historical Thomas Hardy in the margin. As the two soldiers touch the history of Napoleon, so Hardy touches them, and becomes, through them, a bystander in his own poem. (Hardy even makes for himself a home in the poem's border, through a reference to "Max Turnpike" [I,ii,v,52], which in 1805 was a Dorchester landmark. In eighty years Hardy would build there Max Gate, where, twenty years afterwards, he would be living and writing *The Dynasts*.)

These obscure but "historical" persons share the margin of the drama with other equally obscure ones who appear in Hardy's fiction. There are the two Saarlander hussars who were shot as deserters four years before the drama opens—subject of a short story, "The Melancholy Hussar of the German Legion," and of a mention in *The Dynasts*

(I,ii,iv,48); there is Private Cantle of the Locals (I,ii,v and III,v,vi), whose "challengeful" character is familiar to readers of *The Return of the Native*; and "Bob Loveday of Overcombe" (I,v,vii,107), a crew member on the *Victory* and one of the main characters of *The Trumpet-Major*. Both groups, the historical and the imaginary, rub off on one another something of their respective qualities: the fictional characters acquire a quasi-factual status by being linked to those in the historical record; the factual characters are given a kind of datelessness by being placed in a work of imagination. We can go further and say that all of Hardy's other Wessex characters stand behind Cantle and Loveday in the shadows, and that their various "pastoral" worlds touch the edges of the epic-historical world of *The Dynasts*.

Through these glimpses out to other worlds, the poem is enlarged to a universe of many dimensions and designs. All of them are moved by the same single Unconscious Energy; the three perspectives we have thus far discussed take that as their common theme and testimony. But not all of these worlds have their consciousness wholly commanded by the war against Napoleon, and not all of them are shaken with equal force by the historical currents of the Will: that difference is what this fourth perspective sees and shows.

An example of people minding their own business, their minds and lives hardly touched by the reality of war, are the Spanish peasants who happen to look up from their work to see Napoleon's army advancing over the Pyrenees into their land: "Along the great highway through Biscay the wondering native carters draw their sheep-skinned ox-teams aside, to let the regiments pass, and stray groups of peaceable field-workers in Navarre look inquiringly at the marching and prancing progress" (II,ii,i,181). No more is seen of these people, but we may assume, without word in the drama to the contrary, that the war will come and go under the direction of famous men like Marmont and Wellington, passing by these laborers, who will instinctively draw aside into the landscape and escape notice. Like the "man harrowing clods" and the maid who comes whispering with her "wight" in Hardy's lyric, "In Time of 'The Breaking of Nations,' " like the landscape itself and its regular workings, they and their kin "will go onward the same/ Though Dynasties pass" (CP, p. 511).

Later, when the war is brought by the Allies to Paris, other marginal characters put into words their view on life from the drama's edge. The instinct of self-preservation is at work to enable even the insignificant and lowly to survive: "The storm which roots the pine spares the p—s—b—d," says one of the servants in the Tuileries, "girding on his armour," the white cockade that will proclaim that his knee bends once more to the Bourbons even as it did to Napoleon (III,ɪv,iii,407). And even as men bow and shrink aside, the instinct of curiosity invites them to take in the show, to "look inquiringly at the marching and prancing progress," and to marvel at the fortunes of dynasts, whose ups and downs are amusing if one is seated safely on the sidelines.

SECOND SERVANT

Well, well! There's rich colours in this kaleidoscopic world!

THIRD SERVANT

And there's comedy in all things—when they don't concern you. . . .

(III,ɪv,iii,408)

The examples above were set on the European continent, where ordinary people witnessed the actions of war with their own eyes. The England of Hardy's Wessex is farther away from dynastic events: the scenes Hardy stages there give a more rounded view of "low life" in that part of the world, and convey more than did the examples in France and Spain the recognizable sound and flavor of ordinary people in a particular locality—here, the part of the world that Hardy knows best as fact and fiction.

Two scenes show Wessex folk fixing their gaze toward the distant Napoleon. Early in the drama (I,II,v) citizens on the Rainbarrow Mound of Egdon Heath watch anxiously to spread the alarm should Napoleon with his army land on their coast. Towards the end of the action, after the escape from Elba, a "rustic" comes breathlessly into view at Caster-bridge expecting to see Napoleon haled up out of Caster-bridge Jail ("the natural retreat of malefactors"—II,v,vi, 450) and burned to death on Durnover Green. The joke—and serious truth—underlying both scenes is that rural Wessex, in the eyes of the untutored inhabitants whom Hardy uses as its "natural" spokesmen, considers itself an important center in the mainstream of life and therefore a logical place for Napoleon and epic history to "discover" sooner or later, as Austerlitz and Trafalgar were "discov-ered." But in the poem Wessex remains a backwater that keeps its basic traditional and conservative character even though it too is washed by the churning currents of the time.

Recent criticism has made us aware that Wessex in the novels is not a pastoral preserve immune to the touch of time, and that Hardy does depict the processes of economic and social change there.[11] But those processes, being more gradual than war's convulsions, are not discernible in *The Dynasts'* vision of "Europe in throes." Wessex in this work serves as a place that "will go onward the same/ Though Dynasties pass": its tenacious conservatism alive in the shrewd realism of people in touch with the practical truths of traditional human experience, and borne out, as we shall

[11] The first critic in recent times to call attention to this element in Hardy was Douglas Brown, *Thomas Hardy*. Since then, Raymond Williams, "Thomas Hardy," pp. 341–51, has written convincingly; and Mervyn Williams, *Thomas Hardy and Rural England*, has provided additional data.

see, in their local dialect, in which colorful archaisms are still functional and vital.

These country people show the same curiosity and amusement that the lower classes in other countries exhibited in the behavior of dynasts under all sorts of circumstances ("But shall I zee en die? I wanted to zee if he'd die hard," exclaimed the Stourcastle rustic; III,v,vi,450). But their commonsense saves them from being swept into any assumption that Napoleon or any dynast or any man is above the common reactions of human nature. ("He should have the washing of 'em a few times; I warrant 'a wouldn't want to eat babies any more!" reflects Private Cantle's wife, putting the rumor that Napoleon breakfasts on the flesh of human infants into the perspective of her own working-knowledge; I,II,v,52.) Commonsense saves them also from the fear that Napoleon or any dynast or any man can save or destroy them or the universe ("Lard, lard, if 'a were nabbed, it wouldn't make a deal of difference! . . . We should rub along some way, goodnow," says a Wessex man watching King George and wondering what the loss of the king would mean to people like themselves; I,II,iv,47).

Finally, their commonsense realism rejects any romantic view of themselves as either "noble savages" or enlightened "men of reason," or as exempt in any way from the mixed truth of human nature. This sense of slipping through definition, defying augury, is what we hear speaking in the following exchange:

VICAR

My dear misguided man, you don't imagine that we should be so inhuman in this Christian country as to burn a fellow-creature alive?

RUSTIC

Faith, I won't say I didn't! Durnover folk have never had the highest of Christian characters, come to that. And I didn't know but that even a pa'son might backslide to such things in these gory times. . . .

PRIVATE CANTLE

Talk of backsliding to burn Boney, I can backslide
to anything when my blood is up, or rise to anything,
thank God for't! . . . (III,v,vi,450–51)

When Hardy transports these country people and their
comic realism over to the Continent and sets them at the
margins of battle, he shows them in scenes that demonstrate
the tenacity of human nature. The forthright Mrs. Dalbiac,
who, more mindful of her pesetas and her propriety than of
her own danger, has followed her husband to Salamanca
and ridden behind him in the battle (Wellington: "Why
that must be Susanna, whom I know—/ A Wessex woman,
blithe and somewhat fair . . ."; III,i,iii,338), exemplifies this
unselfconscious heroism. Other examples are presented in
the scene at the women's camp at Mont Saint-Jean, just
behind the English line at Waterloo. The prose description
setting forth the view of this scene outlines a picture of life
continuing and renewing itself right alongside of destruction:

> On the sheltered side of a clump of trees at the back
> of the English position camp-fires are smouldering.
> Soldiers' wives, mistresses, and children from a few
> months to five or six years of age, sit on the ground
> round the fires or on armfuls of straw from the adjoin-
> ing farm. Wounded soldiers lie near the women. The
> wind occasionally brings the smoke and smell of the
> battle into the encampment, the noise being continu-
> ous. . . . Behind lies a woman who has just given birth
> to a child, which a second woman is holding.
>
> . . . The occupants of the camp take hardly any no-
> tice of the thundering of the cannon. A camp-follower
> is playing a fiddle near.
>
> (III,vii,v,498)

Hardy has a second set of marginal characters come up
and comment upon this first set, and their exchange sums

up the central meaning that this scene contributes to the drama:

LEGH

. . . What will these poor women do?

RICHMOND

God knows! They will be ridden over, I suppose. Though it is extraordinary how they do contrive to escape destruction while hanging so close to the rear of an action! . . . (III,vii,v,501)

We hear several rustic voices in this scene. One is the voice of an officer's servant who translates Waterloo into Biblical allusions and into his own homemade poetry: ". . . up to my knees in mud that had come down like baccy-pipe stems all the night and morning—I have just seen a charge never beholded since the days of the Amalekites! . . . Well, it's the Lord's doing and marvellous in our eyes . . ." (III,vii,v,500). The speech of the women reflects the intimate knowledge of mortality that we would expect from their work with the wounded and dying. Hardy shows them in different degrees of bereavement: one, with a daughter, has been "all through the peninsula," knows the different expressions death can take in a human face, and does not speak of her own man. Another's husband is out of sight with his battalion, and she thinks of him, as on leaving he apparently did of himself, in the past tense: "Yes, poor man! . . . Not but 'a had a temper at times!" (III,vii,v,499). A third has arrived at Waterloo to find that her husband ("as I used to call him for form's sake") died the night before at Quatre-Bras. The tone beneath the words of all of them is self-forgetfully brisk and buoyant. They are living out the drama's ideal of solidarity, extending to those close at hand who need it the help they had come to give to their own men: ". . . says I, 'Widder or no widder, I mean to see this out'" (III,vii,v,499). Their response to devastation helps us understand how and why humanity "contrives to escape destruction."

What is shown at the Mont Saint-Jean camp resembles the two-scene sequence set in a cellar in Spain, looking out upon the road to Astorga. Here, one group of lives carrying on the business of war is set beside another group living out life in the margin. The framing scene is peopled with fugitives from the war, English soldiers and Spanish women and children who huddle together in a state of degradation. They are half-clothed in rags, half-buried under damp straw, shrinking back into cover to hide from the misery and danger outside, drinking themselves to insensibility. The proximity of death and danger seems to intensify the activity of life, as it did at Waterloo: the cellar is a shelter for sex and wenching as well as a cover from the elements and the war. The talk of the men flows with their wine, and in their talk their minds range from present to past and back again. One deserter pictures what would be happening on that very day, New Year's Day, in Bristol, where things are "proper" and "real" and familiar. Another looks at the advantages of the present situation, with its convenient supply of wine and women. Another dreams in his sleep of being again in practice out on the field: "Poise fawlocks—open pans—right hands to pouch—handle ca'tridge—bring it—quick motion—bite top well off—prime—shut pans—cast about—load—" (II,III,i,209).

But always their attention returns to developments on the road outside: they silently pity the men who limp by in demoralized disarray; identify themselves proudly with their fellows as they catch sight of "something more in order"; being thus inspirited, they start to emerge from hiding, when they hear a soldier being shot nearby for pillaging, and so shrink back, shuddering, "wretches in the cellar" once more. When their refuge is discovered and most of them are dragged off with the retreating army, the wine keeps them from minding or resisting very much; and the few who are left behind are indifferent, looking "stolidly" out on the highway. Only the arrival of Napoleon with his high aides in the next scene galvanizes the remaining two men into sobriety ("Good Lord deliver us from all great men, and take me back to humble life!"; II,III,ii,213) and into a resolve to rejoin their regiment and the war.

What emerges from the ruined cellar and the degradation is not only the men themselves, alive, but also certain lively qualities over and above the strict requirements of the Will. There is the vitality of their language: "snoaching," "cruity," "doxy," "nipperkin of 'Bristol milk.'" There is the quickness of wit in the series of meanings that they ring on one sound: the "doxy" who is the only one safe and sound because she is securely dead; the true doxology versus "foreign doxies" and "a proper God A'mighty instead of this eternal 'Ooman and baby." There is feeling—solicitude for the women ("Pity the women, captain, but do what you will with us!"), and the feeling, in retrospect, that ordinary life has its pleasures after all, and is to be held onto:

SECOND DESERTER

. . . I know what I feel! Would that I were at home in England again . . .—ay, at home a-leaning against old Bristol Bridge, and no questions asked, and the winter sun slanting friendly over Baldwin Street as 'a used to do! . . . Ay, to-night we should be a-setting in the tap of the "Adam and Eve"—lifting up the tune of "The Light of the Moon." 'Twer a romantical thing enough. 'A used to go som'at like this (he sings in a nasal tone):—

"O I thought it had been day,
    And I stole from her away;
    But it proved to be the light o' the moon!"
                                    (II,III,i,209)

Life does have degrees of freedom—places and times relatively unpressured by will, when one can lean back in peace without having to justify the moment. There is something to be savored in the sun's particular slants as one learns to look for them against a familiar skyline. The second

254

deserter's singing is nasal, and his song is only a bawdy refrain, but what matters is that he is bringing into this scene, out of a more relaxed past, a tune—music.

Hardy presents these facts straightforwardly, without sentimentalizing or claiming too much for them, but also without scorning or belittling them. To help him in *The Dynasts*, he has the ready instrument of the viewing over-world through which he can channel a whole range of mental responses to the human scene, including the two extremes of sentimentality or scorn, by assigning each re-action to its appropriate voice among the phantom intel-ligences. He is thus able to achieve a complex double re-sponse, at once critical and appreciative, to this display of human behavior, with the final weight being given to the appreciative.

SPIRIT IRONIC

Quaint poesy, and real romance of war!

SPIRIT OF THE PITIES

Mock on, Shade, if thou wilt! But others find
Poesy ever lurk where pit-pats poor mankind!

(II,III,i,210)

In other words: however low, degraded, vulgar, buffoonish, or contemptible the life of mankind, still humanity at-taches to itself this extra quality, extra residue, of feeling and value, warmth, and color—that is, poetry.[12]

Hardy wrote down some of his thoughts about ordinary, undistinguished men and women in an essay entitled "The

---

[12] I am sure that T. S. Eliot would have disagreed with what I believe Hardy succeeded in putting into this cellar scene. For him the poetry that would have emerged from its degradation and buffoonery would have to be ironic. For a somewhat partisan but still valuable discussion of the historic opposition between Eliot and Hardy, see Katherine Anne Porter, "Notes on a Criticism of Thomas Hardy," pp. 150–61. She views the opposition as a reenactment of the irreconcilable struggle (going back to the Reformation and, even further, to Old Testament times) between the authority of institutional inspiration (tradition) and that of individual inspiration (conscience).

Dorsetshire Labourer."[13] We will refer to it here, for what it has to say about the people on the periphery of our drama.

At its opening, the article assumes that the reader and the essayist are, alike, "thoughtful persons" who are familiar with the popular stereotype of the rural farm-laborer, "Hodge," but who presumably are also open to learning through the essay that there is a more complex reality. For the person who visits Hodge and spends time in his world, Hodge emerges from behind his uniform stereotype and proves to be a man defined by individuality and color and possessing his inalienable measure of happiness.

At this point in the essay Hardy makes some remarks about vision that have a bearing on this present chapter and of course on the whole of our study of his vision: "As, to the eye of a diver, contrasting colours shine out by degrees from what has originally painted itself of an unrelieved earthy hue, so would shine out the characters, capacities, and interests of these people to him."[14] Thus, the thoughtful viewer "would become conscious of a new aspect in the life around him. He would find that, without any objective change whatever, variety had taken the place of monotony."[15] Now the essay comes around to our immediate subject, the "marginal" characters on the margins of *The Dynasts*:

> The great change in his [the thoughtful viewer's] perception is that Hodge, the dull, unvarying, joyless one, has ceased to exist for him. He has become disintegrated into a number of dissimilar fellow-creatures, men of many minds, infinite in difference; some happy, many serene, a few depressed; some clever, even to genius, some stupid, some wanton, some austere; some mutely Miltonic, some Cromwellian; into men who

[13] Thomas Hardy, "The Dorsetshire Labourer," in *Personal Writings*, ed. Orel, pp. 168–91.
[14] *Ibid.*, p. 170.   [15] *Ibid.*

have private views of each other, as he has of his friends; who applaud or condemn each other; amuse or sadden themselves by the contemplation of each other's foibles and vices; and each of whom walks in his own way the road to dusty death.[16]

Elsewhere Hardy had noted that each mute object in nature has its associations, its story, if they could be sensed and told.[17] Now that observation is extended: each mute object (here, each human life) has its associations, its texture, its poetry. "When you stand by his grave at his funeral and think of him even the most prosaic man's life becomes a poem."[18]

This poetry is primarily one of vision: a sighting of diversity, subdued color, warmth, and power. But there is sound to it also, music in the local and downright sounds of the character's names: Susanna Dalbiac; and the widowed Mrs. Prescott, whom Hardy's sympathetic interest traced beyond the theatre of war to such an unlikely corner of the world as Venice; Keziar Cantle of Bloom's End and Private Cantle of the Locals; Bob Loveday of Overcombe; Thomas Young of Sturminster-Newton; Samuel Clark, buried at West Stafford, Dorset; John Bentley, lately at Chelsea Hospital, once of the Fusileer Guards. Hardy makes us care for the specifics of these lives, makes every particular prosaic detail be of value because it is evanescent, lighted up for a moment with the wonder and warmth of life. (Here, on the drama's margin, "Life" seems a better word for "Will." Hardy explains the difference by saying that on the circum-

16 *Ibid.*, pp. 170–71.

17 Hardy, *Life*, p. 114 (May 30); p. 107 (November 28); p. 153 (May 13 and August); p. 164 (February); p. 285 (February 10).

18 This line, with the simple citation, "T.H.," appears on the title page of Evelyn Hardy's *Thomas Hardy: A Critical Biography*. In her edition of *Thomas Hardy's Notebooks*, p. 37, the remark appears in *The First Notebook*, entry 20, May 29, in a slightly different wording: "The most prosaic man becomes a poem when you stand by his grave at his funeral and think of him."

ference, at a remove from the central impulse, impulsion is to some degree relaxed: ". . . each part has therefore, in strictness, *some* freedom, which would, in fact, be operative as such whenever the remaining great mass of will in the universe should happen to be in equilibrium"; Letter I to Dr. Caleb Saleeby, included in *Life*, p. 449).

Not only the names but the speech of all these marginal characters constitute a basic element of music in the drama. Taken together as a whole, the words and discourse of all of them—those provincials whose proper names are given and those servants and camp-followers and deserters specified only as "first," "second," "third," and so on—make for a collective, more than personal, voice that is vital and humorous, free-flowing and freely resonant. It occupies a subordinate ("marginal") position in the whole but has more than marginal importance. It warms and enriches the drama,[19] which would otherwise concentrate all its dimensions and perspectives upon its urgent vision of unfreedom, with a result so stark and unrelenting that we might feel that the Pities speak for us when they call out to the Years to be relieved from the show:

> I feel, Sire, as I must! This tale of Will
> And Life's impulsion by Incognizance
> I cannot take.
>
> (I,i,vi,36)

By contrast, the speech of the principal dynastic players, although it does strike witty, ironic nuances against the anatomy of reality at the rear of the stage, is itself conspicuously flat and stiff, lacking in color and verve. Once again Hardy's description of the mode of speech he had in mind for the drama can help us to understand this

---

[19] Arthur McDowall, *Thomas Hardy*, pp. 113 and 130, says that the speech of the rustics belongs to "the same air that caught the musings of Silence and Shallow," and that these wise, funny rustics contribute "a collective glow, the warmth of which confirms and liberates the story."

juxtaposition of lively and uninhibited talk next to speech that is relatively lifeless and conventional:

> In respect of such plays of poesy and dream a practicable compromise may conceivably result, taking the shape of a monotonic delivery of speeches, with dreamy conventional gestures, something in the manner traditionally maintained by the old Christmas mummers, the curiously hypnotizing impressiveness of whose automatic style—that of persons who spoke by no will of their own—may be remembered by all who ever experienced it. . . . (Preface, p. xi)

The dynastic speakers, then, speak as though under hypnosis, because they, more than others in this drama, are driven more deeply into the dream of life, and they speak their lines by rote, while half-remembering a long-ago time when they were free from such compulsion. The Phantom Intelligences speak in another kind of dream speech—that of disembodied vision, free (and "required") to look upon events and to be intellectually moved by what they see.

Hardy associates them—or at least one of them, the Pities—with "the spectator idealized of the Greek chorus" (Preface, p. ix). Let us borrow his phrase: the peripheral characters in *The Dynasts* make up another voice in the whole chorus: not the "Universal Sympathy of human nature," his definition for the Pities (*ibid.*), but the universal *body* of human nature. Their combined voices bear witness, in part to the events witnessed by the Spirit Intelligences, but even more to the fact of the experience of a body, every body, however short-lived: to the fact that body has its warmth, its seasons, a variety of colors and textures and tones, and surprising one-of-a-kind dialects and perceptions. The dream-voices of the peripheral characters are resonant and witty like the tones of the intelligences and the dynasts; but these voices animate, where those other voices, monotonic and disembodied, hypnotize.

Weaving together, all the dream voices—will, mind, and body—blend into one song, for (let the reader choose) sleeping or waking.

Place as "Framework to the Stagery"

The settings of many of Hardy's scenes are interesting in themselves because they convey more of the sense of a particular place than is strictly required for the "locating" of a scene—convey it so vividly that, again, some of our attention is turned from life on the stage to the life that frames the stage. The prose description that gives the setting for the scene at Rainbarrow's Beacon on Egdon Heath will serve as a useful opening illustration: "Night in mid-August of the same summer. A lofty ridge of heathland reveals itself dimly, terminating in an abrupt slope, at the summit of which are three tumuli. . . . Something in the feel of the darkness and in the personality of the spot imparts a sense of uninterrupted space around . . ." (I,II,v,48).

"The personality of the spot": when we think back on all of Hardy's writing—in this drama the carefully located scenes with their carefully located points of view, and in the novels and stories the slow and often powerful descriptions of places—we appreciate how intently he brings to the mind's eye each theatre of action.

How is the "personality of the spot," any spot, realized? In the passage above, the world is realized through all the bodily senses: sight, touch and perhaps sound, and something like the animal-like intuition that comes from all the faculties working together to transmit the feel of open space when darkness keeps the eyes from fully functioning. The Spirit Watchers do not need to piece impressions together in this way, for they are able to apprehend cognitively the facts of a scene. But with their superior intelligence spirits miss something: the pleasure of feeling the stirrings of life through flesh's sensitive extensions.

By communicating the feel of a place through all the senses, Hardy establishes the presence of other vivid scenes.

Moscow is realized visually as a composition of shapes and planes and lights:

> Herefrom the city appears as a splendid panorama, with its river, its gardens, and its curiously grotesque architecture of domes and spires. It is the peacock of cities to Western eyes, its roofs twinkling in the rays of the September sun, amid which the ancient citadel of the Tsars—the Kremlin—forms a centre-piece. (III,i, vii,346–347)

Madrid's colors are conveyed to the eye and its heat conveyed to whatever parts of the body derive impressions from temperature and weather:

> The view is from the housetops of the city on a dusty evening in this July, following a day of suffocating heat. The sunburnt roofs, warm ochreous walls, and blue shadows of the capital, wear their usual aspect except for a few feeble attempts at decoration. (II,ii, iv,196)

The towns and places on Marie Louise's wedding journey are each imagined in a single word: "vine-circled Stuttgart, flat Carlsruhe, the winding Rhine, storky Strassburg . . ." (II,v,v,279), and together they convey a palpable sense of the earth's texture.

It is true that this particular power of imagining and communicating the unique reality of places is not to be found in Hardy alone; many good writers have it. But the point is that this power testifies against his own statements in the poem about the "Monistic theory of the Universe" (Preface, p. viii). It does not refute the theory itself: Hardy would tell us that the objective truth of materialism still allows for subjective impressions of itself to be held in the intelligences of its "subjects." Like the deserter with his homesickness for Bristol, so too the inhabitants of the Moscows or Madrids, the Viennas or Brussels of this world, are entitled, even in a monistic universe, to think their centers uniquely real and beautiful and precious. But for us as unattached readers to react in that unobjective way to place after place in the poem, and for Hardy to show them in that way, with the lamps lighting up the evening or "the winter sun slanting friendly over Baldwin Street," speaks against some of the poem's most frequent representations about the worthlessness and tedium of existence in such a universe. These representations, which occur in most of the direct comments of the Spirits on the Will, assert that life's patterns are "inutile all" (Years, After Scene, 522); that its phonomena are fantastic and unreal; and that the whole of creation, when its pointlessness is truly perceived by the intelligence, is a "tedious" conjuring-show of "vain and objectless monotony" (Shade of the Earth, I,i,ii,15).

This theme of monotony and revulsion is only one part of the poem's complex response to its own dioramic vision of life. When we discussed the transparencies in Chapter One, we noted the emergence of another response, unstressed but telling, that bore witness to beauty (without using that word), in the Will's "strenuously transmutive bent," "incalculable artistries," and "ceaseless artistries in circumstance." This view sees with the eye of Hardy's diver, to which, "from what has originally painted itself of unrelieved earthy hue," a variety of colors and hues gradually shines forth and declares itself.

When this eye views the phenomena of creation (at first of "unrelieved earthy hue," but in time revealing variety and brightness), the phrase "vain and objectless monotony" does not seem to tell the whole story. The Shade of the Earth's phrase has an emotional impact beyond its immediate context in the poem, so let us see if it applies to the show as we have experienced it. "Monotony": the word does not do justice to the lively interest and uniqueness of each natural phenomenon, each an original center on the universe's surface. "Objectless"? To the Shade of the Earth and to the Spirit of the Years at the very opening of the poem, "patterns, wrought by rapt aesthetic rote," whose only object is themselves and which are not the result of some larger purposive pattern, must be said to be object-less. Art as the object of art is not enough. But what if we allow for the word "art" to acquire fuller and fuller force in the course of time, until it acquires both an ethical *and* an aesthetic meaning? Some such rounding-out, it seems to me, is achieved over the course of the poem when it ends with the word "fair." The diorama has shown beauty and injustice woven together in the same "mistimed" fabric. For the mental spectator who has witnessed and felt that incongruity, the word "fair" must ring with two meanings, the aesthetic one provided for to the full capacities of his senses and beyond them, the other, ethical one, still to be satisfied. To this mental spectator, art, the accomplishment of full fairness, *is* the proper object of art.

We turn then to "vain"—or empty, futile, useless. That sentiment is uttered by two Spirits: the Shade of the Earth said it in the phrase from early in the drama we have been analyzing ("vain and objectless monotony"); and the Spirit of the Years says it again, in effect, with his word "inutile" in the After Scene:

> Yet seems this vast and singular confection
> Wherein our scenery glints of scantest size,
> Inutile all—so far as reasonings tell.
> (After Scene, 522)

This judgment, coming from this Spirit at this time, carries a weight of authority in the poem. He is, as always, offering an "impression" only, which represents his view up to that moment and is subject to change. But since it is offered at the close of the drama and is the last view that this Spirit expresses, it has the gravity of a conclusion. Further-more, this is the same Spirit who earlier in the drama ex-horted all viewers of the drama to stay with the show, to keep watch, to draw no premature conclusions:

> O heap not blame on that in-brooding Will;
> O pause, till all things all their days fulfil!
> (I,v,iv,100)

The word "inutile" coming from him, then, would seem to confirm the testimony of travailing Earth.

Yet the reader must consider again. This last statement is taking place in Hardy's crucial and tactful After Scene, where words and positions are carefully weighed. Thus in the Years' concluding assessment, reason may be carefully stating the extent and limits of its reach, acknowledging, as reason does at its best, that there are stirrings and resonances given off by phenomena that it must miss if it is to remain true to its own being. It can recognize the possibility that Art and Beauty are present with their own autonomous "reason" in force, by such features as singularity, workmanship ("confection"), glintings, and apparent "inutility."

Therefore words like "inutile," and Earth's use of "vain," above, and all such words that judge conclusively that works of creation are finally and forever vain, not worth the spark of life—such words are met by the counterword of "poesy," which, speaking for sentiment and sensation, testifies that creation is not in vain.

Neither voice can conclude in any but a tentative manner. Reason, through the Spirit of the Years, must say "seems" (inutile); and Art, speaking in the last chorus through the Spirit of the Pities, must say that the stirring which it senses is "like to" sounds of joyance. Each counter-voice can only point to its own impressions of phenomena. But the phenomena we have been describing in this chapter and section at least ensure that there is not just one prevailing, monotonous view.

Other Gratuitous Phenomena[20]

It can be argued that the phenomena noted in the section above, communicating the physical experience of place, are

---

[20] I am using the term "gratuitous" in several senses: the everyday connotation of unnecessary, unwarranted, or uncalled-for, applies to the fact that the phenomena in this perspective do not serve Hardy's stated theme, their status is "free"; the sense, derived from *gratus*, of pleasure-

there in each instance to "locate" incidents in the drama, or, by serving as sympathetically or ironically reflecting background, to bring them out more clearly. That argument, a version of the line of criticism with which I took issue at the opening of this chapter, can be made, although I believe it would not finally hold. But the phenomena we shall be looking at in this section cannot be defined as functional; they can only be described as being present in the poem gratuitously. In this sense, of a formal function within the poem, they really are "inutile all."

This distinction between functional and gratuitous becomes more clear and persuasive when we turn to the passages in which these phenomena appear—bearing always in mind this practical qualification, that something of the refreshment they give us as we read along and are surprised by them in context must inevitably be lost in even the most careful act of transfer from the experience of reading to the experience of thinking critically about our reading, one remove away. For an illustration, take a particular visual effect in a picture of Napoleon sitting by a campfire in front of that much-watched and watchful cellar near Astorga. The passage goes: "He unfolds a dispatch, and looks for something to sit on. A cloak is thrown over a log, and he settles to reading by the firelight. The others stand round. The light, crossed by the snow-flakes, flickers on his unhealthy face and stoutening figure . . ." (II,III,ii,212). For advancing the plot, and advancing also the theme of monism (by keeping the focus limited to what could be seen by the firelight, and by keeping it trained upon the vital Energy, health, and potency of the Will in Napoleon—as discussed in Chapter One), it would have sufficed if the last sentence had read, "The light . . . flickers on his unhealthy face and

giving, applies to the nature of these phenomena; and the suggestion in "gratuitous" of the theological term "grace," separately derived from *gratus*, very much applies to the unpredictable power of these phenomena to act as (non-theological) "extras," and to surprise, relieve, and transform.

stoutening figure." Something to that effect we would have expected and approved of. The presence of the phrase "crossed by snow-flakes" adds an extra movement of life, a visual effect that arrests and interests, an unexpected element of beauty that is gratuitous and unnecessary.

With this distinction clear, let us apply it to a few more examples. In an early one, Hardy is setting the scene for the military review about to take place on the South Wessex downs before the king and his court and local spectators. His description moves from the sweeping view to the small detail:

> The down commands a wide view over the English Channel in front of it, including the popular Royal watering-place, with the Isle of Slingers and its roadstead, where men-of-war and frigates are anchored. The hour is ten in the morning, and the July sun glows upon a large military encampment round about the foreground, and warms the stone field-walls that take the place of hedges here. (I,II,iv,46)

The morning sun warming the stone walls: that silent detail brings to consciousness the reader's own experience of similar phenomena, making him aware that, yes, the physical world always does work in this way—which, come to think of it, is a beautiful way.

We come upon another effect of the touch of sunlight upon the earth when we look down from an aerial position over the upper Rhine and watch the Allied armies moving upon France: "It is the morning of New Year's Day, and the shine of the tardy sun reaches the fronts of the beetling castles, but scarcely descends far enough to touch the wavelets of the river winding leftwards across the many-leagued picture from Schaffhausen to Coblenz" (III,IV,i,397). Dull waves ready to be made shining by the sunrise, the movement of a January sun that is different from the sun in

July: manifestations of life like these, which are simply
noted in passing, help to give to human beings disgusted
with the "whole curst show" a means of relief from being
dominated always by the vision of futility at the heart of
things. There is relief in observing the movements of life at
the surface, each of which represents an interweaving of
circumstances different from any other, holding still only
long enough to be noted.

A different phenomenon: when Napoleon's army crosses
the Pyrenees, one of the details that is noted from the
scene's aerial vantage-point is "the whitey-brown tilts of
the baggage-waggons" (II,II,i,181). What is the effect of this
little piece of visual description? We can say that it demonstrates the intensity of Hardy's imagination, showing
that he sees what he describes as though it were actually
before him; but its main effect is to direct attention, not to
Hardy, but to the sight itself, as being quick and interesting
and beautiful.

Then there is a rather ordinary phenomenon, the uneven
levels of housetops and uneven textures of roofs to be seen
alongside the route of Marie Louise's wedding procession:
"After many breaks and halts, during which heavy rains
spread their gauzes over the scene, the roofs and houses of
Munich disclose themselves, suggesting the tesserae of an
irregular mosaic" (II,v,v,279). We include it in our survey
because it illustrates the fact that this perspective is trained
upon distinctions, irregularities, and texture, where the
other three perspectives dissolved them.

Finally, there are the peripheral phenomena seen and
heard during the two historic debate-scenes. In Part One:
"The candle-snuffers go round, and PITT rises. During
the momentary pause before he speaks the House assumes
an attentive stillness, in which can be heard the rustling
of the trees without, a horn from an early coach, and the
voice of the watch crying the hour" (I,I,iii,19). And in Part
Three:

LONDON. THE OLD HOUSE OF COMMONS.

The interior of the Chamber appears as in scene III.,
Act I., Part I., except that the windows are not open
and the trees without are not yet green. (III,v,v,443)

Another perspective (the linking one we discussed in
Chapter Three) also gave a glimpse of life going on outside
the windows of the halls of dynasts:

Behold Tomorrow riddles the curtains through,
And labouring life without shoulders its cross anew!
(II,vi,vii,321)

There the glimpse to the side was brought in to provide another example of suffering, necessitated life, and thus to
reinforce the theme of the drama. But in these examples
life is not perceived as suffering. The visual and auditory
effects by which they are presented to us do not "function"
to advance the plot or theme; they simply "are." And their
simply "being" serves to remind us that life is going on out
there—outside the web that interweaves the people in the
Napoleonic drama, and outside the web being woven out of
ourselves. It is just audible and visible during moments of
remission, when "willed" attention relaxes and allows phenomena on the periphery of vision to register. Trees not
yet green or trees with leafage rustling; the sound of traffic
and of a man's voice announcing that it is a certain hour
on the human clock and all is well: such phenomena put
into perspective the diorama they border. They testify that
each scene, each drama, is partial when it is set against the
infinite, incomprehensible whole; and that stress is only a
part of the rhythm of life, in which every systole has its
diastole, every beat its relaxations and compensations.
    The gratuitous phenomena recalled in this section are
only the few that this reader happened to notice out of
many scattered in the poem like chips of mica among stones,
to flash up and surprise other readers at other times. Mica
in stone, light and color in darkness—these are the figures

we reach for to describe the effect of these small phenomena on the tone and temper of Hardy's vision in *The Dynasts*. That they make an impression far beyond their number and size and position in the world, we have seen; and yet we would not claim that they transform or cancel out the sadness and somberness that is there. Lively though they may be, they sport on the periphery of an animated slide-show that reveals thousands perishing.

Another image comes to mind, the figure of two transecting lines that Hardy describes to make clear to us one of the Waterloo battlefields:

THE FIELD OF QUATRE-BRAS

The same day. The view is southward, and the straight gaunt highway from Brussels (behind the spectator) to Charleroi over the hills in front, bisects the picture from foreground to distance. Near at hand, where it is elevated and open, there crosses it obliquely, at a point called Les Quatre-Bras, another road that comes from Nivelle, five miles to the gazer's right rear, and goes to Namur, twenty miles ahead to the left. At a distance of five or six miles in this latter direction it passes near the previous scene, Ligny, where the booming of guns can be continuously heard. (III,vi,vi,475)

The starkness and exactitude of these details, and the basic simplicity of the cross-figure described, remind us again that Hardy was an architect, with an architect's feel for the foundations and joinings and key-beams and pressures of a construct. This trained sense carries over to the rigid schematism people have remarked upon in his writing —the predictable sets of antithetical characters, the counterthwarts of circumstance, the relentless curve of events. Life as Hardy shows it is like the battlefield drawn here: stark, unsparing, itself unspared—flattened out like Europe in the poem's opening, itself impaled upon itself. It is a scene for an impersonal tragedy without a savior for mankind, no Prometheus and no Christ. But we can compare the cross-

269

figure to a Christian cross. Without Jesus, life takes over all the roles: suffering victim, rigid frame of suffering; Judas and Pilate, Jew and Gentile; love warring with justice and injustice. One oppressive factor is that Calvary is often an everyday affair, working through small, prosaic, quotidien details not taken care of, or connections wrongly made; and so, warding it off requires a grey, strenuous vigilance. To this gaunt bisecting shape are attracted birds and animals, spiders and moths; nests are raised and lichens accrete; quaint grotesque fancies and illusions suggest themselves; sun and shadow play over it, and water and wind and weather run along its sides. All of these visitants have an effect: they soften the figure's gauntness, fill out and shade in the schematism, relieve the starkness. Until universal deliverance comes or the cross is dismantled, they perform the minor deliverances of art, which, against this somber, elemental field of vision, are not minor, but considerable.

2. LIMITS ON THE VIEW

All the things of life shown in the perspective of the periphery are gratuitous in another sense: they are of no use to the characters in the poem, who never notice them; they appear and disappear noticed only by the poet and ourselves. But we have seen that for our minds these phenomena, while peripheral, exert a considerable relieving force upon the whole. What does it mean that the minds in the poem who all, in one way or another, have a care and an interest in the show of life, and who all would be affected by a full knowledge of the possibilities as well as the restrictions that life holds forth, the "goods" as well as the pain and evil—what does it mean that they should all be denied the sight of this part of the full picture?

We can only infer back from effects; but, then, one effect of seeing these phenomena go unremarked by the Spirits is to support the logic by which Hardy sets off spirits from

persons in his cast of characters. The Spirits receive the
world in an intellectual picture; by intellection they "understand" what Hardy puts into his universe. Thus they
see *facts* on the periphery that we miss. They are existences
in space:

>   web Enorm
> Whose furthest hem and selvage may extend
> To where the roars and plashings of the flames
> Of earth-invisible suns swell noisily,
> And onwards into ghastly gulfs of sky,
> Where hideous presences churn through the dark—
> Monsters of magnitude without a shape,
> Hanging amid deep wells of nothingness.
>
> (After Scene, 522)

And they have seen existences back to the beginnings of
human history, against whose long and deep scroll of suffering this drama is but an instant point:

SEMICHORUS II OF IRONIC SPIRITS (aerial music)

> Beheld the rarest wrecked amain,
> Whole nigh-perfected species slain
> By those that scarce could boast a brain;

SEMICHORUS I

> Saw ravage, growth, diminish, add,
> Here peoples sane, there peoples mad,
> In choiceless throws of good and bad;

SEMICHORUS II

> Heard laughters at the ruthless dooms
> Which tortured to the eternal glooms
> Quick quivering hearts in hecatombs.

CHORUS

> Us Ancients, then, it ill befits
> To quake when slaughter's spectre flits
> Athwart this field of Austerlitz!
>
> (I,VI,iii,119–120)

These suffering existences are the correlatives of the particular unsuffering brooks and towns and people and sunbeams we have been looking at, because both are located on the selvage, just visible, of this design. But the phenomena that come to us through our senses are missed by the Spirits. In a monistic universe, Hardy would hold, mind is an outgrowth of body; but in *The Dynasts* these outgrowths have become refined so far beyond unconscious body that raw sensations and physical experience are strange and alien to them. Even the Pities, for all their capacity to sympathize with the pangs that flesh assumes when it takes on life, here miss the obverse of those pangs, flesh's keen pleasures of sensation.

Hardy must have assigned these various modes of perception with some deliberation, giving careful thought to this subtle distinction between the abstract perception available to the Spirit Intelligences and the sense perception available to the fleshly characters. For while we find an interest in perception and memory elsewhere in his writings (presented straightforwardly in the *Life*, ironically in the short stories, appreciatively in the shorter poems),[21] nowhere else is it as developed and articulated as it is through the levels of *The Dynasts*. We do find that Hardy's collected poems offer us a comparable picture of a mind looking upon experience from a detached mental view; but in them that mind and its detachment are characterized in temporal terms only.[22] *The Dynasts* provides Hardy with the space and the means to make discriminations that are at once more subtle and more explicit. The Phantoms in his Overworld possess the freedom to see the phenomena along the framework but not the body with

[21] J. Hillis Miller, *Thomas Hardy*, gives the most extended analysis of perception and memory in Hardy. His book discusses the novels and poems but does not provide extensive treatment of *The Dynasts*.

[22] See especially the following lyrics: "Self-Unconscious" (CP, pp. 311–12), "Joys of Memory" (CP, p. 410), "The Rambler" (CP, pp. 252–53), "The Absolute Explains" (CP, pp. 716–19), and "In Front of the Landscape" (CP, pp. 285–87).

which really to see them. From their disengaged positions they see lines without sensing surfaces, and so their perception is not complete. Below, the human characters have the opposite problem: they possess experiencing bodies, real enough, and are ideally positioned for sensations to stir their physical senses; but the drama pictures them always in relation to the struggle with Napoleon and thus always under stress. In distress, Hardy would seem to suggest, one's consciousness is directed, with the rest of one's energies, on the object against which or for which one is struggling; too little is left over to take in what is unrelated to that drama and simply free.

Virginia Woolf is one critic who has noticed how the attention of Hardy's protagonists is wholly directed upon struggles and concerns (their own or those of others): "They need all their strength to deal with the downright blows, the freakish ingenuity, the gradually increasing malignity of fate. They have none to spend upon the subtleties and delicacies of the human comedy."[23] And so, in an irony we can be sure Hardy appreciated, those who have time and place for the sight of beauty cannot benefit from it; those who would benefit from it lack the right place and time. The experience of joy and the full apprehension of joy are separated—another example of "mistiming" in the fabric.

But that irony does not pertain throughout. Like the backward-looking poet of the lyrics, the flesh-and-blood characters in *The Dynasts* do recognize the physical joy of physical existence—retrospectively. In the present, impressions of life's beauty are pushed to the edges of consciousness by life's pressures; but in memory these impressions are released and they pour with pent-up force into the center. And so *The Dynasts* shows these "inutile" phenomena being approached and recovered by indirection, in backward and side glances, in retrospective and peripheral vision.

23 Virginia Woolf, "The Novels of Thomas Hardy," p. 228.

We see this backward look at work when the dying Nelson asks Captain Hardy what thoughts come to his mind at such an hour of extremity:

HARDY (waking from a short reverie)
Thoughts all confused, my lord—their needs on deck,
Your own sad state, and your unrivalled past;
Mixed up with flashes of old things afar—
Old childish things at home, down Wessex way,
In the snug village under Blackdon Hill
Where I was born. The tumbling stream, the garden,
The placid look of the grey dial there,
Marking unconsciously this bloody hour,
And the red apples of my father's trees,
Just now full ripe.

NELSON
                    Ay, thus do little things
Steal into my mind, too.

                              (I,v,iv,97)

The Captain's speech delivers here a pastoral elegy for Nelson's sweetness of nature; but at large, into the whole poem, it delivers forth the kind of phenomena we have been describing: things continuing on placidly, unconscious of human battles; beloved places; the look of ripened apples and the sound of a tumbling stream—"old childish things."

And we remember other times in the drama when men close to fighting and death found their minds ranging back to happier days back home, with freshly discovered appreciation. At Astorga, it is Bristol that is conjured up; at Vitoria, the hussars call up pleasant summer days past at Budmouth. Their reminiscing "suddenly bursts into melody" (III,ii,i,366), a song about the joys of the prime of life when men and women go pranking, pacing, clinking, challenging, a time that can never again be entered except in memory, song, or dream. Retrospection, dream (Captain

274

Hardy's "reverie"), art (the songs)—all three open into one another and grant to human beings temporary release from the stresses of present experience. The mind slips into a realm of experience that is beyond the touch of the Will's pulsations. Here, where time is stilled, the mind can select, reorder, make and uncover symbols, relive and transmute whatever the unconscious has "noticed."

In the anatomizing perspective that we studied in our first chapter, art was limited in tone and subject-matter. All of the images of life in it—the tableaux, the songs, the epigrams—seemed to be parodying some ironic version of the drama's theme of determinism: "we are free" or "we are puppets"; "we are sleepwalking" or "we dream." But the songs that represent art in this perspective are freely creative, even to the point of transcending, at certain disinterested moments of perception, the somber limitations inherent in being alive. We can draw this basic distinction: Hardy's more emphatic and dominant perspectives focussed on those conditions which obstruct and limit the sphere of life, while this unstressed one focusses instead on what still remains within the limits of the sphere of life. To borrow from Auden's elegy on Yeats, this perspective makes "a vineyard of the curse."

The Spirits, and the human beings directly above the beat of life, are denied the full sight of these "noticings." But we as readers have the sight of them, and the benefit of sharing every vantage-point inside and outside the poem, including the vantage-point of the poet. Because, when we read, we are somewhat sheltered from the beat of our own lives, we can perhaps take note of Hardy's witness and his own example: become sensitive to these silent phenomena on the periphery; bring to full view that which we usually relegate to the unconscious and appreciate only in hindsight; and contemplate a vision of life as rounded and developed as the one Hardy delivers to us here. When we put down the book and take up our own lives again (our lives, which Hardy says we go through half-consciously, as though in a dream), we may even carry over into them the memory of some of these dispelling recognitions.[24]

3. THE VIEW'S EXTENT: NATURE, VISION, AND POETRY

We recognize that this perspective is shown to our eyes and not to any other set of eyes within the poem; and we can make out a logic in that selectiveness. But what are we to make of the fact that these phenomena are only *shown* to us, and no more? For certainly, had Hardy chosen to make more of them, ample means lay within the poem for making this perspective a more dominant element in his pattern. He had the instrument of the Phantom Intelligences for calling attention (intellectual attention) to sights of peace along-side the scene of war, recreation alongside travail. If he had wanted to bend an entire world into his picture of "in-utile" suffering (the theory of Eliot and Blackmur to which we took exception at the beginning of this chapter), the Intelligences could have cited these instances of busy uncon-sciousness to "comment ironically on the human condition" (Pinion). Sometimes Hardy does draw ironic meanings from such phenomena. Mrs. Yeobright's look down on the ant world in *The Return of the Native* and Knight's sight into the fossil world in *A Pair of Blue Eyes* are notable instances of sudden, surprising views of Nature's unqualified power and indifference, where the views did act to diminish the significance of his human characters, even in their dying

---

[24] In "Self-Unconscious" (CP, pp. 311–12) the poet describes a man walking along in reverie, musing upon the future and failing to note the beauty in "The moment that encompassed him." The poem ends with regret for this man: those evanescent phenomena passed away, and they were "all that mattered." It would have been good had such a man been able to have stood "At a clear-eyed distance, and conned the whole." To have seen oneself with whole vision while *in* the mo-ment, while enveloped by the airs, lights, sounds, colors, motions, and lives of Earth, would have been to apprehend the best meaning of life, to experience the infinite in the finite.

moments. But, while the theme of human insignificance is certainly present in *The Dynasts*, and is voiced by all of the Spirits, Hardy did not enlist these phenomena in its service.

Let us take this hypothesis further. We have suggested in our reading that the diorama reveals a counter-element to the primary and tragic one in Hardy's vision. We have made much of the plea of the Spirit of the Years that we hold back from too hasty a condemnation of the defendant, Life:

> O heap not blame on that in-brooding Will;
> O pause, till all things all their days fulfil!
>
> (I,v,iv,100)

And we have said that even though the Overworld debate is left open, the Spirit of the Pities does dominate it at its close, with his triumphant assertion that life's "unscanted scope" makes possible all things, even unprecedented things, and is the source of "final Hope" (After Scene, 523). If Hardy had wanted to strengthen the element of affirmation we have seen in his pattern, certainly these phenomena, as examples of that "unscanted scope," would have been useful to the Spirit of the Pities when he came to make his final hymn of tentative and wondering praise of Life, the "Might."

And so, the hypothesis would have us conclude, if Hardy did indeed mean for us to view these aesthetic phenomena as we have, as positive revelations of life's inexhaustibility, he would have pointed to them more clearly and unequivocally. In Blackmur's phrase, he would have made them "count." A Spirit Intelligence, either the Spirit of the Pities speaking in his mood of hope, or some separately conceived faculty—perhaps a "Spirit Aesthetic" or a "Spirit Affirmative"—could have cited them as important elements and changed the whole course of the mental debate about the drama. The carefully qualified hopefulness in the poem's conclusion would have been made decisive and emphatic. Our own reading—the full and diverse visual pattern we have attempted to delineate—could have been offered much more forthrightly, without being tissued in speculation and conditions.

But we return from hypothesis to *The Dynasts* as we have it. Hardy could have, but did not, make this perspective something other than peripheral; did not, in the sight of the reader, attach to it any of the repeated "meanings" that run like strophes and anti-strophes through the Over-world's brooding music—not to either of the "negative" or "affirmative" responses we have suggested as crude alternatives, nor to any other.

And even as we try to imagine how these peripheral phenomena might have been given more explicit attention by the Phantom Intelligences, we sense that such harnessing would have weakened the poem. To have enlisted them to support a view of optimism would have been untrue to Hardy; to have drawn them into a more thoroughgoing pessimism would have flattened out a whole dimension of *The Dynasts* and taken away its free suggestiveness.

Virginia Woolf describes this sense of free suggestiveness which is part of the experience of reading Hardy:

"The novels . . . are full of inequalities; they are lumpish and dull and inexpressive; but they are never arid; there is about them a little blur of unconsciousness, that halo of freshness and margin of the unexpressed which often produce the most profound sense of satisfaction. It is as if Hardy himself were not quite aware of what he did, as if his consciousness held more than he could produce, and he left it for his readers to make out his full meaning and to supplement it from their own experience."[25]

A fine description, and one that stirs us to further thought: are we talking about an unconscious lack of finish, one of those not-unhappy effects brought about by the carelessness of genius? "Blur of unconsciousness" may put us on our guard, because it echoes a word in Hardy's closing directions in the Preface ("Gauzes or screens to blur

25 Woolf, "The Novels of Thomas Hardy," p. 225.

outlines might still further shut off the actual"), where we see him fully conscious, fully aware of what he was doing, and in full imaginative control of the connections between his poetic conception and the effects they would produce upon the reader. Woolf catches beautifully the wonderful result of Hardy's "lack of finish," which we shall have more to say about. But we may disagree with her speculation: "as if Hardy were not quite aware of what he did." We cannot settle questions of conscious or unconscious intent, and should not try, but we can offer suppositions about what "he could [and did] produce," and point to our evidence for them.

One piece of evidence for the supposition that Hardy may have been conscious of these effects lies in a statement made early in the *Life*. In it the young poet shows that he was aware that there were effects to be gained from an artist's holding back one hand with the other:

> Am more and more confirmed in an idea I have long held, as a matter of common sense, long before I thought of any old aphorism bearing on the subject: "Ars est celare artem." The whole secret of a living style and the difference between it and a dead style, lies in not having too much style—being, in fact, a little careless, or rather seeming to be, here and there. It brings wonderful life into the writing:
>
> > A sweet disorder in the dress . . .
> > A careless shoe-string, in whose tie
> > I see a wild civility,
> > Do more bewitch me than when art
> > Is too precise in every part.
>
> Otherwise your style is worn like half-pence—all the fresh images rounded off by rubbing, and no crispness or movement at all. (*Life*, p. 105)

Hardy is speaking of matters of cadence, "inexact rhymes and rhythms" in verse and prose, which, as instances of art-

ful imprecision, are of a different order from the unarticu-
lated perceptions we have been wondering about in *The
Dynasts*. But the statement shows a conscious attitude that
could have become a matter of practice when it came to
other artistic choices between precision and imprecision,
between drawing the strings tight or leaving them loose.[26]

Hardy's lyrics provide a good testing-ground for our instinct that we are dealing with a consciously achieved effect. For many of them, like the lyric "Afterwards" cited
at the beginning of this chapter, deal with the phenomena
we have noted in the margins of *The Dynasts*: impressions
of weather, of flora and fauna, of the texture and individuality of living things. Some lyrics make poetry out of
names—the names of places (for example, "A Death-Day
Recalled," CP, p. 329) or of people ("To Lizbie Browne,"
CP, pp. 118–20, and "Friends Beyond," CP, pp. 52–54) or of
pieces of music ("Reminiscences of a Dancing Man," CP,
pp. 201–02, and "A Church Romance," CP, p. 236). Other
lyrics address the common joys of life: autumn, in "Shortening Days at the Homestead" (CP, p. 771); different kinds
of rains, in "Weathers" (CP, p. 533); cider-drinking, dancing, love-trysting, in "Great Things" (CP, pp. 445–46); the
sweeping, pulsing music of existence, in "Lines to a Movement in Mozart's E-Flat Symphony" (CP, p. 430). Such
lyrics remind us that Hardy "noticed" and derived conscious pleasure from these physical contacts with life. And
then there are the love poems of 1912–1913, in which the
poet's unconscious seems to be speaking, and which are
Hardy's most moving tributes to the beauty offered up by
life along with the sorrow. In so far as beauty seems to
outlive sorrow in memory, it would seem, at least in these
triumphant poems, to constitute an exception to the hard
law voiced so forbiddingly in "Yell'ham Wood's Story"
(CP, p. 280): "Life offers—to deny!" What is remarkable

---

[26] See also Hardy's important remarks on his "Gothic" attitude to
irregularity and spontaneity, carried from his training in architecture
over to his work in verse: *Life*, pp. 300–01.

about all these lyrics in praise of the beauty of life is that Hardy does not supply in them any modifier that tells us in what way or to what degree these phenomena are "fair" in his eyes. Except for his good-humored "great" in "Great Things" and his "liking" in "Weathers," their fairness comes out only through the beauty transmitted and the exhilaration communicated in his renderings of them.

Next let us look at a pair of poems that present an illustration of human inattention while displaying alongside it the phenomenon that is being missed—setting the two alongside each other without any explanation or remark. Because they duplicate, in their silent presentation, the treatment of phenomena we are trying to understand in *The Dynasts*, they would seem useful evidence for our friendly debate with Woolf as to whether Hardy was in conscious control of the effects he produced. The lyrics are "The Fallow Deer at the Lonely House" (CP, p. 566) and "Coming Up Oxford Street: Evening" (CP, p. 680). In each poem there is a difference in meter and line-length and in degree of onomatopoeic sound that sets off the two sides of the picture. In "The Fallow Deer" the lines that depict the dreamy human beings are longer, the meter more slow and regular; the two short concluding lines that describe the doe seem to reproduce in the meter (the dactyls "Wondering," "Fourfooted") and the words ("aglow," "tiptoe") her shining eyes, her tentative alert footings, and the brevity and lightness of her presence as compared to the heavy human building. The first part of "Oxford Street" traces the illumination of a setting sun, a silent movement of light much like those we have seen presented silently and effectively in *The Dynasts*. The four opening repetitions of "sun" imitate the forcefulness of direct glare; next, the modulation from "sun" to "sun-mirrorings, too" shifts the poem's focus to the sun's indirect reflections; finally, the open-voweled verbs "explores" and "solves" bring to view the warm, lambent rays at the sunlight's edges. After this passage come longer lines, more mechanical in meter, which depict a homeward-bound clerk whose spirit is so constricted by his work that the sun's intricate effects are to him just one more instance of the tedium of life.

In both these poems the two elements, the slower "civilized" and the quick "wild," the unobserving mind and the unobserved body, are set side by side, without comment. And yet, perhaps Hardy is not entirely noncommittal here. For is there not an authorial and poetic comment—a testimony, as it were, to the inspiriting power of nature—in the successful closeness and quickness with which the physical phenomena are rendered? The testimony—if it is that—is as impersonal as is the object described. Since we find that such lyrics hold back in their borders some of the same meanings that are held back in *The Dynasts*, and hold them back by similar methods, they support our sense that the "margin of the inexpressed" is for Hardy a matter of long-standing poetic instinct and practice. "It brings wonderful life into the writing."

The strongest support for our opinion that Hardy's carelessness is a careful effect lies in *The Dynasts* itself. The transparencies provide a parallel instance of the poet's holding back from an acknowledgment of beauty, leaving it silent in the poem and leaving it for his readers to, as Woolf put it above, "make out his full meaning and to supplement it from their own experience." When we discussed Hardy's transparencies in our first chapter, we noted that two modes of language were used to describe them: first, a technical and scientific vocabulary; second, emerging at the end of the third transparency and in the fourth, words having to do with creation and artistry; and both modes woven together in the sixth transparency in a mutually appropriate image of dream. The second, artistic vocabulary did much to reconcile us to the Will's blind pulsations, we said, by instilling in us a sense of the presence of wonder and beauty. But this sense was supplied by ourselves: at no point in his language for the transparencies did Hardy use the reconciling word "beauty." And yet, the words he did use—"sublime," "strenuously transmutive," "Creation's prentice artistry," "Express . . . Tentative dreams," "Mangle its types, reknead the clay/ In some more palpitating way" (Ironic Spirits, I,vi,iii,118–119); "like breezes made visible, the films . . . that pervade all things . . . moving them to Its inexplicable artistries" (III,i,i,330) —came so close to "beauty" as to move *us* to supply the missing word. We feel the satisfaction of having contributed, with Hardy, to the world's witness: of having adjusted an imbalance and brought to light an unrealized, not quite accounted for, fairness.

What Hardy has done—and not done—with the transparencies should help us to understand what he is about in the prose stage directions, where most of the peripheral phenomena are presented. This part of the poem is the only direct outlet in the drama for his narrative voice, after that powerful[27] instrument has been dramatically objectified and divided among the various onlooking Intelligences. When, in the course of a prose stage direction or scene description, he introduces one of the peripheral phenomena we have been considering, Hardy never insinuates, by as little as the addition or modulation of a few words, what his own reaction to it may be. We are not told whether the fact that the Maceira river trickled "unconcernedly" by humankind is in his view a grim or gladdening one. By maintaining reserve even here, and presenting the drama of action, he channels his intellectual and moral reactions into their spirit conduits and leaves sense phenomena latent, like an untapped secret. By eschewing authorial hints and not breaking into his own voice as rhetorical "speaker of the epic" or lyrical "lover of life's

---

[27] J.I.M. Stewart, *Thomas Hardy*, p. 81, speaking of the tendency of that narrative voice to press upon the reader Hardy's antitheses and examples, calls it "the technique of the nudge" and finds it at work throughout Hardy's novels. We could call what we are describing the technique of a "counter-nudge," except that it is more subtle and suggestive than that.

shows," he allows this undeveloped portion of his design to be entered into and completed by us.

This reticence and reserve achieve certain paradoxes: the "inutile" is more effective than if it were directly harnessed; nature, left silent in the wild, communicates in her own ways to each of us. And we ourselves are left at liberty: left not to see, like the human beings under pressure in the drama and the phantoms watching it; or to see, draw our own conclusions, make our own connections, and fashion things fair in our own eyes. Surely the case can be made, and maintained, that Hardy's poetic vision combines a steadfastly bleak reading of ultimate things with this silent, noncommittal registering of the beauty and individuality of things that are near and familiar. It is all the more eloquent because it is not quite articulated, and more heuristic because it stimulates the reader to extend and irradiate its weave.

Up to now, in analyzing the "margin of the unexpressed" in Hardy's poetic vision (translating Woolf's "unexpressed" into "shown but not articulated"), we have spoken of its practical effect on us as we read. We have seen that this effect is, basically, an aesthetic pleasure. We have speculated, also, as to Hardy's awareness of this effect of free suggestiveness, and pointed to what might have been his practical motive and method: "Ars est celare artem." To complete our analysis, we turn to certain of Hardy's theoretical reasonings that would seem to accord with this effect in his writing-practice. If we can perceive how in this instance theory, practice, method, and effect work together in *The Dynasts*, we may more fully recognize the art of this great poem and gain a sense of "the unity and wholeness of Hardy's vision, regardless of the genre in which he chose to write."[28]

The theories that bear here are part of what we called in our Introduction Hardy's poetics of vision. He established

[28] Gerber and Davis, "Introduction," *Thomas Hardy: An Annotated Bibliography*, p. 18.

his poetics, we said,[29] squarely on the variety and relativity and "idiosyncrasy" of human sight.

> . . . in life the seer should watch that pattern among general things which his idiosyncrasy moves him to observe, and describe that alone. This is, quite accurately, a going to Nature; yet the result is no mere photograph, but purely the product of the writer's own mind. (*Life*, p. 153)

The idiosyncratic pattern (which this poet well knows is only a temporary impression of reality) is reproduced emphatically: by selection, simplification, exaggeration, distortion, leaps of fancy, and all the devices of poetic license, some of which we have detailed in this study.

> Art is disproportioning—(i.e. distorting, throwing out of proportion)—of realities, to show more clearly the features that matter in those realities, which if merely copied or reported inventorially, might possibly be observed, but would more probably be overlooked. (*Life*, p. 229)

In *The Dynasts* the pattern that is thus thrown in stark outline, like a shadow-skeleton upon a wall, assumes the form of the unconscious universal brain, beating out spasmodically its electric signal-patterns, weaving and unweaving itself, blankly dealing pain to its parts and screaming earlessly from that pain. The dissolving light of Hardy's imagination, we said, not only revealed that stark pattern to us, but reconciled us to the sight by its pure, impersonal beauty. Certainly Hardy was conscious of the reconciling pleasures of pattern:

> There is enough poetry in what is left [in life], after all the false romance has been abstracted, to make a sweet pattern. . . . (*Life*, p. 114)

[29] See Introduction, Section 3, "Hardy's Thoughts on Vision."

So, then, if Nature's defects must be looked in the face and transcribed, whence arises the *art* in poetry and novel-writing? . . . I think the art lies in making these defects the basis of a hitherto unperceived beauty, by irradiating them with "the light that never was" on their surface, but is seen to be latent in them by the spiritual eye. (*Life*, p. 114)

In Hardy's pattern there are two elements of pleasure: the beauty of the irradiated line, and the beauty of the spaces between the lines. Under the penetrating gaze of a spiritual eye, the eye of imagination, the body's denser, harder tissues—the form-setting ones—stand out more emphatically than do the softer, more yielding tissues they contain. But each element gives off its own radiance: the one brilliant and monochromatic, striking the back of the eye at its central defining focal point; the other luminous and softly colored, touching the walls of the eye at the sides, where sharp focus is relaxed and colorings register. In the vision of a different, less deliberately idiosyncratic poet, the two elements might have been differently harmonized and might appear less provocative to us. But because Hardy's design has thrown the "realities" into what seems a "disproportioning," we may be irritated by his pattern, we may be disturbed, but we are affected by it to look and look again.

A brief comparison will illustrate this point. Both Hardy and Wordsworth in their poems were in touch with sense-experience and prized it: again and again natural phenomena give to Wordsworth, as they do to Hardy, a renewed vision of life's upwelling powers. For Wordsworth such phenomena become the fulcrum of a poem, cracking the glaze of convention to show the springs of life beneath, and lifting the poet's spirit from anxiety to joy in that act of revelation. The levering phenomenon is directly addressed and assessed by Wordsworth, where in Hardy it is left to the side of the poem, to do its great work of lifting in its own way.

"Resolution and Independence" and *Tess of the d'Urber-villes* are both poetic works according to Wordsworth's standard in his Preface to the *Lyrical Ballads*, because in both "the passions of man are incorporated with the beautiful forms of nature."[30] (Hardy knew "Resolution and Independence" well, and even listed it as one of his "Cures for Despair" when he was a young man; *Life*, p. 58.) Both works present a character whose fortitude under adversity inspires the author and the reader. But they conclude so differently. Because Wordsworth supplies his own poetic person as a vehicle adequate to the emotions raised and transmuted over the course of the poem, we consent to enter that person and relive his ritual experience as he does. When at the poem's end he resolves that in future times of depression and anxiety "I'll think of the Leech-gatherer on the lonely moor!" his conclusion speaks for us. We accept, as life-giving images of power for ourselves in our own tranquility or anxiety, the phenomena he delivers to us in the poem: and we fail to achieve full enjoyment of Wordsworth's poetry if at any point we refuse to meet his earnestness with a correspondingly earnest acceptance.

The reader of *Tess* has a more perplexing time. The beauties of setting and sense phenomena and human character are all present; but the author chooses to leave out of his authorial assessments the power that these have to console. Hardy does not claim that the harmony and beauty of Tess's life as she moves through the landscape of her world somehow compensate for the suffering she undergoes. Such a claim might have been too neat, might, in its turn, have left too much out of its account. But we never have a chance to contemplate it, for he concludes with the opposite claim:[31] that her life was a cruelly protracted freak of circumstance, relieved only when it was cancelled out. As readers we rise up, provoked, to supply the side of

[30] This point of continuity was noted by Edmund Gosse, "Mr. Hardy's Lyric Poetry," p. 273.
[31] See the first sentence of the last paragraph of the novel.

the story left silent: Tess's purity of spirit,[32] and the winter and summer beauty of the earth.[33] These harmonies triumph over the dissonance of circumstances and of human capacity to harm—and even, in retrospect, take those troubling notes into their swell and make music the more moving in our ears. By becoming an advocate, against the narrator, for Tess, for nature, for life, the reader is more deeply involved than he would be if Hardy had done all the work.

But it must also be said: if this conscious provocation were a calculated device only, if we suspected that Hardy's bitter protests at Tess's unmerited sufferings were not meant as truthfully and seriously as was the evidence for her transfiguration, the work as a whole would not trouble and move us as it does.[34] If we felt that our adjustment of his vision were not a free act, our experience of collaborative reading would not continue to yield up, when we look back on it, what Woolf called "the most profound sense of satisfaction."

[32] Stewart, *Thomas Hardy*, p. 168, says of her: "Tess Durbeyfield herself is as the sun at noon"; and, on p. 170: her appetite for joy, "inseparably mingled with her suffering, establishes her so unshakably among the very greatest characters in English fiction." I agree.

[33] Virginia Woolf, in "The Novels of Thomas Hardy," p. 225, praises "that sense of the physical world which Hardy more than any novelist can bring before us; the sense that the little prospect of man's existence is ringed by a landscape which, while it exists apart, yet confers a deep and solemn beauty upon his drama."

Walter de la Mare, "*The Dynasts*," in *Private View*, agrees: "Few English novelists can compare with Mr. Hardy in the depth and significance he gives to life by unifying it with the great world without" (p. 33); "It is a deep and spacious beauty that survives in memory . . ." (p. 32).

[34] Ian Gregor, *The Great Web*, pp. 196–204, describes the urgency created by the constant tension between the narrative and the narrator's glosses, a tension that "keeps altering the relationship between the reader and the text," in his fine analysis of the conclusion to *Tess*. On p. 203 he speaks of the author's "honesty," which accords to his narrative the plurality of contrary responses that it demands. This last point could also apply to *The Dynasts*.

For what has enabled us to be critics, not of Hardy's vision in the work but of his incomplete and partial interpretation of it, is the fact that he has controlled not us but himself. Because he has kept vision and interpretation distinct, so can we.[35] Two gifts in one are delivered to us by this self-restraint and reserve. First is the pleasure we take in the way that Hardy's sense phenomena quicken the senses and imagination. The second satisfaction comes once we have been stirred into testifying to the silent beauty we witnessed, when we realize that we have presumed to take over from Hardy the interpretation of his vision, that we have become co-authors, poets and seers, with him. It is an indication of this author's objectivity that he would share his powers with us, and that he should even, in his artful, art-concealing way, set us ahead of himself. He sets us free to discover inside his work, while in the experience itself, that our own ordinary minds have the power to find and create for ourselves, in the face of testimonials to the contrary, such beauty.

Hardy believed that man's awakening to the powers of the the human imagination could be a source of joy equal almost to the old belief in a conscious God:

> I do not think there will be any permanent revival of the old transcendental ideals; but I think there may gradually be developed an Idealism of Fancy; that is, an idealism in which fancy is no longer tricked out and made to masquerade as belief, but is frankly and honestly accepted as an imaginative solace in the lack of

[35] As this 1917 entry in the *Life* shows, Hardy believed that Wordsworth did not always keep vision and interpretation distinct, and he considered that this confusion constituted a difference between himself and Wordsworth, a difference he thought became more pronounced as Wordsworth grew older: "I hold that the mission of poetry is to record impressions, not convictions. Wordsworth in his later writings fell into the error of recording the latter" (*Life*, pp. 377–78). We should remember, though, that this is the "later" Hardy speaking about the later Wordsworth—not about the Wordsworth of "Resolution and Independence," a poem that, as we saw, was esteemed by the young Hardy.

any substantial solace to be found in life. (Letter written in 1901, quoted in *Life*, p. 310)

"Modern" as this statement appears, it is different from the modernist faith in art that it seems to anticipate: holding back from Wallace Stevens' conviction that sense experience constitutes a sufficiency, even an empire, for man; temperamentally unwilling to clap hands and sing, like Yeats, at man's bare and beggarly situation; too protestant to try to assume the mantle of artist-priest-schoolmaster, as did, in their various ways, Joyce and Pound and Eliot. For Hardy's words "frankly and honestly" in the passage above have a double thrust. They seem to declare a new faith in the human imagination come into adulthood, frankly recognizing and enjoying its position as creator and center of the subjective universe. And yet they also declare a sense of second-best, and an acknowledgment of the need for consolation. To Hardy, subjective "imaginative solace" is by definition a lesser thing than objective "substantial solace."[36] The rhythms of art and the pleasures of sensation divert and console the mind from its pain; but so long as the source of pain persists in the very composition of flesh, true solace —the healing of substance or flesh—will always lie in the future, unaccomplished.

The reservation in Hardy's endorsement of "Fancy" gives us one more way of understanding where he places and how he places his marginal phenomena. The deliverance they effect is just beginning, still on the edges of the universal task of deliverance that must be complete before all is fair. In the meantime the patient naturalist "notes Life's conditions" ("On A Fine Morning," CP, p. 118), collects his observations, records his sensations, and offers them as data toward the faroff unpredictable resolution of the universal experiment: "Unadjusted impressions have their value, and the road to a true philosophy of life seems

[36] For one impression of what Hardy thought of a purely aesthetic justification of human existence, see the irony in the lyric, "On a Fine Morning," CP, p. 118.

to lie in humbly recording diverse readings of its phenomena as they are forced upon us by chance and change."[37]

Let us return to the word "latent" because it reminds us
of many things. Latency allows for the evolutionary hope
that within the stuff of life lies unborn form, groping in the
direction of harmony and consciousness. The eductive new
heroes, of whom the poem approved, respected "latency"
and resisted heavy-handed dictatorial ways. The poem introduced those heroes as

> Men surfeited of laying heavy hands
> Upon the innocent,
> The mild, the fragile, the obscure content
> Among the myriads of thy family.
>
> (Fore Scene, p. 3)

These lines apply as well to Hardy's artistic witness: to the
self-restraint with which he set aside those relatively free
areas in his design, where beauty of form and substance
are shown by implication only, unactualized and unartic-
ulated and untamed by the artist's hand. For Hardy's
moral and aesthetic sensitivity are of a piece. Even as he
explicitly protests against injuries to flesh, he implicitly
demonstrates by his own counter-practice his sensitivity
towards flesh in all its aspects: its powers of sense, its vulnerability, and the potential contained in its very formless-
ness to yield up, in the fullness of time, its own "immanent
form."

This compound of expression and inexpression, hardness
and softness, emphasis and relaxation, which is spun out
large in *The Dynasts*, is in the very weave of Hardy's
shorter poems as well. Their forms, seemingly unstudied
and careless, prove to be the products of complex experi-
mentation,[38] with interlocking rhymes, subtle repetitions,

[37] Hardy, Preface to "Poems of the Past and Present," in *Personal
Writings*, ed. Orel, p. 39.

[38] The *Life*, pp. 300–301, so states, and an examination of any group
of lyrics bears this statement out.

cunningly irregular rhythms. The sounds of the long lines weaving in with short ones, and of the driving rhythms alternating with receding ones, are reminiscent of the intricate dance-steps set to "simple" country airs that the boy Hardy and his father used to set into motion with their fiddles. Like dance patterns, a number of the lyrics were measured out in the past before their living word-substance was poured into them. Hardy tells us this remarkable fact in the *Life* ("verse skeletons," "mostly blank"—*Life*, p. 301), and the matter-of-fact statement accords with the many other times he employs the form-content dichotomy, in *The Dynasts* and in his reflections elsewhere:

> Poetry is emotion put into measure. The emotion must come by nature, but the measure can be acquired by art. (*Life*, p. 300)

> His vision had often been that of so many people brought up under Church of England influences, a giving of liturgical form to modern ideas, and expressing them in the same old buildings . . . [modifying] the liturgy by dropping preternatural assumptions out of it. . . . (*Life*, p. 376)

Cast into these apparently pre-set, finished molds, and held in counterpoise by them like plasm in a vial, is the freshness of Hardy's words: the crabbed and harshly consonantal, which make his language seem, like Wyatt's and Donne's, to shrug off courtly smoothness and surface; the dialect words and neologisms, each differently derived but alike in result in that each strikes our ears as unworn, newly plucked or newly hewn; the many "-ing" words— verbals or compound verbs that seem in their dropping trochaic or dactyllic meters to preserve the wetness and give and fertility of new life; the onomatopoeic words that bring natural sensations close to us. Such words, as one critic said, "strike, bite in, caress, disturb, unveil the truth, quicken the curiosity."[39] They make a language liquid

[39] Edmund Blunden, *Thomas Hardy*, p. 265.

enough to flow freely within Hardy's constraining stanzas and buoyant enough to "upbear" his recalcitrant expressions—the circumlocutions, the learned abstractions, the remnants of nineteenth-century poetic diction (those unabashedly uplifting terms like "Charity" and "Lovingkindly," "Poesy" and "sublime").

In *The Dynasts*, with a vision so inclusive and a frame so complex, the elements that give refreshment are broadly represented, registering less as individual words counterpointed to formal requirements than as peripheral observations counterpointed against central foci. But it is as true in *The Dynasts* as elsewhere in the lyrics that the quality that makes Hardy's language live, besides the freshness of the words themselves, is the effect it gives of living *for* something—an impression that the very things that seem to be out-of-place or strained or idiosyncratic in it— the quirkish loppings-off of parts of words ("plashings," "Byss," "ope"), the awkward-looking changes of grammatical forms ("onwardly," "usward," "warely," "Foregone" as a noun for the past), the neologisms ("uptrips," "upthroated," "unknow," "unsee," "inexist," "unclosing" her eyes, "enghosted," "philosopheme," "magnipotent," "homuncules") and archaisms ("yclept," "slitten," "shotten," "mire-bestrowed")—are there to be looked *through* to the more important reality they are reaching to and describing, and present only incidentally to be looked at or dwelled upon. Hardy's aim, we feel, is the same as the one he recognized in his friend William Barnes, who also, as Hardy explained, strained the resources of language available to him, pushing dialect and archaisms to their limit to achieve "closeness of phrase to his vision."[40]

And Hardy himself achieved this closeness: "the word formed with primitive intensity upon the thing indicated, is his mark and his command."[41] As readers, we feel that his

[40] Hardy, Preface to "Select Poems of William Barnes," in *Personal Writings*, ed. Orel, p. 80.
[41] Blunden, p. 266.

language always refers to something seen by him so intensely and clearly that we too can almost see it outside the
verse, and can almost check the verse against it—as though
against nature, against experience, against an accessible
and shareable "objective reality." Even if we had not read
his thoughts about vision and "disproportionings," we
would tacitly allow, as have all Hardy readers, friendly
and otherwise,[42] that his irregularities and idiosyncrasies
constitute and recreate an act of seeing, that they are what
they are out of an urgency and a reaching-out for the truth
they see and strive to give form to.

"Latency" can take us one step further: Hardy is enacting, by his self-restraint with his material, his respect for
our minds. He is treating his readers as he would have the
"Will" treat its creatures: that is, with regard for feelings,
histories, memories, and capacities to discover and create.
The openings he has left to the Will in his picture, the
possibilities for a gradual and free coming-to-consciousness,
he similarly leaves to us. Because our minds, yoked metaphorically with that cosmic mind, are treated as though
they were that "other," every time we respond creatively and
sympathetically, a small part of "It" does also.

When we look back to the diorama-model that has
framed this discussion, we discover that latency lies at the
heart of Hardy's vision as its power and purpose. Latency
awaits the reader's discovery and expression, not only in this
last perspective on the periphery, but in the other perspectives we have also studied. The powers of the Phantom-
Spectators are our guide here as elsewhere. The Spirits
shared with us the substance of the perspectives discussed
in our first three chapters. They controlled the "mode" of
visualization, but again and again those Spirit Intelligences

[42] A reading of Gerber and Davis' *Annotated Bibliography* shows that
through the years, when readers singled out Hardy's views or "impressions of life" for attention, they would criticize them on grounds
of correctness or tact but not on those of sincerity or fidelity of representation.

did not fully comprehend all that their "mode" apprehended. When we looked through to the back of the stage, at the monistic views of the Will, we were required to intervene, as readers, to append the transforming word "beauty" to the qualities that emerged in the transparencies. The same interceding was necessary at the front of the stage: when Pity's own eye failed to note that Napoleon was to be pitied as well as condemned, we have to amend that vision, make it more true to itself. And similarly with the phenomena in the lateral aspects of Hardy's vision: the urgent examples of unfreedom needed to be balanced and completed by impressions of life enjoying relative freedom. In every direction the act of vision is adjusted and completed by Hardy's reader.

The phenomena of this fourth chapter, then, are seen and not seen by the Intelligences that Hardy projects for us onto the Overworld. These phenomena make their impressions, not upon the conscious level, as did the phenomena in the first three chapters, but below, somewhere in the subconscious, where they are stored as data—to be recovered in the future by Everyman's backward-looking mind, or to be converted in the present by the individual reader's mind. As we read, we deliver up this aspect of life from subconsciousness to consciousness.

Thus latency lies before us wherever we look in Hardy's poem, persuading us that it does the same in life. It implicates us in the workings of the diorama and makes our vision intersect, intervolve, and become one with the poem's great field of vision. That, finally, is why Hardy's peripheral phenomena are left unexpressed in the marginal reaches of the dreaming mind: they lie in waiting there, noted subconsciously only, until we enter the scene, "called" by Hardy to draw subconscious and conscious together.

Let us listen one more time to Hardy reflecting on poetic vision. It will serve as his parting word to us on how the universe and man, objective reality and subjective trans-

mutation of reality, cosmos without and cosmos within, require each other for the act of creation:

> The exact truth as to material fact ceases to be of im-
> portance to art—it is a student's style—the style of a
> period when the mind is serene and unawakened to the
> tragical mysteries of life; when it does not bring any-
> thing to the object that coalesces with and translates
> the qualities that are already there,—half-hidden, it
> may be—and the two united are depicted as the All.
> (*Life*, p. 185)

And so we come back to the image that has guided this
essay—the diorama, a device that uses cloth screens and
weaving lights to produce a show of reality. From big to
little, from its overall conception to its smallest units of
words, *The Dynasts* is like a diorama: a series of gauzes,
veils, or screens, exhibiting, sometimes filtering, sometimes
blurring, sometimes quite blotting out the "actual," in
order to deliver the "real." And the diorama, in turn, is
like the theatre of our visioning, where impressions of experience are delivered by the senses to the brain, where
they are ordered and interpreted and adjusted with our
previous impressions. We should expect the optical me-
chanics to be somewhat creaky and dusty in an antiquated
seeing-machine modelled after Daguerre; but, irradiated
by that dateless "light that never was," they deliver their
vision. If we consent to pay the price of admission, if we
bend, enter the dark room, outstay our initial impressions
of remoteness and estrangement, we come to experience the
most penetrating, pure, fresh and restoring effects.

And who knows but whether the poem does not deliver
us into the frame of the diorama, after all? It may be that
Hardy, in his reach for the unreachable objective All, depicts his poem in the very act of almost achieving it. There
are no "curtaining" phenomena to close off Hardy's After
Scene, and the diorama, from our view—no beautiful effects of weather, smoke, mist, fog, darkness, thickenings of

night. In the final stirring that "thrills the air," does the show break its self-enchantment, become show no longer? Or are we dissolved into the All, darkled to "extinction swift and sure"? Our eyes, grown used to the lighting, keep musing on these visual perspectives, keep watching the lights and images reflected from surfaces, over and over, on and on.

BIBLIOGRAPHY

Abercrombie, Lascelles. *Thomas Hardy: A Critical Study.* London: Secker, 1912; rpt. New York: Russell and Russell, 1964.

Agenda (Thomas Hardy Special Issue), 10 (Spring–Summer, 1972). Ed. Donald Davie.

Archer, William. "Real Conversations: Conversation I.—With Mr. Thomas Hardy." *Critic,* 38 (April, 1901), 309–18.

Auden, W. H. "A Literary Transference." *Southern Review* (Thomas Hardy Centennial Edition), 6 (Summer, 1940), 78–86.

Bailey, J. O. "Evolutionary Meliorism in the Poetry of Thomas Hardy." *Studies in Philology,* 60:3 (July, 1960), 569–87.

———. *The Poetry of Thomas Hardy: A Handbook and Commentary.* Chapel Hill: Univ. of North Carolina Press, 1970.

———. *Thomas Hardy and the Cosmic Mind: A New Reading of "The Dynasts."* Chapel Hill: Univ. of North Carolina Press, 1956.

Bailey, John. *The Continuity of Letters.* London: Oxford Univ. Press, 1923.

Baker, Howard. "Hardy's Poetic Certitude." *Southern Review* (Thomas Hardy Centennial Edition), 6 (Summer, 1940), 49–63.

Barber, D. F., ed. *Concerning Thomas Hardy: A Composite Picture from Memory.* London: Charles Skilton, 1968.

Barzun, Jacques. "Truth and Poetry in Thomas Hardy." *Southern Review* (Thomas Hardy Centennial Edition), 6 (Summer, 1940), 179–92.

Beach, Joseph Warren. *The Technique of Thomas Hardy.* Chicago: Univ. of Chicago Press, 1922; rpt. New York: Russell and Russell, 1962.

Blackmur, R. P. "The Shorter Poems of Thomas Hardy," in *Language as Gesture*. New York: Harcourt, Brace, 1952. Pp. 51–79.

Blunden, Edmund. *Thomas Hardy*. London: Macmillan, 1951.

Bowra, C. M. *The Lyrical Poetry of Thomas Hardy*. Nottingham: Nottingham Univ., 1946. Rpt. in *Inspiration and Poetry*. London: Macmillan, 1955. Pp. 220–41.

Brennecke, Ernest, Jr. *The Life of Thomas Hardy*. New York: Greenberg, 1925.

————. *Thomas Hardy's Universe: A Study of the Poet's Mind*. London: T. Fisher Unwin, 1924; rpt. New York: Russell and Russell, 1966.

Brooks, Jean R. *Thomas Hardy: The Poetic Structure*. Vol. 1 of *Novelists in their World*, ed. Graham Hough. Ithaca, New York: Cornell Univ. Press, 1971.

Brown, Douglas. *Thomas Hardy*. London: Longmans, 1961.

Carpenter, Richard. *Thomas Hardy*. New York: Twayne, 1964.

Cecil, Lord David. *Hardy the Novelist: An Essay in Criticism*. London: Constable, 1943.

Chakravarty, Amiya. *"The Dynasts" and the Post-War Age in Poetry*. London: Oxford Univ. Press, 1938.

`hapman, Frank. "Hardy the Novelist." *Scrutiny*, 3 (June, 1934), 22–37.

Chew, Samuel C. *Thomas Hardy, Poet and Novelist*. New York: Knopf, 1921.

Child, Harold. *Thomas Hardy*. New York: Holt, 1916.

Chilton, Eleanor Carroll and Herbert Agar. *The Garment of Praise: The Necessity for Poetry*. New York: Doubleday, 1929.

Church, Richard. "Thomas Hardy as Revealed in *The Dynasts*." *Essays by Divers Hands: Being the Transactions of the Royal Society of Literature*, n.s. 29 (1958), 1–17.

Clifford, Emma. "The Impressionistic View of History in *The Dynasts.*" *Modern Language Quarterly*, 22 (March, 1961), 21–31.

————. "Thomas Hardy and the Historians." *Studies in Philology*, 56 (October, 1959), 654–68.

————. "The 'Trumpet Major Notebook' and *The Dynasts.*" *Review of English Studies*, n.s. 8 (May, 1957), 149–61.

————. "*War and Peace* and *The Dynasts.*" *Modern Philology*, 54 (August, 1956), 33–44.

Collins, Vere H. *Talks with Thomas Hardy at Max Gate, 1920–1922.* London: Duckworth, 1928.

Cox, R. G., ed. *Thomas Hardy: The Critical Heritage.* New York: Barnes and Noble, 1971.

Daguerre, Louis Jacques Mandé. *An Historical and Descriptive Account of the various processes of the Daguerréotype and the Diorama.* London: McLean, 1839. New York: Kraus Reprint, 1969.

Davidson, Donald. "The Traditional Basis of Thomas Hardy's Fiction." *Southern Review* (Thomas Hardy Centennial Edition), 6 (Summer, 1940), 162–68.

Davie, Donald. *Thomas Hardy and British Poetry.* New York: Oxford Univ. Press, 1972.

Deacon, L. and T. Coleman. *Providence and Mr. Hardy.* London: Hutchinson, 1966.

De la Mare, Walter. "*The Dynasts.*" *The Bookman* (June, 1908), 110–112.

————. *Private View.* London: Faber and Faber, 1953.

Dobrée, Bonamy. "*The Dynasts.*" *Southern Review* (Thomas Hardy Centennial Edition), 6 (Summer, 1940), 109–24.

————. "Thomas Hardy," in *The Lamp and the Lute: Studies in Six Modern Authors.* Oxford: Clarendon Press, 1929; 2nd ed. New York: Barnes and Noble, 1964. Pp. 18–37.

Drabble, Margaret, ed. *The Genius of Thomas Hardy.* New York: Knopf, 1976.

Drew, Elizabeth, *The Enjoyment of Literature*. New York: W. W. Norton, 1935.

Duffin, Henry Charles. *Thomas Hardy: A Study of the Wessex Novels, Poems, and "The Dynasts."* Manchester: Manchester Univ. Press, 1937.

Eliot, Thomas Stearns. *After Strange Gods: A Primer of Modern Heresy*. New York: Harcourt, Brace, 1934.

Elliott, Albert Pettigrew. *Fatalism in the Works of Thomas Hardy*. Philadelphia: pvtly. ptd., 1935; rpt. New York: Russell and Russell, 1966.

Elliott, George R. "Hardy's Poetry and the Ghostly Moving-Picture." *South Atlantic Quarterly*, 27 (July, 1928), 280–91.

———. "Spectral Etching in the Poetry of Thomas Hardy." *PMLA*, 43 (December, 1928), 1185–95.

Exideuil, Pierre d'. *The Human Pair in the Works of Thomas Hardy*. London: Humphrey Toulmin, 1930.

Fairchild, Hoxie Neale. "The Immediate Source of *The Dynasts*." *PMLA*, 67 (March, 1952), 43–64.

———. *Religious Trends in English Poetry*. 5 vols. Vol. 5: *Gods of a Changing Poetry, 1880–1920*. New York: Columbia Univ. Press, 1962.

Fairley, Barker. "Notes on the Form of *The Dynasts*." *PMLA*, 34 (September, 1919), 401–15.

Firor, Ruth. *Folkways in Thomas Hardy*. Philadelphia: Univ. of Pennsylvania, 1931; rpt. New York: Barnes and Noble, 1962.

Forster, E. M. *Aspects of the Novel*. New York: Harcourt, 1927.

Garwood, Helen. *Thomas Hardy: An Illustration of Schopenhauer*. Philadelphia: John C. Winston, 1911; rpt. Folcroft, Pennsylvania: Folcroft Press, 1969.

Gerber, Helmut E. and W. Eugene Davis. *Thomas Hardy: An Annotated Bibliography of Writings About Him*. Vol. 3 of The Annotated Secondary Bibliography Series on *English Literature in Transition, 1880–1920*.

Ed. Helmut E. Gerber. DeKalb, Illinois: Northern Illinois Univ. Press, 1973.

Gittings, Robert. *Young Thomas Hardy*. Boston: Little, Brown, 1975.

Gosse, Edmund. "Mr. Hardy's Lyrical Poems," *Edinburgh Review*, 227 (April, 1918), 272–93.

Gregor, Ian. *The Great Web: The Form of Hardy's Major Fiction*. Totowa, New Jersey: Rowman and Littlefield, 1974.

Guerard, Albert, J., ed. *Hardy: A Collection of Critical Essays*. Englewood Cliffs, New Jersey: Prentice Hall, 1963.

———. *Thomas Hardy*. New York: New Directions, 1964.

Halliday, F. E. *Thomas Hardy, His Life and Work*. Bath: Adams and Dart, 1972.

Hardy, Emma. *Some Recollections by Emma Hardy with Notes by Evelyn Hardy Together with some Relevant Poems by Thomas Hardy with Notes by Robert Gittings*. New York and London: Oxford Univ. Press, 1961.

Hardy, Evelyn. *Thomas Hardy: A Critical Biography*. London: Hogarth Press, 1954.

———, ed. *Thomas Hardy's Notebooks, and Some Letters from Julia Augusta Martin*. London: Hogarth Press, 1955.

— and F. B. Pinion, eds. *One Rare Fair Woman: Thomas Hardy's Letters to Florence Henniker, 1893–1922*. Coral Gables, Florida: Univ. of Miami Press, 1972.

Hardy, Florence Emily. *The Life of Thomas Hardy, 1840–1928*. London: Macmillan, 1962.

Hardy, Thomas. *Collected Poems*. London: Macmillan, 1930.

———. *The Dynasts: An Epic-Drama of the War with Napoleon*. London: Macmillan, 1924.

Harper and Brothers, eds. *Thomas Hardy: Notes on His Life and Work*. New York: Harper, 1925.

Hedgcock, F. A. *Thomas Hardy: Penseur et Artiste*. Paris: Libraire Hachette, 1911.

Hickson, Elizabeth Cathcart. *The Versification of Thomas Hardy*. Philadelphia: pvtly. ptd., 1931.

Holloway, John. *The Victorian Sage: Studies in Argument*. London: Macmillan, 1953.

Hopkins, Annette B. "*The Dynasts* and the Course of History." *South Atlantic Quarterly*, 44 (1945), 432–44.

Hornback, Bert G. *The Metaphor of Chance: Vision and Technique in the Works of Thomas Hardy*. Athens, Ohio: Ohio Univ. Press, 1971.

Horsman, E. A. "The Language of *The Dynasts*." *Durham University Journal*, n.s. 10 (December, 1948), 11–16.

Howe, Irving. *Thomas Hardy*. New York: Macmillan, 1967.

Hynes, Samuel L. *The Pattern of Hardy's Poetry*. Chapel Hill: Univ. of North Carolina Press, 1961.

Johnson, Lionel. *The Art of Thomas Hardy*. London: Mathews and Lane, 1894; aug. ed. London: Lane, 1923.

Kay-Robinson, Denys. *Hardy's Wessex Re-appraised*. Newton Abbot, Devon, England: David and Charles, 1972.

Korg, Jacob. "Hardy's *The Dynasts*: A Prophesy." *South Atlantic Quarterly*, 53 (January, 1954), 24–32.

Kramer, Dale. *Thomas Hardy, The Forms of Tragedy*. Detroit: Wayne State Univ. Press, 1975.

Lawrence, D. H. *Movements in European History*. London: Oxford, 1925.

———. "Study of Thomas Hardy," in *Phoenix: The Post-humous Papers of D. H. Lawrence*. Ed. Edward D. McDonald. London: Heinemann, 1936. Pp. 398–516.

Lea, Hermann. *Thomas Hardy's Wessex*. London: Macmillan, 1913.

Leavis, F. R. "Hardy the Poet." *Southern Review* (Thomas Hardy Centennial Edition), 6 (Summer, 1940), 87–98.

———. *New Bearings in English Poetry: A Study of the Contemporary Situation*. London: Chatto and Windus, 1932.

Leavis, Q. D. "Hardy and Criticism." *Scrutiny*, 11 (1943); rpt. in *A Selection from Scrutiny*, Vol. 1. Ed. F. R. Leavis. Cambridge: Cambridge Univ. Press, 1968. Pp. 291–98.

Lee, Vernon. *The Handling of Words, and Other Studies in Literary Psychology*. London: John Lane, 1927; rpt. Lincoln, Nebraska: Univ. of Nebraska Press, 1968.

Lerner, Laurence and John Holmstrom, eds. *Thomas Hardy and His Readers: A Selection of Contemporary Reviews*. London: Bodley Head; New York: Barnes and Noble, 1968.

Lewis, C. Day. "The Lyrical Poetry of Thomas Hardy." *Proceedings of the British Academy*, 37 (1951), 155–74. Rpt. as *The Lyrical Poetry of Thomas Hardy*. London: Cumberledge, 1957.

McCaffrey, Isabel Gamble. "Hardy's *The Dynasts*: A Study in Aesthetic Unity." B.A. Thesis, Swarthmore College, 1946.

McCormick, Benedict, O.F.M. "Thomas Hardy: A Vision and a Prelude." *Renascence*, 14 (Spring, 1962), 155–59.

Macdonnell, Annie. *Thomas Hardy*. London: Hodder and Stoughton, 1894.

McDowall, Arthur. *Thomas Hardy: A Critical Study*. London: Faber and Faber, 1931.

Marsden, Kenneth. *The Poems of Thomas Hardy: A Critical Introduction*. London: Athlone; New York: Oxford Univ. Press, 1969.

May, Charles E. "The Hero in Thomas Hardy's *The Dynasts*." *Research Studies*, 40 (1972), 251–59.

Meisel, Perry. *Thomas Hardy: The Return of the Repressed*. New Haven: Yale Univ. Press, 1972.

Miller, J. Hillis. *Thomas Hardy: Distance and Desire*. Cambridge, Mass.: Harvard Univ. Press, 1970.

Millgate, Michael. "Hardy's Fiction: Some Comments on the Present State of Criticism." *English Literature in Transition*, 14 (1971), 230–38.

Millgate, Michael. *Thomas Hardy: His Career as a Novelist.* New York: Random House, 1971.

Mizener, Arthur. "*Jude the Obscure* as a Tragedy." *Southern Review* (Thomas Hardy Centennial Edition), 6 (Summer, 1940), 193–213.

Modern Fiction Studies, 6:3 (Autumn, 1960). Thomas Hardy Number.

Morrell, Roy. *Thomas Hardy: The Will and the Way.* Singapore: Univ. of Malaya Press, 1965.

Muir, Edwin. "The Novels of Thomas Hardy," in *Essays on Literature and Society.* London: Hogarth Press, 1949. Pp. 110–19.

Muller, Herbert J. "The Novels of Hardy Today." *Southern Review* (Thomas Hardy Centennial Edition), 6 (Summer, 1940), 214–24.

Murry, John Middleton. "The Poetry of Mr. Hardy," in *Aspects of Literature.* London: Collins, 1920. Pp. 121–38.

Nevinson, Henry W. *Thomas Hardy.* London: Allen and Unwin, 1941; rpt. Folcroft, Pennsylvania: Folcroft Press, 1967.

Orel, Harold. "*The Dynasts* and *Paradise Lost.*" *South Atlantic Quarterly*, 52 (July, 1953), 355–60.

———. "Hardy and the Epic Tradition." *English Literature in Transition*, 9:4 (1966), 187–89.

———. *Thomas Hardy's Epic-Drama: A Study of "The Dynasts."* Lawrence, Kansas: Univ. of Kansas Press, 1963.

———, ed. *Thomas Hardy's Personal Writings: Prefaces, Literary Opinions, Reminiscences.* Lawrence, Kansas: Univ. of Kansas Press, 1966.

———. "Trends in Critical Views Toward Hardy's Poetry." *English Literature in Transition*, 14:4 (1971), 223–29.

Perkins, David. "Hardy and the Poetry of Isolation." *Journal of English Literary History*, 26 (June, 1959), 253–70.

Pinion, F. B. *A Hardy Companion: A Guide to the Works of Thomas Hardy and their Background*. London and Melbourne: Macmillan; New York: St. Martin's Press, 1968.

Pinto, Vivian de Sola. "Hardy and Housman," in *Crisis in English Poetry*. London: Hutchinson House, 1951. Pp. 36–58.

Porter, Katherine Anne. "Notes on a Criticism of Thomas Hardy." *Southern Review* (Thomas Hardy Centennial Edition), 6 (Summer, 1940), 150–61; rpt. in *The Collected Essays and Occasional Writings of Katherine Anne Porter*. New York: Delacorte Press, 1970. Pp. 3–13.

Purdy, Richard Little. *Thomas Hardy: A Bibliographical Study*. London, New York, Toronto: Oxford Univ. Press, 1954; rpt. 1968.

Ransom, John Crowe. "Honey and Gall." *Southern Review* (Thomas Hardy Centennial Edition), 6 (Summer, 1940), 1–19.

————. "Thomas Hardy's Poems, and the Religious Difficulties of a Naturalist." *Kenyon Review*, 22:2 (Spring, 1960), 169–93.

Roberts, Marguerite. *Hardy's Poetic Drama and the Theatre*. New York: Pageant Press, 1965.

Roppen, Georg. *Evolution and Poetic Belief: A Study in Some Victorian and Modern Writers*. Oslo: Oslo Univ. Press, 1956.

Rutland, William R. *Thomas Hardy*. London: Blackie, 1938.

————. *Thomas Hardy: A Study of his Writings and their Background*. Oxford: Blackwell, 1938; rpt. New York: Russell and Russell, 1962.

Schwartz, Delmore. "Poetry and Belief in Thomas Hardy." *Southern Review* (Thomas Hardy Centennial Edition), 6 (Summer, 1940), 64–77.

Scott-James, R. A. *Thomas Hardy*. London: Longmans, Green, 1951.

Sherman, George Witter. "The Influence of London on *The Dynasts.*" *PMLA*, 63 (September, 1948), 1017–28.

Southerington, F. R. *Hardy's Vision of Man.* London: Chatto and Windus, 1971.

Southey, Robert. *The Life of Nelson.* Boston: Houghton Mifflin, 1916.

Southworth, James Granville. *The Poetry of Thomas Hardy.* New York: Columbia Univ. Press, 1947.

Stedmont, J. M. "Hardy's *Dynasts* and the Mythical Method." *English*, 12 (Spring, 1958), 1–4.

Stevenson, Lionel. *Darwin Among the Poets.* New York: Russell and Russell, 1932.

Stewart, J.I.M. "Thomas Hardy," in *Eight Modern Writers.* Vol. 12 of *The Oxford History of English Literature.* Ed. F. P. Wilson and Bonamy Dobrée. New York: Oxford Univ. Press, 1963. Pp. 19–70.

———. *Thomas Hardy.* London: Allen Lane, 1971.

Symons, Arthur. *A Study of Thomas Hardy.* London: Charles J. Sawyer, 1927.

Tate, Allen. "Hardy's Philosophic Metaphors." *Southern Review* (Thomas Hardy Centennial Edition), 6 (Summer, 1940), 99–108.

Van Doren, Mark. "The Poems of Thomas Hardy." *Four Poets on Poetry.* Ed. Don Cameron Allen. Baltimore: The Johns Hopkins Press, 1959. Pp. 83–107.

Van Ghent, Dorothy. "On *Tess of the d'Urbervilles,*" in *The English Novel: Form and Function.* New York: Holt, Rinehart and Winston, 1953. Pp. 195–209.

Wain, John. "Introduction." *The Dynasts: An Epic-Drama of the War with Napoleon,* by Thomas Hardy. New York: St. Martin's Press, 1965. Pp. v–xix.

Waldock, A.J.A. "Thomas Hardy and *The Dynasts,*" in *James, Joyce, and Others.* London: Williams and Norgate, 1937. Pp. 53–78.

Warren, R. P. *Selected Essays.* New York: Random House, 1966.

Webb, A. P. *A Bibliography of the Works of Thomas Hardy, 1865–1915.* New York: Franklin, 1916.

Weber, Carl J., ed. *"Dearest Emmie": Thomas Hardy's Letters to his First Wife.* London: Macmillan, 1963.

———. *Hardy of Wessex: His Life and Literary Career.* New York: Columbia Univ. Press, 1940; 2nd ed., New York: Columbia Univ. Press, 1965.

———, ed. *The Letters of Thomas Hardy.* Waterville, Maine: Colby College Press, 1954.

Webster, Harvey Curtis. *On a Darkling Plain: The Art and Thought of Thomas Hardy.* Chicago: Univ. of Chicago Press, 1947.

Weygandt, Cornelius. *The Time of Yeats: English Poets of Today Against an American Background.* New York: Appleton, 1937.

White, R. J. *Thomas Hardy and History.* New York: Barnes and Noble, 1974.

White, William. "Dreiser on Hardy, Henley, and Whitman: An Unpublished Letter." *English Language Notes,* 6:2 (December, 1968), 122–24.

Williams, Harold. *Modern English Writers: Being a Study of Imaginative Literature, 1890–1914.* London: Sidgwick and Jackson, 1918.

Williams, Mervyn. *Thomas Hardy and Rural England.* London: Macmillan, 1972.

Williams, Raymond. "Thomas Hardy." *Critical Quarterly,* 6 (Winter, 1964), 341–51.

Wing, George. *Thomas Hardy.* New York: Grove Press, 1963.

Woolf, Virginia. "The Novels of Thomas Hardy," in *The Second Common Reader.* London: Hogarth Press, 1932; rpt. New York: Harcourt, Brace, 1932. Pp. 266–80.

———. *A Writer's Diary: Being Extracts from the Diary of Virginia Woolf.* Ed. Leonard Woolf. London: Hogarth Press, 1952.

Wright, Walter F. *The Shaping of "The Dynasts": A Study in Thomas Hardy*. Lincoln: Univ. of Nebraska Press, 1967.

Zabel, Martin Dauwen. "Hardy in Defense of his Art: The Aesthetic of Incongruity." *Southern Review* (Thomas Hardy Centennial Edition), 6 (Summer, 1940), 125–49.

Zachrissen, Robert Eugen. *Thomas Hardy's Twilight View of Life*. Uppsala and Stockholm: Almquist and Wiksells, 1931.

Zietlow, Paul. *Moments of Vision: The Poetry of Thomas Hardy*. Cambridge, Mass.: Harvard Univ. Press, 1974.

INDEX

Abercrombie, Lascelles, 9, 9n, 33n, 112, 112n
aerial perspectives, 22, 65-66; and mind's freedom, 68; virtuosity of, 66. *See also* perspectives
"After-Scene" (of *The Dynasts*), 31, 63, 164-66, 195, 213, 262, 296; as conclusion to debate, 32-34, 33n, 61, 117, 165-66, 243, 243n, 263-64, 277
Agar, Herbert, 33n
Alexander the Great, 135
analogizing perspective, 41, 198-235; basis of, 211, 223; and battles, 198-204; as dealing with masses, 210-11; as linking man and earth, 214-15; and remoteness of view, 209-10; and sensory linkings, 205-209; thematic results of, 198, 215-19, 219ff, 228-29, 232-35; as yielding abstract patterns, 210n. *See also* perspectives
anatomizing perspective, 39-40, 48-117. *See also* perspectives
Arrowsmith, J., 37
Auden, W. H., 275
Augustine, 187
authorial sympathy, *see* Hardy, Thomas: authorial sympathy of. *See also* sympathy

Bailey, J. O., 32n, 112, 112n, 114, 114n, 168, 168n
Barnes, William, 293, 293n
Barzun, Jacques, 113n
battles, 198-204
Beatty, Dr. C. J. P., 155
Bergson, Henri, 113

Blackmur, R. P., 231n, 238, 238n, 276-77
Blunden, Edmund, 35n
Bowra, C. M., 35n, 64n
brain, 116-17, 164; dream as activity of, 55; as image for the Will, 39-40, 48-55, 65, 80, 116-17, 164; universal and human, 55-57, 63-65
Brennecke, Ernest, Jr., 11n
Brooks, Jean, 10n, 168, 168n, 173n
Burke, Edmund, 11

Carlyle, Thomas, 26, 26n
Carpenter, Richard, 10n
Chakravarty, Amiya, 32n, 168, 168n, 173n, 230, 230n
characters, Hardy's types of, 21-22, 122-24
Chaucer, Geoffrey, 175-76
Chew, Samuel C., 11n
Chilton, Eleanor, 33n
Clifford, Emma, 19n
Clodd, Edward, 34, 225
consciousness/unconsciousness, 46, 56, 110-11, 117, 158-63, 169-70, 173, 193-95, 232-35, 273, 278-79, 281, 291-92, 291n, 294-95; Hardy's views of, 185, 187-88; and Hardy's *Life*, 15; limitations of, 111-13, 115-16; moral value of, 163-67; and sleep, 193-95; traditional views of, 186-88

Daguerre, Louis Jacques Mandé, 37, 65n, 296
Darwin, Charles, 11, 205, 229-30
Davis, W. Eugene, 36n, 57n, 294n
de la Mare, Walter, 9, 9n, 57n, 62, 62n, 174-75, 175n, 288n

death scenes: Moore, 154-56;
Nelson, 155-56, 162; Pitt, 152-54,
156-57; Villeneuve, 112n, 152
determinism, 169-73, 186, 211; and
dream, 188; and freedom, 116;
in Hardy and Chaucer, 175-76;
in Hardy and Dreiser, 88-89;
images of, 98-107; perspectives
on, 39-41; and responsibility,
185; roll calls as patterns of,
171-72
diorama: and authorial sympathy,
176, 185, 196-97; description of,
36-38; dissolving light of, 37,
43-44, 48, 62, 176-78, 185, 195,
198, 201, 285, 297; and The
Dynasts, 36-43, 105, 164, 176,
196, 238, 296; and Hardy's
vision, 196, 238, 294-96; and
reader's mind, 44-45, 56, 65, 105,
294-96. See also perspectives;
vision
dissolving vision, see vision: dissolving. See also diorama
Dobrée, Bonamy, 33n, 57, 57n,
64n, 213-14, 213n, 214n, 237,
237n
Donne, John, 292
drama: The Dynasts as, 29, 31, 35;
in reader's mind, 44-45
dream, 24n, 36, 40, 43, 54-55, 61-
63, 93, 105, 115, 209, 211, 274-
76, 282; and anomalies in The
Dynasts, 61-63; and brain image, 55; and determinism, 188;
in Hardy's critical writings, 188-
90; in Hardy's other works, 36;
and human action, 186-95; and
Napoleon, 160-61, 192-95;
references to in The Dynasts,
190-92
Dreiser, Theodore, 88-89, 89n
Drew, Elizabeth, 10n

dualism, 81, 112-14. See also
monism
dumb shows, 110
Dynasts, The, 5n; aerial perspectives in, 22, 65-66; characters
in, 21-22, 122-24; conclusion of,
32-34, 32n, 33n, 61, 117, 164-66,
243, 243n, 263-64, 277; criticisms
of, 3-4, 3n-4n, 7-9, 18-19, 43-44,
57, 189; and diorama, 36-43, 105,
164, 176, 196, 238, 296; as discussed in the Life, 14ff, 20, 22,
22n; as drama, 29, 31, 35; and
dream, 61-63, 190-92; dualism
in, 81, 112-14; as epic, 10n, 56-
57; evolving composition of,
14-24; generic approaches to,
10-11; Hardy's narrative voice
in, 3, 283; history in, 3, 17-20,
19n, 23, 23n, 104-105, 245-47;
hope in, 33-34, 166, 243-44, 277-
78; imaginative unity of, 9, 44-
45; language of, 4, 35, 35n, 49-
55; meliorism in, 32-35, 65, 111-
12, 117, 164-69; modernity of,
5-6, 11, 21, 32n, 56-58, 156, 173;
monism in, 5, 14, 81, 112-14,
261; as morality play, 124; Napoleon as subject of, 3, 17; and
oral history, 23, 23n; perspectives of, 39-42; and philosophy,
11-14, 11n-12n; as poem, 28-31;
as poem staged in the mind, 45,
56ff, 65, 105, 188; reader as col-
laborator in, 11, 31, 31n, 32-35,
44-47, 56-57, 105, 282-84, 287-
89, 288n, 294-95; and visual
images, 17-19; visual interpretation of, 24, 36; visualization
of scenes in, 65-80

"Elegy Written in a Country
Churchyard," 108
Eliot, George, 37

Library of Congress Cataloging in Publication Data

Dean, Susan, 1937-
  Hardy's poetic vision in The dynasts.

  Based on the author's thesis, Bryn Mawr College.
  Bibliography: p.
  Includes index.
  1. Hardy, Thomas, 1840-1928. The dynasts.
2. Napoleón I, Emperor of the French, 1769-1821, in
fiction, drama, poetry, etc.   I.   Title.
PR4750.D8D4   823'.8   76-45895
ISBN 0-691-06324-9